QUICK ESCAPES® SERIES

QUICK ESCAPES® DETROIT

Third Edition

26 WEEKEND TRIPS FROM THE MOTOR CITY

BY

KHRISTI SIGURDSON ZIMMETH

The Globe Pequot Press

GUILFORD, CONNECTICUT

Photo Credits: p. 1: Courtesy of Michigan Travel Bureau; p. 7: © Bob Brodbeck; p. 18: by Robert De Jonge, courtesy Michigan Travel Bureau; p. 33: courtesy Traverse City Convention and Visitors Bureau; p. 65: courtesy Ann Arbor Hands-On Museum; p. 74: courtesy Marshall Area Chamber of Commerce; p. 125: Peter J. Schulz, courtesy of the City of Chicago; p. 131: Javet M. Kimble, courtesy of the city of Chicago; p. 139: courtesy of the Greater Cincinnati Convention and Visitors Bureau; p. 143: courtesy Maumee Bay State Park; p. 152: courtesy of the Kerr House; p. 160: by Dan Feicht, courtesy of Cedar Point; p. 173: by Joan Tuefei, courtesy of the Convention and Visitors Bureau of Greater Cleveland; p. 183: courtesy of the Ohio Department of Development; p. 219: courtesy of Convention and Visitors Bureau of Windsor-Essex; p. 225: courtesy of Metropolitan Toronto Convention and Visitors Association; pp. 257, 261: © Banayote Photography

Cover design by Laura Augustine
Cover photo by Gordon R. Gainer/The Stock Market
Page design by Nancy Freeborn
Maps by Maryann Dubé

Quick Escapes is a registered trademark of The Globe Pequot Press.

Library of Congress Cataloging-in-Publication Data
Zimmeth, Khristi Sigurdson.
    Quick escapes Detroit : 26 weekend trips from the Motor City /
by Khristi Sigurdson Zimmeth. — 3rd ed.
        p. cm. — (Quick escapes series)
    Includes index.
    ISBN 0-7627-0917-0
    1. Detroit Region (Mich.)—Guidebooks. 2. Middle West—Guidebooks.
I. Title. II. Series.
F574.D43Z56 2001
917.704'34—dc21
                                                        00-069622
                                                        CIP

Manufactured in the United States of America
Third Edition/First Printing

To Maria Shaw, who got me into the business; to Ron Garbinski, who kept me in it; and to Susan Alpert, whose love of travel inspires me still.

.

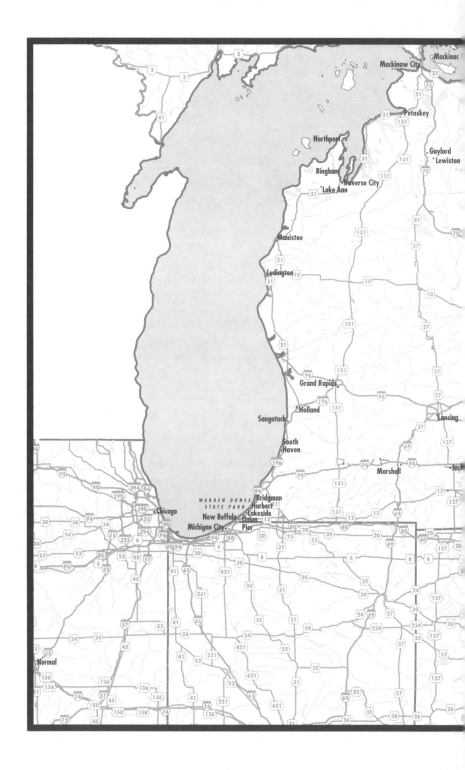

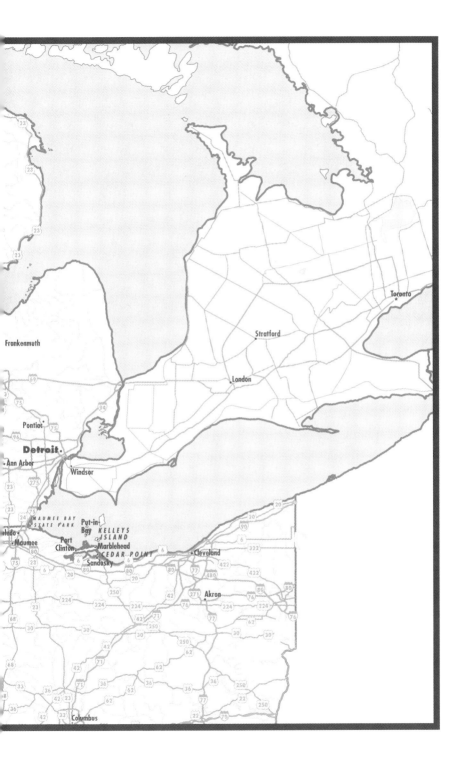

CONTENTS

ACKNOWLEDGMENTS

Thanks are due to a number of people who helped me during the process of putting this book together: my sister, Kerry Sigurdson Hoffmann, who babysat; and my husband, John, and my children, Nate and Claire, who were supportive in more ways than I can count.

Help Us Keep This Guide Up to Date

Every effort has been made by the authors and editors to make this guide as accurate and useful as possible. Many things can change after a guide is published, however—establishments close, phone numbers change, facilities come under new management, and much else.

We would love to hear from you about your experiences with this guide and how you feel it could be improved and be kept up to date. Though we may not be able to respond to all comments and suggestions, we'll take them to heart, and we'll also make certain to share them with the author. Please send your comments and suggestions to this address:

The Globe Pequot Press
Reader Response/Editorial Department
P.O. Box 480
Guilford, CT 06437

Or you may e-mail us at:
editorial@globe-pequot.com

Thanks for your input, and happy travels!

INTRODUCTION

Some say that Henry Ford indirectly invented the weekend getaway when his first horseless carriage rolled off the assembly line. Before that, huge ships and slow-moving railways took well-off vacationers and countless overstuffed steamer trunks on holidays that lasted at least a month, sometimes two or three. There was no such thing as "traveling light."

With the invention of the automobile, however, shorter trips were possible and soon became popular. Travel became less expensive and more accessible to a wider range of people. Months at the shore or on the continent were replaced by weekends by the beach, at the cottage, or soaking up the sights in a nearby city. By the mid-1950s, almost everyone could enjoy that delicious, otherworldly feeling of "being somewhere else" which pleasure travel provides.

Whether we were the first to enjoy them or not, metro Detroiters have certainly perfected the art of the weekend getaway. Half the state's population lives in the Detroit metropolitan area, but an excellent network of freeways and secondary roads allows us to zip easily out of the city to the surrounding countryside. And zip we have. As our area belched out the fast-moving cars we became known for and built more and more factories, we've increasingly escaped to the bucolic lands in the western and northern parts of the state.

"If you seek a pleasant peninsula, look around you," the state motto asserts. And pleasant it is—from charming small-town Marshall, with its treasure trove of nineteenth-century architecture and antiques shops, to increasingly cosmopolitan Traverse City. Great weekends beckon throughout the state, each with its own attractions and flavor. For that reason, the majority of the getaways described in this book are right here in our own backyard.

Although Michigan offers an incredible variety of adventures, Detroit also has the enviable position of being at the heart of the Midwest. Within a 300-mile radius (the limit for this book and, I think, for a comfortable weekend drive) are some of the region's most fascinating cities, including Chicago, Illinois; Cincinnati, Ohio; and Toronto, Ontario. All make easily accessible, quick escapes for metro Detroiters.

This book (now in its third edition) includes some of my favorite short trips, ones I've enjoyed as an editor at *Michigan Living Magazine* and during more than thirty years of residing in the Wolverine State. Some I've enjoyed as a footloose single traveler; others have seen me accompanied by a husband and laden with two kids, two Labs, and a Chrysler Town & Country minivan full of swim toys. There are benefits to both, of course, and so I've tried to give you an assortment of escapes, some family friendly, others for adults only.

A word or two about prices: For restaurants, a meal is considered inexpensive if entrees are less than $10; moderate when $10 to $15; and expensive when $15 and up. I've attempted to be as accurate as possible with other fees, but prices change often, and many vary with the season.

A few caveats: Unless you're an avid skier, you'll agree that Michigan and most of the Midwest are at their best in the milder seasons. Therefore, a number of these trips are geared toward fair weather, although they are certainly available to travelers year-round. I have also tried to seek out getaways that can be enjoyed during other seasons and note that whenever possible. There are many more great destinations than space to accommodate them in these pages, however. If this book doesn't include your favorite, let me know and I'll do my best to include it next time. Finally, be aware that the information herein was current as of September 2000. As with any business, change occurs rapidly, and the hotel or restaurant that was once extraordinary may now be just average—or may not be there at all. It's always a good idea to call ahead to avoid disappointment.

Let me know if I've missed any of your favorites or if you have comments or corrections. In the meantime, there's enough here to keep you busy for at least the next few years—or until the fourth edition hits the bookstores.

Happy Traveling!

> The information listed in this guidebook was confirmed at press time. We recommend, however, that before traveling you call establishments to obtain current information.

MICHIGAN
ESCAPES

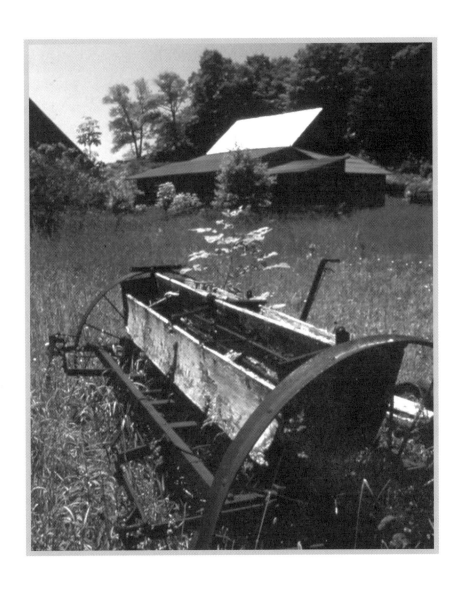

Mackinac Island

AN ISLAND IDYLL

4 NIGHTS

Bicycling • Beaches • History • Sight-seeing

A nineteenth-century Fort Mackinac physician was known to prescribe stays on Mackinac Island for those "suffering from overworked brain or muscle." A century later, the island is still a favorite tonic for anyone looking to escape the hassles of modern living. Once on the island, visitors discover that the nonmotorized pace is just what the doctor ordered and the perfect antidote to work-week stress and other twenty-first-century trials and tribulations.

In summer, the population of this 3-mile-long island swells from just 500 year-round residents to thousands of day-trippers, also known as "fudgies" (from their fascination with the island's fudge shops) who try to cram the many attractions into a frantic, daylong stay.

Savvy travelers prefer to stay at least a weekend (some stay the whole summer), which allows them to slow down enough to enjoy the island's pace and peace. If you're looking to really escape the crowds, consider a visit in fall, when the air cools, the leaves turn (colors peak from mid-September to mid-October), and rates fall dramatically in the island's often-expensive hotels.

Another good time to visit is late in spring, when the Lilac Festival attracts travelers and lovers of this heavenly shrub. For other useful tips, consider picking up a copy of *Mackinac Connection: An Insider's Guide* by local author Amy McVeigh, available in the Island Bookstore or by special order.

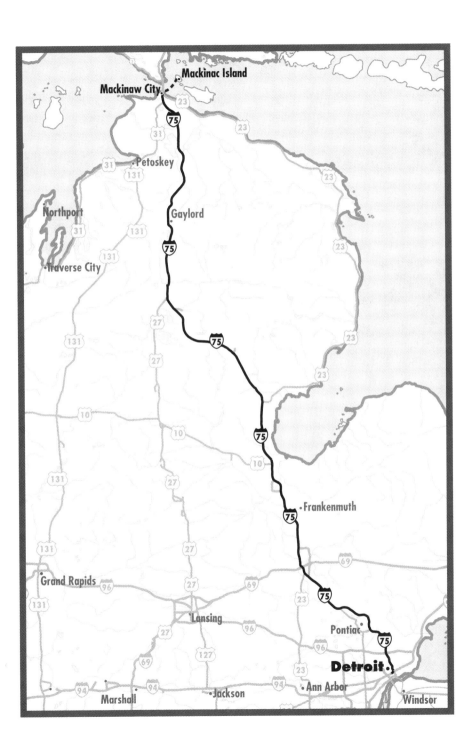

DAY 1

Afternoon

From Detroit, Mackinac (rhymes with "Saginaw") Island is a fairly lengthy drive of approximately 280 miles. To get there, take Interstate 75 north to exit 337, 338, or 339. Plan to spend at least three full days on the island to build in time for relaxing and to make the drive worthwhile. Catch dinner somewhere on the way.

LODGING: A good idea is to spend the first night in Mackinaw City. The **Hamilton Inn Select—Beachfront** (701 South Huron Street; Mackinaw City, MI 49757; 231–436–5493) was built in 1995 and was quickly awarded three diamonds by AAA. It features 300 feet of sandy beach, private balconies, and free continental breakfast. It's also closest to the ferryboats and offers handy discount coupons for island attractions. Skip the city's nightlife, however, for you'll be catching the first ferry next morning. Rates: $68–$198 per night, including continental breakfast.

DAY 2

Morning

BREAKFAST: Hamilton Inn Select—Beachfront, Mackinaw City (it's included in your room rate). After, it's time to strap on your sea legs. Mackinac Island is accessible only by ferry or seaplane, and three companies offer frequent ferries from Mackinaw City in the Lower Peninsula and St. Ignace in the Upper Peninsula. The oldest and largest is the **Arnold Line,** which has been serving the island since 1878. **Shepler's** is the second largest and is known for its personal service (they'll even fill up and wash your car and do minor repairs while you're on the island). **Star Line** is the newcomer. All take approximately fifteen minutes to make the trip and offer incredible vistas along the way.

Once on board, be sure to take an outside seat for the best views. Along the way you'll pass the **Mackinac Bridge,** which joined the state's Upper and Lower Peninsulas in November 1957. Known as "Mighty Mac," it's the world's longest suspension bridge and took years of planning and $96 million to complete. Today it features 4 miles of uninterrupted steel superstructure and is considered one of the world's marvels of human engineering.

Afternoon

Once on the island, reserve the remainder of the first day for relaxing and checking out your hotel. Linger over refreshments in Mission Point Resort's **Point Dining Room** or take in a movie in the resort's 575-seat theater. There's plenty of time to see the sights tomorrow.

LUNCH: A rustic yet comfortable place for lunch on the island is the **French Outpost** (Cadotte Avenue, across from the Little Stone Church, Mackinac Island, MI 49757; 906–847–3772). The menu is mostly soups, salads, pizza, or sandwiches; but there's also an excellent raw bar. You can choose from three dining areas—the main restaurant, the deck overlooking the straits, or the screened-in porch. Moderate.

LODGING: With its signature red roof and white-clapboard sides, **Mission Point Resort** (1 Lakeshore Boulevard, Mackinac Island, MI 49757; 906–847–3312 or 800–833–7711) blends well with the island's Victorian architecture. Surprisingly, it was built in the 1950s and 1960s as a home for the Moral Rearmament, a Christian activist group. Perfect for travelers with or without children, this sprawling resort is spread out over eighteen acres. It is located near enough to Main Street to be convenient but far enough away to be relaxing. And unlike the more famous Grand Hotel, its prices are palatable.

Included in the room rates ($139–$339 per night) are use of the 3,000-square-foot health club (with sauna, steam rooms, and massages as well as bike rentals and in-line skates), cassette tours of the island, and tennis and volleyball courts. The 236 newly redecorated guest rooms sport a "rustic lodge meets English country inn" decor, with rich, dark colors. The hotel's signature space, however, is the breathtaking Great Hall, built to resemble a sixteen-sided, 36-foot-tall teepee. If you've brought the kids, Mission Point has an innovative Kid's Klub program, with an extensive menu of activities, including an Indian powwow, scavenger hunts, freighter watching, and a new 3,000-square-foot activities center. An added bonus: Kids eat free in the hotel's three restaurants.

DINNER: If you have kids in tow, tonight's the night to take advantage of the hotel's Kid's Eat Free deal. But if you're adults looking for something a little more atmospheric, stroll through downtown (you'll be amazed how much quieter it is in the evening) to the **Carriage House** (906–847–3321). Tucked inside the Hotel Iroquois, many consider it the island's best restaurant. This relaxed but elegant waterfront restaurant offers fine food in an intimate setting. There's a great view of the straits as well as fresh and imaginative fare that includes broiled whitefish and fettuccine Alfredo with morels, a chef's specialty. Reservations are always a good idea. Moderate to expensive.

After dinner you can opt to take in a play back at the resort. Mission Point operates the only live theater on the island. Performances are offered six nights a week in season and range from comedies to dramas.

DAY 3

Morning

BREAKFAST: Your room rate at Mission Point includes the generous breakfast buffet. Served in the dining room, it includes both hot (eggs, bacon, hash browns) and cold (yogurts, fruits, juice) items, as well as baked goods (bagels, croissants, toast). If you sleep in and miss the buffet, the resort's **Freighters Deli** has croissants and cappuccino and is decorated with old photos of Great Lakes ships. It's also an ice-cream parlor and serves the only Pizza Hut pizza on the island, something you may want to remember if you have kids or are prone to late-night cravings.

A good way to get your bearings and an orientation to the island is to take a carriage tour. More than thirty local families pooled their resources forty years ago to start this cooperative business; today they operate about seventy-five carriages, with three hundred horses that take visitors on tours that last either forty-five minutes or an hour and a half. Both tours include all the top island attractions, including **Fort Mackinac** and **Arch Rock** (with stops to let you get out and enjoy the view) as well as an optional drop-off at the Grand Hotel at the end of the tour. Call (906) 847–3573 for information.

LUNCH: Many of the island's eateries can be expensive, and sometimes the food is average at best. Consider a picnic instead. Pick up your pleasure at **Doud's Mercantile** (906–847–3551) at Main and Fort Streets. Enjoy it overlooking the water and the marina's many beautiful boats. Inexpensive.

Afternoon

After lunch is the time to explore on your own. To do so, make your first stop the handy island Visitor's Center across from Marquette Park. It's a good place to pick up information, learn more about the island, and chat with the friendly staff (its well-maintained restrooms are also a good place for a pit stop).

Horse-drawn carriages are one of the most popular ways to get around Mackinac Island.

From the Visitor's Center, turn left on Main Street to take you downtown. Many of the shops are closed on Sundays, so if you plan to exercise your credit cards, do it on Saturday. Main Street has the usual souvenir and gift shops as well as a number of small, independent clothing boutiques that feature all things pricey and preppy. A few more unusual highlights include **Maeve's Art & Antiques** (906–847–3755), with great jewelry and original island scenes. It's owned by Maeve Croghan, whose Irish ancestors lived and worked on the island. Across the street, the **Island Scrimshander** (906–847–3792) is run by three brothers who make their living at this ancient mariner's art. If you're lucky, you'll catch one of them at work.

If exploring the island has piqued your curiosity, learn more at **Island Books** (906–847–6202) in the lobby of the Lilac Tree Hotel (Main Street). Here you'll find good regional titles, current best-sellers, and lots of steamy beach or porch reading.

If you're allergic to T-shirt and gift shops as well as to the ubiquitous fudge shops (most in the world!), you'll prefer Market Street, which runs parallel to Main and reflects the island's quieter side. A street of fishing crews and fur traders, it's a refreshing contrast to the teeming throngs that often crowd Main Street. Some fourteen historical buildings are furnished in 1880s style; many offer tours and a glimpse of a bygone way of life.

DINNER: Reserve one night for an all-out splurge at the 330-room **Grand Hotel** (906–847–3331 or 800–33–GRAND), indisputably the most famous spot on the island. One of the classic pleasures of a weekend on Mackinac is getting all dressed up and walking or biking to the Grand, as travelers have been doing for more than a century. The classic white Greek Revival structure (the world's largest summer-only hotel) was built in 1887 by steamship and railroad barons. It sits high on a bluff overlooking fifty acres of Victorian gardens and the town below. Its veranda is one of the most photographed sites in the state. It's 660 feet long and holds more than a dozen white rockers. (Be forewarned, however: There's a $10.00 fee per person just to stroll the porch and explore the hotel if you're not staying or eating there. A swim in the famous serpentine pool costs $8.00 per person.) Rooms, of course, are decorated with antiques and command prices of up to $460 per night. Even the least expensive room is $275 in the off-season. New in 1998 were eight suites dedicated to America's first ladies, and a suite named in honor of the movie *Somewhere in Time*. Partial revenues from the suite are donated to the American Paralysis Association in honor of Christopher Reeve, a star of the film.

The Grand is also the only place in Northern Michigan where you're still expected to dress after 6:00 P.M. and at dinner (men must wear a coat and tie). The main dining room has an unmatched setting, along with drill teams of uniformed waiters at your beck and call. The food is surprisingly good despite the fact that the large dining room serves so many at a time, with a popular five-course feast that includes seafood cocktail with mustard sauce, smoked salmon, fresh whitefish, and aged prime rib. Dinner is included for hotel guests; non-guests pay a fixed per-person price of $70. It's well worth it for this once-in-a-lifetime experience.

After dinner, watch the sun set from the hotel's rooftop piano bar, with its breathtaking view of the straits. If you're on a budget or you've brought the kids and you'd still like to experience the Grand, consider having breakfast or lunch in one of the hotel's other eateries, including Carlton Teas, which serves breakfast and light lunches; the Geranium Bar; or the Jockey Club Grand Stand.

DAY 4

Morning

BREAKFAST: Mission Point. Time to work off some of last night's Grand Hotel meal with a little exercise, island style. As two days on Mackinac have revealed, bikes are more at home here than cars. Take advantage of the fresh air and burn a little energy with a trip around the island on a bike. Check out the ones built for two, or if you're really ambitious (and in good physical condition), consider renting in-line skates from the hotel.

Bike rentals can be found at Mission Point or at a number of places along Main Street (try Rybas, 906–847–3829, with three locations; or Island Bike Rental, 906–847–6288, on Livery near the Shepler Dock). Or you can bring your own wheels and pay an extra $3.00 to ferry them across.

A good route for beginners and families is the **South Bicycle Trail,** which takes in most of the island's natural highlights, including dramatic limestone Arch Rock, which rises to 146 feet and is the site of awe-inspiring vistas. From there, take Rifle Range Road inland and turn right on Garrison Road to Skull Cave. Legend has it that a British trader spent the night here during an Indian attack, only to find it full of bones. Continue on Garrison past the cemeteries, then turn right on Fort Holmes Road to Fort Holmes. The incredible view from the stockade alone is worth the trip. From there, the road leads to British Landing, about 2 miles, or left into town.

British Landing, roughly halfway around the island on the western shore, has a half-mile nature trail, a bluff with a good bridge view, and a friendly and informative on-duty naturalist. Nearby is the Croghan Water Wetland Area, home to a variety of native flora and fauna. British Landing is also where, in winter, an ice bridge forms across to St. Ignace to allow year-round residents to snowmobile off the island.

Another popular cycling choice is the 8-mile shoreline route around the island. Insiders, however, agree that to really experience Mackinac's magic, you have to explore its interior. You'll bike along wooded trails, explore ancient geological formations, and spot bald eagles along island bluffs. A free map at the Visitor's Center details this and other worthwhile routes.

The majority of the natural and historical attractions and some 80 percent of the island itself are set aside as the **Mackinac Island State Park** (906–847–3328). Congress made the island the country's second national park in 1875; in 1894 much of it became Michigan's first state park, thereby protecting it from extensive development. More recently, *National Geographic*

Traveler named it one of the top ten parks in the nation. Its highest point is Fort Holmes, which offers great views.

Another fort worth checking is **Fort Mackinac** (906–847–3328), located high on a bluff overlooking the harbor. This restored eighteenth- and nineteenth-century British and American outpost is now preserved as a museum. All the 1780 buildings are original and include period furnishings, audiovisual presentations, and costumed guides. Kids love the Children's Discovery Room, where they can roll hoops and play other nineteenth-century games and pose for silly photos in authentic military costume. The whole family will love the stirring military music, battle reenactments, and cannon and rifle demonstrations. Admission is $7.25 for adults, $4.25 for children ages six through twelve, $21.00 for a family.

LUNCH: The fort is also the site of a charming tearoom, with a terrace that offers great views of the straits. The food is made by the Grand Hotel and includes soups, salads, personal-size pizzas, and hearty sandwiches. Afterward, indulge in the popular pecan fudge ice-cream ball, which is big enough for two. Inexpensive.

Afternoon

Charming St. Anne's church, the island's largest parish, has a pretty public garden and a basement full of artifacts that relate to the island's history. From there, you can cut through the garden path and head for McGulpin Street, where the **Mackinac Island Butterfly House** (1308 McGulpin Street; Mackinac Island, MI 49757; 906–847–3972) is a favorite spot for visitors of all ages. Hundreds of species in free flight fill the house. It was for sale at press time—call ahead to confirm before visiting.

If architecture is your thing, don't miss a walk past the island's "summer homes" located on Front Street. The row of Victorians includes the governor's warm-weather digs, built in 1909 in the shingle style. The state bought the governor's home for just $15,000 in 1945; it's worth at least $1 million today. It's open for tours on Wednesday mornings only.

DINNER: The **Island House** (Lakeshore Drive, Mackinac Island, MI 49757; 906–847–3347) across from the marina is known for its fine Governor's Room restaurant. Entrees include specialties such as Barbarie duckling in Beaujolais wine sauce and slow-roasted prime rib. There's also a popular breakfast buffet (All-U-Can-Eat for just $15) and the casual Garden Grill, a handy place for a burger, ribs, or chicken. Moderate to expensive.

Besides late dinners and watching the breathtaking sunsets, the island isn't known for its scintillating nightlife. One notable exception, however, is the **Pink Pony Bar & Grill** (adjacent to the lobby, in the Chippewa Hotel on Main Street; 906–847–3341), long a favorite of yachtsmen and women competing in the Port Huron-to-Mackinac and Chicago-to-Mackinac races. Recently doubled in size, it still has the trademark pink steed outside the front window and still serves up outstanding views of the marina and the straits. The one-hundred-year-old serpentine bar and live entertainment attract crowds after dinner; in summer, diners spill outside to a new, two-tiered deck. Popular dinner choices include Chicago-style baby back ribs, herb-crusted whitefish, and spicy Caribbean-inspired shrimp. Moderate.

If the kiddies are in tow, skip the bar and head back to Mission Point in time for the nightly hayride. You'll enjoy a memorable—if a bit bumpy—ride as well as a different perspective on this timeless island.

DAY 5

Morning

BREAKFAST: Enjoy the view and a leisurely meal before hitting the ferry and heading home. Don't forget to pick up some of that famous fudge!

THERE'S MORE

Freighter Watching. A free and fun pastime for the entire family is watching the many freighters from around the world that pass through the straits. Many freighter fans, much like bird-watchers, keep a log.

Gaming. Mission Point arranges nightly junkets to nearby Kewadin Casinos in St. Ignace and Sault Ste. Marie. You can take the 11:30 P.M. ferry back to the resort or plan to stop on your own once you leave the island.

Golf. The Mackinac Straits area has six championship courses, including one at the Grand Hotel. For more information, contact the Mackinac Island Chamber of Commerce at (906) 847–6418 or (800) 454–5227.

Horseback Riding. The back of a steed is another way to explore the island. Try Cindy's Riding Stable (906–847–3572) or Jack's Livery Stable (906–847–3391).

Sailing and Fishing. Sailing cruises with departures from Mackinac Island marina yield bountiful catches of king salmon, whitefish, perch, and chinook. Ask your hotel concierge about charters and other offerings.

SPECIAL EVENTS

June. Lilac Festival, Mackinac Island
  Mackinac Island Chamber Music Fest

July. Fireworks, Mackinac Island
  Chicago-to-Mackinac and Port Huron-to-Mackinac Yacht Races

August. Bike Races, Mackinac Island

September. Labor Day Bridge Walk, St. Ignace

OTHER RECOMMENDED RESTAURANTS

Mustang Lounge (Astor Street; 906–847–9916) is an island staple and a good spot for burgers and beer. Inexpensive to moderate.

Village Inn (Hoban Street; 906–847–3542) is a favorite watering hole for island natives and an excellent spot for cozy family dining. It's known for its steakburger, planked whitefish, and outdoor patio. Moderate.

Watersmeet (below the Lilac Tree Hotel; 906–847–3806) serves up tasty pastas, Mexican-inspired dishes, and salads, all with a great view. Moderate.

OTHER RECOMMENDED LODGINGS

The Chippewa Hotel (Main Street; Mackinac Island, MI 49757; 906–847–3341) has been an island landmark since 1902. It recently received a $2.5 million renovation, updating its guest rooms and doubling the size of its popular Pink Pony Bar & Grill. Accommodations are in thirty-five standard rooms and twenty-six waterfront suites, all with oak trim, marble, wicker, and brass. Rates: $145–$300 per night.

The Island House (800–626–6304 or 906–847–3347) has 97 rooms in a renovated four-story 1852 hotel across from the marina. The island's oldest hotel, it offers Victorian guest rooms and three two-bedroom suites with private veranda. There's also a new indoor pool as well as the respected Governor's Dining Room. Rates: $99–$400 per night.

Lilac Tree Hotel (906–847–6575) is a newer, all-suite hotel in the heart of downtown. Twelve rooms have Jacuzzis; all feature antiques and reproductions. The Lilac Tree is one of the few hotels to have winter packages. Rates: $145–$250 per night.

FOR MORE INFORMATION

Mackinac Island Chamber of Commerce, Mackinac Island, MI 49757; (906) 847–6418.

Leelanau County

MICHIGAN'S LITTLE FINGER

3 NIGHTS

Beaches • Restaurants • Shopping • Wineries

Whole books have been written about the Leelanau Peninsula, the area known as Michigan's Little Finger, located on the Lower Peninsula northwest of Traverse City. For many, Leelanau is "Up North" at its best, with 100 miles of Lake Michigan shoreline overlooked by sandy bluffs and challenging dunes, picturesque back roads full of fruit farms, beaches, and historic lighthouses as well as charming country towns, most of which still cater more to residents than tourists (the county didn't even get its first traffic light until 1991, a result of encroaching sprawl from Traverse City).

Summers can be a bit crowded, with tourists who are heading for the beaches or the casino clogging the main roads. Slip off to a back road, however, and you're virtually assured of solitude and scenery that's sure to take your breath away. Or consider a trip in the off-season, when the towns and the area's signature cherry orchards are blanketed in a shroud of snow. Whenever you come, you're sure to agree with the original Native American inhabitants, who named this peninsula *Leelanau*—"Land of Delight."

If you're looking for a longer stay, consider combining Leelanau County with Traverse City (Michigan Escape Three). Although geographically close to each other (it's just 30 miles from Traverse City to Suttons Bay in Leelanau County), each offers more than enough to fill a weekend—or longer.

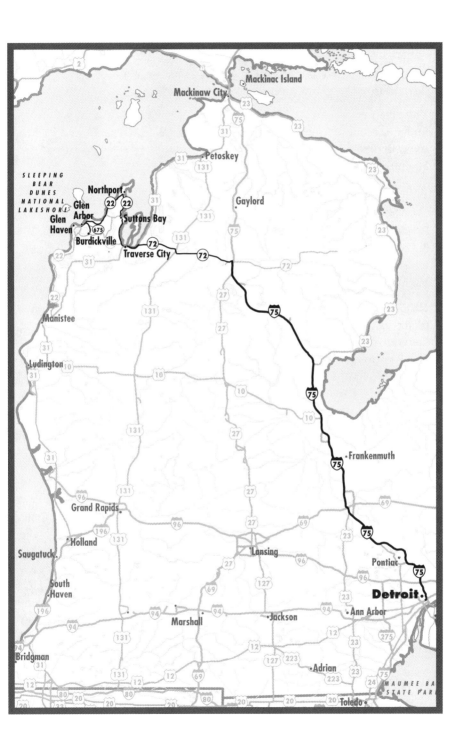

DAY 1

Morning

The peninsula is about 275 miles northwest of Detroit. Get an early start on Friday morning to beat the weekend gridlock on Interstate 75 and plan to arrive in time for a late lunch. To get to the peninsula, take I–75 north to State Highway M–72, then north on M–22 to Glen Arbor.

Afternoon

LUNCH: Poppycock's (128 East Front Street; Traverse City, MI 49636; 231–941–7632) is a good place to stop on your way to Leelanau. This colorful storefront restaurant has an innovative menu based on available fresh foods. Inexpensive to moderate.

LODGING: One of the many pleasures of the peninsula is its lack of anonymous chain hotels. The majority of rooms are in charming bed-and-breakfasts, upscale condominiums, or full-service resorts. One of the best places to stay in the area is the **Homestead** (Wood Ridge Road, Glen Arbor, MI 49636; 231–334–5000), with more than 300 spacious condo-like units and 1 mile of breathtaking Lake Michigan waterfront. Surrounded by the Sleeping Bear Dunes, the resort includes outdoor pools, water slide, clay tennis courts, and a noted golf academy as well as biking, hiking, and children's programs. Its central location makes exploring the rest of the peninsula easy. Rates start at $140 for a one-bedroom condo.

After checking in, you may choose to explore nearby Glen Arbor, just a few miles south on State Highway 22, or hang out on the Homestead's beautiful beach. Glen Arbor has just one main street, but it's full of intriguing shops such as **Leelanau Interiors** (231–334–4754), with interesting things for the home; the **Cottage Book Shop** (5970 South Lake Street, Glen Arbor, MI 49636; 231–334–4223), full of good reads; and the **Lake Street Studios** (5968 South Lake Street, Glen Arbor, MI 49636; 231–334–6112), which exhibits the work of local artists, including Suzanne Wilson. It also has one of three outpost galleries of area jewelry designer **Becky Thatcher** (5975 South Lake Street, Glen Arbor, MI 49636; 231–334–3826); the others are in Leland, Michigan, and Key West, Florida.

If you'd like a workout, you can rent mountain bikes at **Bear Bikes** (231–326–6100) or try your luck at canoes, kayaks, or tubes at **True North**

(231–334–3090). True North also stocks snacks and other goodies to fill your cooler.

DINNER: For a true culinary treat, take M–675 to nearby Burdickville, where you'll find **La Bécasse** (9001 South Dunns Farm Road, Burdickville, MI 49636; 231–334–3944). Home to fine French country fare, including cassoulet and bouillabaisse. It's expensive—but worth it.

DAY 2

Morning

BREAKFAST: Fuel up with a hearty breakfast in your condo at the Homestead or at the **Good Harbor Grill** (6584 Western Avenue, Glen Arbor, MI 49636; 231–334–3555). Good Harbor specializes in fresh and natural homemade fare made with local produce and whole grains. You won't go wrong with one of the three-egg omelettes, the vegetarian eggs Benedict, or the "Big Bear" breakfast—three eggs, bacon, sausage, and hash browns cooked in a skillet and topped with melted cheese. If you're looking for something a little lighter, try the multigrain pancakes or the maple-almond-crunch granola. Inexpensive to moderate.

You'll need that early-morning energy for your next stop: the **Sleeping Bear Dunes National Lakeshore** (9922 Front Street, Empire, MI 49630; 231–326–5734. The 70,000-acre park is just south of your hotel off State Highway 109. If you have kids, this will be the thing they'll tell their friends about when they get home. A masterpiece of ice, wind, and water, the dunes are named after a Chippewa Indian legend about a mother bear and her two bear cubs who attempted to cross Lake Michigan to escape a forest fire. The two cubs drowned and are today represented by the Manitou Islands. The massive Sleeping Bear dune represents where the mother waited for her offspring.

For a good overview of the park, stop at the handy Visitors Center operated by the National Park Service. A slide program, books, and free maps offer information about the dunes and their history. There's also a snack bar where you can get something to drink after your climb. Depending on how ambitious you are (and what kind of shape you're in), you may choose to climb the dunes or take the car on the 7.1-mile route known as the **Pierce Stocking Scenic Drive.** If you choose to use your oxygen power, you'll be rewarded with a great cardiovascular workout as well as a breathtaking view of Glen

The Sleeping Bear Dunes are a challenge even for the most physically fit.

Lake and the Manitou Islands. Choices for hikers range from the 130-foot **Dune Climb** (maybe they should have called it the "Dune Crawl") to the Dunes Trail, a 3.5-mile round trip, or the 2.8-mile walk to Sleeping Bear Point. Be forewarned: No water or shelter are provided, and it's easy for kids to get lost in the expanse of sand at the top. It's best to wear sturdy shoes and take a map and a canteen of water. A $7.50 admission fee per car gets you in to all the park attractions. Call (231) 334–2000 for more information.

If you prefer to drive, the scenic Pierce Stocking offers panoramic views of the dunes, Glen Lake, and Lake Michigan. It's open from mid-April through mid-November, weather permitting, and can get a little crowded on peak summer weekends. The route is also a breathtaking—if challenging—bike trail.

Afterward, stop at the **Coast Guard Maritime Museum** on Sleeping Bear Point in Glen Haven. The museum (included in park admission) recounts the region's maritime history and houses a replica of a Great Lakes steamer pilothouse, shipwreck artifacts, and other relics of the area's shipping past, including remains of boats that fell prey to Lake Michigan's legendary fury. Other things to do at the Dunes: Hike Pyramid Point off Port Oneida Road for a great vista of wind and water; seek out the views of Inspiration Point off the southwest side of Glen Lake; laze on the sand and take a dip in the clear but cold Lake Michigan at one of the beaches within the park, including **D. H. Day Park** in Glen Haven, North Bear Lake, and Good Harbor Bay; hike the Empire Bluffs off Wilco Road south of Empire and canoe along the Platte and Crystal Rivers, both within park boundaries. Crystal is a short, shallow river that's ideal for beginners or families with young children; the Platte is also gentle, while the Upper Platte is fast and for experienced canoers only. In winter, the park has 50 miles of marked cross-country ski trails.

Afternoon

LUNCH: If you're starving, stop at **Boone Docks** (5858 South Manitou Boulevard, Glen Arbor, MI 49636; 231–334–6464), where you can enjoy a rustic setting and homemade soups, sandwiches, and seafood. Try the patio if the weather permits, where live music is featured on summer weekends. Moderate. Otherwise, hold off until you get to Leland, about 25 miles up Highway 109.

The most famous eatery in Leland is the **Blue Bird** (102 River Road, Leland, MI 49636; 231–256–9081). This casual Northern Michigan institution is known for its huge cinnamon rolls as well as its homemade soups and Great Lakes whitefish. Moderate.

Leland is one of the peninsula's main tourist towns, with shops that range from tacky to trendy. If you're looking for some good beach reading, don't miss **Leelanau Books** (109 North Main Street, Leland, MI 49636; 231–256–7111), which was recently enlarged and stocks a wide selection of titles for both children and adults. Other shops along Main Street worth a look include **Tampico** (112 North Main Street, Leland, MI 49636; 231–256–7747), importers of Central American goods; **Ragamuffin** (113 North Main Street, Leland, MI 49636; 231–256–9675), with adorable and affordable clothes for kids; and **Becky Thatcher Designs** (110 North Lake Street, Leland, MI 49636; 231–256–2229), with high-quality Native American–inspired jewelry crafted of local materials such as the popular Petoskey stone. Farther down Main Street you'll find **Stone House Breads** (407 South

Main, Leland, MI 49636; 231–256–2577), owned and operated by Bob Pisor, whom Detroit-area TV watchers will remember from the Channel 4 news.

Leland is also home to **Fishtown,** set along Lake Michigan. Fishtown is a tad touristy for some tastes, but is worth a stop if only for its breathtaking location. Here old fishing shanties-turned-shops have been renovated to sell leatherworks, candy, baked goods, pottery, and a bevy of other merchandise.

DINNER: To escape the crowds downtown, head for the serenity of the **Leland Lodge** (565 Pearl Street, Leland, MI 49654; 231–256–9848). The Leland Room is a quiet New England–style spot that offers elegant dining with a great view overlooking the adjacent golf course and Leelanau valley. (There's also an adjacent lodge with hotel rooms and efficiency apartments.) Moderate to expensive.

DAY 3

Morning

BREAKFAST: Grab a bite at your hotel before setting off to explore. Today's itinerary includes tours of North Leelanau and the peninsula's other towns as well as a stop at the Native American–run casino near Suttons Bay.

From the Homestead you'll want to head north on Highway 22. You'll pass through Leland and can stop if you missed anything the day before. Otherwise, continue to Northport, a charming town at the tip of the peninsula. Resist the urge to stop and shop, however, until you've visited a few sites at the peninsula's tip. The drive alone is worth the trip, winding through beautiful countryside beside blue water.

Ready for a healthy snack? Stop at **Kilcherman's Christmas Cove Farm** (Christmas Cove Road/DeLong Road, off Route 201; 231–386–5637), just north of Northport, home to two-hundred varieties of apples. Many are historic varieties that date back as far as 1600. It's one of the few antique apple farms in the country.

Head another 3 miles north, and you'll find another not-to-be-missed attraction, the **Grand Traverse Lighthouse,** registered as a National and State Historic Site. The lighthouse is 5 miles north of the village of Northport in the 1,300-acre **Leelanau State Park** (231–386–7553). Visitors are free to roam the grounds and explore the buildings as well as climb to the top of the historic structure. From it you can see Charlevoix, a popular resort town that's some 77 miles away by car but just 17 miles by sea. Other favorite stops include Peterson Park, site of some of the peninsula's best sunsets, and the rocky yet scenic Northport Point.

Afternoon

LUNCH: Stubb's Sweetwater Grill (115 Waukazoo, Northport, MI 49670; 231–386–7611) is a casually elegant eatery that specializes in regional cuisine such as freshly prepared fish and local wines. Once a bar and grill, it was purchased a few years ago by two Culinary Institute of America graduates, who have transformed it into Northport's best restaurant. Moderate.

After lunch is the time to explore Northport. The tiny village nestles into the tip of the peninsula and remains much as it has for centuries, save for a few new shops and restaurants. Streets are lined with tidy homes and bed-and-breakfast inns; restaurants are casual and friendly. A few highlights include **Barb's Bakery** (112 North Mill Street, Northport, MI 49670; 231–386–5851), where you can grab a freshly baked pastry (try the doughy cinnamon twists) and some fresh coffee while chatting with the owner; **North Country Gardens** (6700 North Matheson Street, Northport, MI 49670; 231–386–5031), a large gift shop with unusual merchandise by local artists in a restored building (the building also is home to the local chamber of commerce, where you can pick up brochures and other information); and **Bird 'N' Hand Antiques** (123 East Nagonaba Street, Northport, MI 49670; 231–386–7104), which features vintage clothing and vintage-inspired millinery by owner-designer Barbara Pare (Northport also has seven other antiques stores). And if art's your thing, Northport is home to two worthwhile spaces: **Zoon Gallery** (122 West Nagonaba, Northport, MI 49670; 231–386–5937), featuring art and crafts by Cranbrook graduate Char Bickel that revolve around whimsical animal themes; and **Joppich's Bay Street Gallery** (109 North Rose, Northport, MI 49670; 231–386–7428), a seasonal spot that features local Michigan artists. A few steps away is the local marina, where you can ogle the sailboats from as far away as Florida and relax with an ice-cream cone from the nearby **Ship's Galley** at the public beach and park.

From Northport, head south on Highway 22 to **Suttons Bay.** Another popular resort town, Suttons Bay is the largest town on the peninsula's eastern shore. Originally called Suttonburg and Pleasant City, it was named after Harry C. Sutton, who came to the area in 1854 to clear the woods and supply fuel for wood-burning steamboats. By 1876 the town had grown, with three hotels that did a flourishing summer business and a number of shops (one, Bahle's Department Store, remains today and is run by the original family).

Suttons Bay is a pretty port town with good shopping and restaurants from family-style to fancy (the town's trademark red phone booths were imported from England to add a dash of color). It also has some of the peninsula's best shopping, with wearable art by local artists at the **Painted Bird** (216 St. Joseph Street; 231–271–3050); funky fashions at the **Lima Bean** (222 St. Joseph Street, Suttons Bay, MI 49682; 231–271–5462); and everything for the palate at **Bacchus and Brie,** with a wide selection of wines as well as pastas, cheeses, and coffees. Others also worth a stop include **Hats and Haberdashery** (310 St. Joseph Street, Suttons Bay, MI 49682; 231–271–5226), and the historic **Bahle's Department Store** (210 St. Joseph Street, Suttons Bay, MI 49682; 231–271–3841).

If the kids need to let off steam or you've a mind to take a dip, the city park and marina has an attractive sand beach and a playscape for kids. Want to take in a movie? Suttons Bay has one of the few cinemas on the peninsula, **The Bay Theater,** housed in a historic storefront (216 St. Joseph Street, Suttons Bay, MI 49682; 231–271–3772).

DINNER: Suttons Bay also has some of the most diverse dining on the peninsula. If you're feeling like splurging, there's no better place than **Hattie's** (111 St. Joseph Street, Suttons Bay, MI 49682; 231–271–6222), which serves up fine dining in a simple and elegant atmosphere of tiny, twinkling lights. Specialties include the unusual morel ravioli as well as grilled range hen with barbecue sauce, Thai-style scallops, and the signature dessert, Chocolate Paradise with Raspberries. Expensive.

If the kids are along, you might feel more at home at the casual **Boone's Prime Time Pub** across the street (102 St. Joseph Street, Suttons Bay, MI 49682; 231–271–6688), an outpost of the popular Boone's Long Lake Inn in Traverse City. It's known for its family dining, specializing in steaks, shrimp, and tasty sandwiches. Get here early or there will be a wait. Moderate.

Feeling lucky? After dinner you may want to head for the nearby **Leelanau Sands Casino** (2521 North West Bay Shore Drive [Highway 22], Suttons Bay, MI 49682; 888–951–8946). Owned and operated by the Grand Traverse Bay band of Chippewa Indians, the casino offers blackjack, craps, Caribbean stud poker, live keno, and 450 slot machines from 25 cents to $5.00. The casino is open seven days a week and is open until 3:00 A.M. nightly. (There's also a bingo palace, restaurant, and lodge.) You must be at least eighteen years old to enter and twenty-one to play craps, blackjack, and Caribbean stud poker.

DAY 4

Morning

BREAKFAST: The **Leelanau Country Inn** (149 East Harbor Highway, Lake Leelanau, MI 49653; 231–228–5060) is halfway between Glen Arbor and Leland off Highway 22. The 110-year-old inn has been cited as the area's best restaurant as well as the best Sunday brunch, with more than fifty homemade items, as well as the region's largest selection of locally produced wines. Reservations are always a good idea. Moderate. (In addition, there are four comfortable, country-style guest rooms, each hand-stenciled and a bargain at $50 to $65 per night.)

Oenophiles who have had a chance to taste the fruits of the area may want to use their final day to explore the wineries themselves. The Leelanau Peninsula and nearby Traverse City area are perfectly situated on the 45th parallel, halfway between the equator and the North Pole, and have rich soil as well as four distinct seasons. That makes it the perfect climate for growing and harvesting premium wine grapes. The region boasts seven renowned wineries, four of which are on the Leelanau Peninsula.

Boskydel Vineyards (7501 East Otto Road, Lake Leelanau, MI 49653; 231–256–7272) is owned by Bernie Rink, who began testing hybrid grape vines in 1965 and installed Leelanau County's first bonded wine cellar. Today it produces French-American hybrid grapes that combine French wine quality with disease-resistant American roots. The winery is best known for its Vignoles, Seyval Blanche and De Chaunac, Boskydel red, white, and rosé blends—and for its atmosphere, which is reminiscent of Germany's Rhine region and New York's Finger Lakes. It's off South Lake Leelanau Drive between State Highway 204 and County Road 633 and is open from 1:00 to 6:00 P.M. year-round for tours and tastings.

Good Harbor Vineyards (34 North Manitou Trail West, Leland, MI 49654; 231–256–7165) is known for its white grape varieties grown on the premises and aged in French oak barrels and stainless-steel vats. Favorites include Trillium, named after the ubiquitous local wildflower, Fishtown, and Northern Lights. Self-guided tours and tastings are available, as are the vineyard's acclaimed products, such as the 1991 Good Harbor Riesling. Located 3 miles south of Leland on M–22, behind the Manitou Farm Market; open from 11:00 A.M. to 5:00 P.M. during the week and noon to 6:00 P.M. weekends from May through October; call for November through April hours.

On the other side of the peninsula are the remaining two local wineries. **Leelanau Wine Cellars** (County Road 626 and Kalchik Road, Omena, MI 49674; 231–386–5201) is a 65,000-gallon winery that produces a full line of vinifera, hybrid, and fruit wines. Try the Vis-à-Vis or the Chardonnay. Tasting facilities are open daily year-round (call for hours) at the winery itself as well as in Empire and Leland.

L. Mawby Vineyards (4519 Elm Valley Road, Suttons Bay, MI 49682; 231–271–3522), the smallest of the local wineries, produces fewer than 3,000 cases of estate-grown table and méthode champenoise sparkling wines from their vineyards on the hills overlooking Suttons Bay. Wines are filtered only when necessary, creating a unique method for wines that mature and develop in the bottle. Worth noting are the 1996 Vignoles and the Cremant Brut NV. Tastings and sales are available from May through October, Thursday through Saturday from 1:00 to 6:00 P.M. or by appointment.

Whichever vineyard you visit and wine you choose, all make sweet reminders of your weekend in the Leelanau Peninsula to savor long after you've returned home.

THERE'S MORE

Canoes. The Crystal River Canoe Livery (6052 West Harbor Road, Glen Arbor, MI 49636; 231–334–3090) takes adults and children on two-and-one-half-hour excursions along the easy yet scenic Crystal River.

Golf. Northern Michigan abounds with excellent courses, including Grand Traverse Resort (800–748–0303) home to The Bear, one of the area's toughest courses; Crystal Mountain Resort (12500 Crystal Mountain Drive, Thompsonville; 800–968–7686), with twenty-seven holes; and Sugar Loaf Resort (800–968–0574), where a new Arnold Palmer course has opened. There are also a number of good public courses nearby, including Matheson Greens in Northport, Mistwood in Lake Ann, and Interlochen Golf Club..

Herbs. Busha's Brae Herb Farm (2540 North Setterbo Road, Suttons Bay, MI 49682; 231–271–6284) is a working herb farm that features a garden of biblical herbs, a Shakespearean garden, a cottage garden, and a production garden, all open to visitors. Teas and herbal luncheons plus a herbal newsletter and catalog are all available on request. Open May through December.

Sailing. Interested in learning more about the science of sailing? The Inland Seas Educational Association (ISEA) offers half-day, full-day, and overnight programs for all ages on board the *Inland Seas*. The association specializes in ecology, aquatic biology, family schoolship, and navigation programs and is based in Suttons Bay. For more information, contact ISEA, 101 Dame Street, Suttons Bay, MI 49682; (231) 271–3077.

If you're looking for something a little more relaxing, consider a three- or six-day Windjammer cruise (13390 Southwest Bay Shore Drive, Box 8, Traverse City, MI 49684; 800–968–8800) on the tall ship *Manitou*. Docked in Northport, it sails to Beaver Island, Harbor Springs, legendary Mackinac Island, and secluded islands and bays to view wildlife. It's the perfect add-on to a weekend getaway if you're looking to extend your trip.

SPECIAL EVENTS

July. Fireworks Celebration, Northport

Harbor Days, Northport

August. Annual Arts Festival, Suttons Bay

Leelanau Peninsula Wine Festival, Northport

OTHER RECOMMENDED RESTAURANTS

Leland

The Cove (111 River Street, Leland, MI 49654; 231–256–9834) is a local landmark that overlooks historic Fishtown. It's known for its signature Fishtown Stew as well as for its freshwater fish, burgers, and sandwiches. Open May through October. Moderate.

Fischer's Happy Hour Tavern (State Highway 22 between Leland and North-port, Leland, MI 49654; 231–386–9923) is an institution that specializes in good food, great service, and a family-friendly atmosphere. It's also one of the few places that's open seven days a week, year-round. Inexpensive to moderate.

Northport

Woody's Settling Inn (117 Waukazoo Street, Northport, MI 49670; 231–386–9933) is a casual, family-style bar and restaurant that's open year-round and known for its cherry-smoked chicken, nachos, and fresh fish. In summer, lunch and appetizers can be eaten on the patio that overlooks downtown Northport. Moderate.

Suttons Bay

Cafe Bliss (420 St. Joseph Street, Suttons Bay, MI 49682; 231–271–5000) serves up vegetarian and ethnic-inspired cuisine in a gray, turn-of-the-century home on the outskirts of town. Moderate.

OTHER RECOMMENDED LODGINGS

Cedar

Sugar Loaf Resort (4500 Sugar Loaf Mountain Road, Cedar, MI 49621; 231–228–5461 or 800–952–6390) is the largest resort on the peninsula, with more than 500 hotel rooms, townhouses, and luxury condos. It also features free golf packages, an all-grass miniature golf course, scenic chair-lift rides (it's also a popular winter destination), and an Arnold Palmer–designed golf course. Rates: $125–$175.

Maple City

Leelanau Country Inn (M–22 south of Leland, Maple City, MI 49664; 231–228–5060) has six rooms in a historic 104-year-old inn between Glen Arbor and Leland. Summer rates start at $55–$65 per night.

Omena

Omena Shores B&B (13140 Isthmus Road, Omena, MI 49674, P.O. Box 154; 231–386–7313) is a lovingly restored 1850s barn full of antiques, wicker, and handmade quilts. Rates: $75–$95 per night.

Suttons Bay

Open Windows B&B (613 St. Mary's Avenue, Suttons Bay, MI 49682; 231–271–4300) is a century-old home with three guest rooms near downtown

Suttons Bay. Room rates ($75–$100) include homemade breakfast served on the porch or in the kitchen.

For more accommodations, see Traverse City (Michigan Escape Three). Snowbird Inn B&B (473 North Manitou Trail West, Suttons Bay, MI 49682; 231–256–9773); Aspen House (1353 North Manitou Trail West, Suttons Bay, MI 49682; 231–762–7736); and Manitou Manor (M–22 West, Suttons Bay, MI 49682; 231–256–7712) are all good bed-and-breakfast choices nearby.

FOR MORE INFORMATION

Traverse City Convention and Visitors Bureau, 101 West Grandview Parkway, Traverse City, MI 49684-2252; (800) 872–8377.

Traverse City

LIFE IS JUST A BOWL OF CHERRIES

3 NIGHTS

Shopping • Sun and Sand • Restaurants • Skiing • Sailing

If Northern Michigan had a capital, it would be Traverse City. The city is the largest in the northern part of the state, and among the most popular with visitors. Besides Florida, this is where downstaters dream of retiring or opening an antiques shop or bed-and-breakfast. Purists claim the city's original charm has been lost to excessive development, but most visitors find Traverse City to be a delightful mix of small-town friendliness and big-city amenities.

The area earned its name from the early French fur trappers. Traveling by canoe across the stretch of open water between the tip of the Leelanau Peninsula and Charlevoix, they would call their venture *la grande traverse,* or "the great crossing." Thus the area became known as Grand Traverse Bay. Lumbermen followed the fur traders, tapping the area's rich resources. Lumbering thrived into the early 1990s, when two other industries—cherry farming and tourism—began to flourish. Both continue to influence the local economy today.

Strategically located at the head of Grand Traverse Bay, Traverse City is also known as the Cherry Capital of the World, and a huge, eight-day festival celebrates the harvest each July. Many of those cherries are grown on the Old Mission Peninsula, where a number of the vineyards are also located.

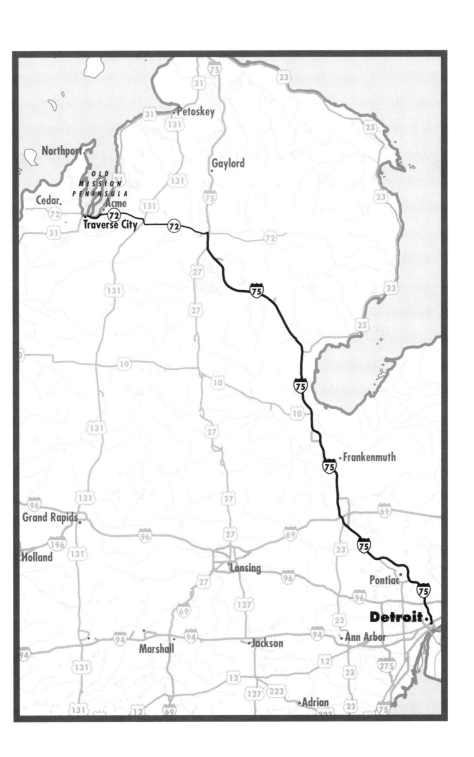

DAY 1

Afternoon

Hit the road in the morning and plan to be in town in time for a late lunch. Traverse City is about a four-hour drive northwest of Detroit. To get there, take Interstate 75 north and exit near Grayling onto State Highway 72, which heads west directly into Traverse City.

LUNCH: One of the best places for lunch is **Cousin Jenny's Cornish Pasties** (129 South Union Street, Traverse City, MI 49686; 231–941–7821), a cozy downtown eatery that serves seven varieties of pasties as well as homemade soups, salads, and scones. Inexpensive.

Spend the afternoon getting your bearings and exploring the nearby downtown. When it's time for dinner, treat yourself to something special.

DINNER: Windows (7677 West Bay Shore Drive, Traverse City, MI 49686; 231–941–0100) is considered by many to be the city's best restaurant. With gourmet French-American cuisine and daily specials, it's a Northern Michigan must. Expensive.

LODGING: Bayshore Resort (833 East Front Street, Traverse City, MI 49686; 231–935–4400 or 800–634–4401) manages to be both elegant and convenient to nearby downtown. (It's also the state's only smoke-free lodging.) The 120 rooms are classically decorated in taupe stripes with rose and teal accents and antique reproduction furniture. Some have a whirlpool bath and/or fireplace. There are also a sugar sand beach, a large indoor pool, and a fitness area. *Tip:* Kids love the rooms on the ground floor that lead directly onto the beach. Rates: $100–$195 per night.

DAY 2

Morning

BREAKFAST: One of the nicest things about a stay at Bayshore is its continental breakfast, served from 6:00 to 10:00 A.M. in a spacious room near the lobby. More than just coffee and a doughnut, it includes self-serve yogurt, fresh fruit, juices, cereals, and your choice of breads and pastries.

After breakfast it's time to wander downtown and start exploring. The compact central city is just a few blocks from your hotel and is lined with well-maintained nineteenth- and early twentieth-century storefronts, where you'll find more than one hundred shops, from fashionable to funky. Be sure to stop at **Horizon Books** (243 Front Street, Traverse City, MI 49684; 231–946–7290), housed in a former J. C. Penney store and considered by bibliophiles to be among the best bookstores in the state. It was also one of the first to have its own in-house coffee bar. Not far away is the **Opera House** on Front Street, a Victorian landmark built in 1891 and one of just eighteen opera houses left in the state. It's still used for occasional concerts and is open for tours by appointment. Call (231) 922–2070.

Other stores worth exploring include **Cali's Cottons** (242 East Front Street, Traverse City, MI 49684; 231–947–0633), where owner, Alison Knowles, stocks comfy 100 percent cotton clothing; **Dandelion** (130 East Front Street, Traverse City, MI 49684; 231–933–4340), known for its adorable and unusual selection of duds for kids; and the **Firehouse Fair** (118 Cass Street, Traverse City, MI 49684; 231–935–4442), which is housed in a former firehouse and stocks a wide assortment of interesting gifts and goodies. Not far away is **Wilson's Antiques** (231–946–4177), near Cousin Jenny's on Union Street, where more than fifty dealers set up shop in booths that are filled with just about every kind of collectible imaginable. If you're looking for souvenirs for the folks back home, don't miss **American Spoon Foods** (231–935–4480), also on Front Street. It's a Northern Michigan institution with a national reputation for its gourmet jams, jellies, and foodstuffs, including a few unusual selections such as cherry salsa and cherry hot pepper jelly. Chocoholics may also want to take home a few of the edibles from **Kilwin's Chocolates** (129 East Front Street, Traverse City, MI 49684; 231–946–2403) as a sweet reminder of a Traverse City stay.

Afternoon

LUNCH: Poppycock's (128 East Front Street, Traverse City, MI 49684; 231–941–7632) is a delightful restaurant in the heart of downtown. Lunch selections include an excellent Front Street Salad (greens, grilled chicken breast, sun-dried cherries, fresh goat cheese, sprouts, and pecans) as well as sandwiches (try the herb-crusted whitefish or the Portabella mushroom stack) and pastas (Poppycock's marinara is made with sun-dried tomatoes, pine nuts, feta cheese, and marinara sauce over whole-wheat fettuccine). Moderate.

After lunch it's time to take in some of the other attractions. One you won't want to miss is the **Dennos Museum Center** (1701 East Front Street, Traverse City, MI 49684; 231–922–1055), not far from your hotel. Part of

Northwestern Michigan University, it's devoted to the hands-on exploration of science, art, and technology. Three changing galleries house temporary and traveling exhibitions. The museum is best known, however, for its spectacular collection of contemporary Eskimo art, one of the best in the country. Here you'll find more than 550 pieces of sculpted soapstone and prints depicting the culture of these fascinating Arctic people in a permanent space known as Inuit Art Gallery. In summer, the museum is also home to the Michigan Ensemble Theater, which performs in the auditorium.

Another local favorite away from downtown is the **Music House** (7377 U.S. Highway 31 North, Acme, MI 49610; 231–938–9300), a "performing museum" of beautifully restored and rare antique musical instruments in an authentic turn-of-the-century decor. The unusual museum features everything from tiny music boxes to a seventy-year-old hand-carved Belgian dance organ. While there, you can trace the history of sound reproduction in the phonograph and radio galleries, listen to a huge Regina Corona Music Box, even sip a soda to the tunes of the Nickelodeons at the in-house Hurry Back Saloon. Open May through October.

DINNER: Head back downtown to catch one of the newest attractions, the **Grand Traverse Dinner Train** (Eighth Street and Woodmere Street, Traverse City, MI 49684; 231–933–3768 for reservations). It winds its way along a 33-mile track, giving diners an incredible view of the bay and the surrounding landscape. Romantic meals are their specialty, served on four 1950s-vintage dining cars that once ran between New Orleans and Los Angeles. The five-course meal costs $55–$62 per person, depending on the season. It's worth the price for appetizers such as smoked salmon pâté, changing soups such as cream of wild morels, and your choice of four entrees, including garlic-roasted prime rib, farm-raised rainbow trout with Château Grand Traverse pan sauce and herb-scented orzo, breast of chicken stuffed with smoked duck and apples, or tri-color pasta with roast vegetable stuffing. Expensive.

If you still haven't had enough of the bay and you'd sooner go by schooner, consider a sail on the **tall ship** *Malabar* (13390 West Bay Shore Drive, Traverse City, MI 49686; 231–941–2000 or 800–678–0383). It's an authentic replica of an eighteenth-century topsail gaff-rigged sailing vessel, with more than 105 feet of pure sailing pleasure. It sails three times daily between late May and early October. Choose a noon sail with a picnic meal, an afternoon sail, or a breathtaking sunset sail with a picnic meal. Reservations are required.

Cherry trees blanket the Traverse City area, and their fruits make popular souvenirs.

DAY 3

Morning

BREAKFAST: If you're looking for something heartier with which to start the day, **Mabel's** (472 Munson Street; Traverse City, MI 49686; 231–947–0252) has raked in the *Traverse Magazine* awards, from "Best Breakfasts" and "Northern Michigan's Top Ten Restaurants" to "Best Place to Bring Kids." The huge morning meals (served all day) include overstuffed omelettes, thick slabs of home-baked French toast, and more. Pick up a few of the famous sticky buns on the way out. Inexpensive. Mabel's is about a half mile from your hotel.

Traverse City is known for its vineyards and its cherries, both of which dominate the scenic Old Mission Peninsula. No visit would be complete without exploring this thin, 18-mile-long spit of land that bisects Grand Traverse Bay. Its hilly topography and rich soil are among some of the finest in the country for growing cherries and grapes, with the bay moderating temperatures and preventing the early spring warming that endangers fruit buds.

Today the western shore is a fashionable address for Traverse City residents. The east shore is less crowded and more scenic. For spectacular vistas and panoramic views, follow State Highway 37 as well as East Shore Road, Bluff Road, and Smokey Hollow Road.

LUNCH: The **Bluewater Bistro** (14039 Peninsula Drive, Traverse City, MI 49686; 231–223–4030) is a clean-lined, nautical-flavored eatery with a spectacular Bowers Harbor marina setting on Old Mission Peninsula. The food is equally good—with a wide range of fare from burgers and salads to innovative daily specials, including fish and pastas. The restaurant's signature popovers come with all meals. Open just two years, the restaurant has recently been discovered and can get crowded on weekends. Reservations are always a good idea. Moderate.

Afternoon

Château Grand Traverse (12239 Center Road, Traverse City, MI 49686; 231–223–7355 or 800–283–0247) is the first winery you'll encounter on the Old Mission Peninsula. Owned by the O'Keefe family since 1974, it's approximately 8 miles from downtown Traverse City along Center Road (Highway 37). With panoramic views of both East and West Grand Traverse Bays, Northern Michigan's largest winery sits on more than 140 acres planted with grapes. An inviting and newly expanded tasting room allows visitors to sample the fruits of the vineyard in a French wine-bar atmosphere. Standouts include the Johannesburg Riesling and the impressive Ice Wine (don't forget to ask how it's made).

Another family-owned winery is **Bowers Harbor Vineyards** (2896 Bowers Harbor Road, Traverse City, MI 49686; 231–223–7615), some 9 miles outside Traverse City. The first thing you'll notice as you approach is the spectacular view of the small hamlet of Bowers Harbor. Owners Jack and Linda Stegenga got into wine making after abandoning careers raising Hereford cows. Today, their small winery is known for its sparkling Riesling Brut, a light and lively fruity wine, as well as for the Chardonnay and the Shiraz.

The newest kid on the block is **Peninsula Cellars** (18250 Mission Road, Traverse City, MI 49686; 231–223–4310), founded in 1994. Located in the village of Old Mission, it has just 4 acres of grapes planted among 180 acres of cherry trees. Winemaker Lee Lutes honed his skills at a Long Island winery and a vineyard in Northern Italy. A Michigan native, he returned a few years ago to help owners Dave and Joan Kroupa get the winery on its feet. Old Mission Cellars is considered a "boutique" winery, with just five wines: two white, one red, and two fruit wines. Try the Chardonnay, the Riesling, or the cherry and apple wines, considered the best in the area.

The most romantic of the vineyards, hands down, is **Château Chantal** (15900 Rue du Vin, Old Mission, MI 49686; 231–223–4110 or 800–969–4009), also a favorite spot for weddings. About 12 miles north of Traverse City on 65 acres overlooking both the east and west bays, this winery began developing its vineyards in 1983 and opened its elegant tasting room and facility ten years later. Named after the owners' daughter, Chantal, it produces wonderful chardonnay, Riesling, pinot noir, and merlot wines. It's open for tastings daily and is the site of a popular Jazz at Sunset series on Friday nights. The chateau is also a bed-and-breakfast, with three wonderful and well-priced rooms overlooking the vineyards and the surrounding countryside. Not surprisingly, guests are encouraged to sip wine and watch the sun set from the chateau's charming patio.

If you're more interested in vintage lighthouses than vineyards, **Old Mission Point and Light** dates to 1870. The original frame keeper's dwelling is still here, as is a pretty beach with good swimming. Across the way you can see Omena on the Leelanau Peninsula and Eastport on Torch Lake. Also worth a visit is the **Old Mission Church,** off Old Mission Road in the hamlet of Old Mission. The church is a replica of a house of worship built in 1839 by a Presbyterian missionary to the Chippewa Indians. The information-packed historical displays are a product of the Old Mission Women's Club, a group of enthusiastic volunteers.

DINNER: After a tour of the vineyards, you'll want to stay on the peninsula and dine at the **Bowers Harbor Inn** (13512 Peninsula Drive, Old Mission Peninsula, Traverse City, MI 49686; 231–223–4222). Many foodies consider this the most romantic eatery in the area, as much for its spectacular view and vintage summer-house setting as for the fine food. The drive along the West Bay to the restaurant alone is worth the trip even if the food weren't good. But it is. Specialties include Fish-in-a-Bag. If you prefer to go casual, the adjacent Bowery serves ribs, rotisserie chicken, and great burgers. Moderate to expensive.

MICHIGAN

DAY 4

Morning

BRUNCH: Park Place Hotel (300 East State Street, Traverse City, MI 49684; 231–946–5000) is known to serve the area's best brunch. It includes both breakfast and lunch items—from cold boiled shrimp to savory pasta salads and freshly baked breakfast items—for under $16. Moderate.

If you've brought the kids, Sunday is a great day to take in the **Clinch Park Zoo** (231–922–4904). Its location along the waterfront makes it one of the prettiest zoos in the country. The tiny zoo specializes in animals that would be found in the woods around Traverse City, including a black bear mom and two adorable cubs, a repetitive crow, playful beavers, otters, and turtles as well as the more ominous coyote, wolf, and bison. Don't miss the chance to take the mini-locomotive for a roundabout view of the bay and beyond. Afterward, if weather permits, laze awhile on the adjacent Clinch Park Beach, one of the city's most popular. The zoo is open daily from April through November. Admission is $2.00 for adults; $1.50 for children ages five through thirteen; free for children under five.

Afterward, you may want to head back downtown to explore anything you missed or spend the rest of the day lazing around the beach before hitting the freeway and heading home. Another option is to head to **Interlochen Center for the Arts,** where music has charms that will soothe the savage breast. The renowned music school has more than 200 performances each year by students, faculty, and big-name entertainers. From outdoor concerts in the open-air pavilion overlooking Green Lake to campus concerts by summer student campers, Interlochen offers a taste of the arts. For ticket information, call (231) 276–7200.

THERE'S MORE

Alden. *National Geographic* called Torch Lake one of the most beautiful lakes in the world. This clear but cold lake is home to great fishing and water sports, as well as to the tiny town of Alden, which is among the state's most charming. Spencer Creek (9166 Helena Street, Alden, MI 49684; 231–331–6147) is a gourmet restaurant on the town's main street, with spectacular sunsets over the lake and fine regional cuisine. Alden is also home to a couple of excellent antiques shops and Talponia Books, one of the most unusual used-book stores in the state, where you'll find vintage beach reading side by side with collectible first editions.

Apples. Amon Orchards (8066 U.S. Highway 31 North, Williamsburg; 231–938–9160) is a family-owned and run fruit farm that's a favorite of family visitors. Trolley tours of the orchards, a farmer's market, and a petting zoo are among the many attractions.

Balloon Rides. You won't need eighty days to get a great view of Traverse City and the Old Mission Peninsula. Spectacular sights are daily fare at Grand Traverse Balloons (225 Cross Country Trail, Traverse City, MI 49686; 231–947–7433), which offers airborne tours in multicolored, seven-story-tall hot-air balloons. Flights are offered at sunrise and sunset, last one hour, and are followed by champagne celebrations.

Golf. The Traverse City area has more than twenty excellent courses on which to tee off. Highlights include A-Ga-Ming in Kewadin (800–678–0122); the Bear and Spruce Run at Grand Traverse Resort in Acme (800–748–0303); High Point Golf Club in Williamsburg (800–753–7888); Mistwood Golf Course in Lake Ann (231–275–5500); and the Legend at Schuss Mountain/Shanty Creek in Bellaire (800–678–4111). For more information, contact the course directly or the Traverse City Convention and Visitors Bureau at (800) 872–8377.

Parasailing. Feeling ambitious? A number of companies take visitors high in the sky on parasailing adventures. Grand Traverse Parasail (231–947–3938) is docked at Bay Winds Restaurant and sails from 11:00 A.M. to sunset in season.

Shopping Outlets. Caught the outlet fever? Horizon Outlets (3639 Marketplace Circle, Traverse City, MI 49686; 231–941–9211) includes more than 40 shops featuring deals and discounted goods. Among the best is the Eddie Bauer outlet, which has great "Up North" resort and casual clothing that you'll wear long after you return home.

SPECIAL EVENTS

May. Blossom Days, Old Mission Peninsula

June. Bay Day, Traverse City

July. Fireworks, Traverse City

Fireworks, Traverse City

National Cherry Festival, Traverse City

Outdoor Art Fair, Traverse City

OTHER RECOMMENDED RESTAURANTS

Old Mission Peninsula

Old Mission Tavern (17015 Center Road, Old Mission Peninsula, Traverse City, 49686; 231–223–7280) serves classic cuisine from Greece, Italy, France, and Poland. Diners flock here for the pierogies served on Thursday and the leg of lamb served on Sunday. Moderate.

Traverse City

Don's Drive Inn (2030 U.S. Highway 31 North, Traverse City, MI 49684; 231–938–1860) is the place for classic-style burgers, fries, and shakes. Inexpensive.

Omelette Shop. Another great choice for breakfast, it's a frequent winner of the "Best Breakfast" category in the *Traverse Magazine*'s reader polls. Two locations: 1209 East Front Street, Traverse City, MI 49684; (231–946–0590), in a strip mall near the Bay Shore Hotel, or 124 Cass Street, Traverse City, MI 49684 (231–946–0912), downtown. Inexpensive.

Schelde's (714 Munson Avenue, Traverse City, MI 49684; 231–946–0981) is known for its family-friendly menu and service. The all-you-can-eat salad bar is a favorite here and at other Schelde's restaurants across the state. Inexpensive to moderate.

Scott's Harbor Grill (12719 South West Bay Shore Drive, Traverse City, MI 49684; 231–922–2114) has one of the best views and patio dining that fills up quickly. The restaurant offers a wide range of salads, sandwiches, and entrees as well as daily specials. Moderate.

Sleder's Family Tavern (717 Randolph, Traverse City, MI 49684; 231–947–9213) is the state's oldest tavern (est. 1882) and well known for its buffalo burgers and Mexican entrees. Moderate.

OTHER RECOMMENDED LODGINGS

Acme

Grand Traverse Resort & Spa (100 Grand Traverse Village Boulevard, Acme, MI 49610; 800–678–1308) has 750 rooms, suites, and condos as well as ten restaurants, lounges, and a shopping gallery. Rates: $115–$325 per night.

Cedar

Sugar Loaf Resort (4500 Sugar Loaf Mountain Road, Cedar, MI 49621; 800–952–6390) is a good choice in winter because of its on-site skiing. In addition to hotel rooms, there are studios and condos. Rates: $115–$175.

Traverse City

Holiday Inn (615 East Front Street, Traverse City, MI 49686; 231–947–3700 or 800–888–8020) is recently renovated and a favorite family spot where kids eat free. Two blocks from downtown, it has 179 rooms on West Bay. Rates: $95–$175 per night.

Park Place Hotel (300 East State Street, Traverse City, MI 49684; 231–946–5000 or 800–748–0133) is the city's only multi-storied hotel right in the heart of downtown. Rates: $125–$165 per night.

Pointes North Inn (2211 U.S. Highway 31 North, Traverse City, MI 49684; 231–938–9191 or 800–968–3422) has fifty-two luxury suites on 300 feet of sandy beach on East Bay. All rooms have water views, with private balcony, Jacuzzi, microwave, refrigerator, and VCR. This is a great spot for families. Rates: $135–$150 per night.

FOR MORE INFORMATION

Traverse City Convention and Visitors Bureau, 101 West Grandview Parkway, Traverse City, MI 49684; (231) 947–1120 or (800) 872–8377.

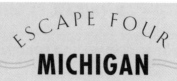
Petoskey/Harbor Springs

PAPA'S PLACE

2 NIGHTS

Shopping • Golf • Arts • History • Nature

Don't wait too long to discover the vintage charms of Petoskey; not long ago the National Trust for Historic Preservation named the city to its list of the top ten endangered places in the United States. Faced with a new Wal-Mart and the suburban sprawl that has transformed Traverse City, many fear that one of the state's most charming areas will be lost.

Long a favorite of travelers, Petoskey and neighboring Harbor Springs became famous in the latter half of the nineteenth century, when they were established as summer resorts. (Settled originally by the Ottawa and Chippewa Indians, Petoskey was named after Ottawa chief Pe-to-se-ga.) Petoskey became the choice of families who found its clean air and relaxed pace a welcome change from the harried city. Harbor Springs, on the north side of Little Traverse Bay, became famous for its excellent harbor and a regular stopping place for large passenger ships (passage to Petoskey from Chicago once went for $15 round-trip). The area's natural beauty also attracted wealthy midwestern families, including the Fords, Upjohns, Gambles (of Proctor & Gamble), and Offields (Wrigley's gum), who built grand homes around the bay in neighboring Wequetonsing and Harbor Point. Attracted, too, was the family of Ernest Hemingway, possibly the most famous summer resident.

Emmet County's two largest towns face each other across Little Traverse Bay and are just 9 miles apart via State Highway 119. Both towns have survived and continue to flourish today as summer resorts. The population swells in warm weather, but the area attracts visitors year-round. Scenic back roads

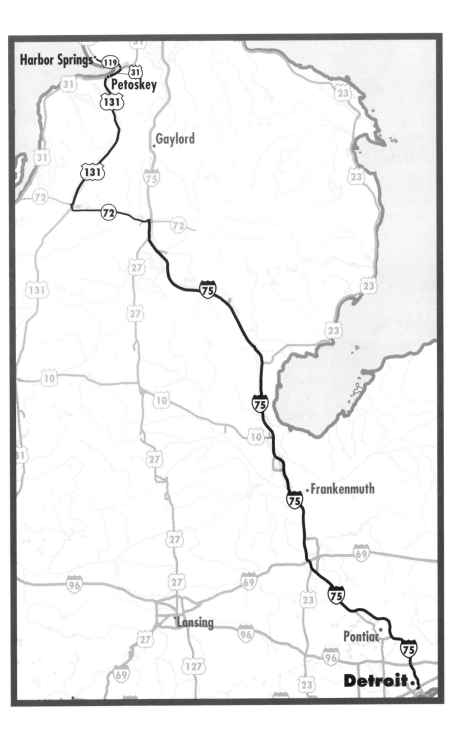

blaze with color in autumn and nearby Boyne Mountain and Boyne Highlands, two of the state's best downhill ski resorts, attract thousands of winter sports enthusiasts.

DAY 1

Morning

Petoskey is approximately 260 miles north of Detroit. To ensure enough time to enjoy the weekend, take Friday off and plan on an early start to beat the midafternoon traffic along north Interstate 75. Take I–75 to State Highway 72 west to U.S. 131 North. U.S. 131 goes right into Petoskey. Plan to be in town early enough for a late lunch and a round of afternoon shopping. With more than seventy historic shops in a six-block area, downtown Petoskey offers a great escape from the mall maul.

Afternoon

LUNCH: Roast and Toast (309 East Lake Street, Petoskey, MI 49770; 231–347–7767) is a fun spot in the middle of downtown that specializes in simply prepared healthy food. *Traverse Magazine* named it one of the top ten places in Northern Michigan for lunch and one of the top three places for great coffee (they roast their own daily). It lives up to its many accolades, with two or three savory soups (try the great tomato-herb minestrone), a full-fledged deli menu, and fresh salads such as the grilled chicken Caesar or the tasty romaine with pecans, blue cheese, and vinaigrette. All baked goods are made fresh daily. Inexpensive.

Petoskey's downtown shopping area is known as the **Gaslight District** and is nationally recognized for its unusual and distinctive boutiques. With decorative nineteenth-century storefronts and vintage gas lamps, they're grouped along a few main streets and are an easy and enjoyable stroll. Some of the exclusive clothing, gift, and jewelry shops are open year-round; others are summer only and move south to West Palm Beach or Naples, Florida, during the long Michigan winter.

If you're interested in the area's fascinating history, head for **McLean & Eakin Books** (307 East Lake Street, Petoskey, MI 49770; 231–347–1180), the city's (and some say the state's) best bookstore. In an era of supermarket–style chains, it's fiercely independent and devoted to remaining so. An armchair in the window is often occupied by the shop's amiable cat or by captivated readers, who head here for the best in children's literature, local and regional publications (there's a great selection of Hemingway's Michigan works and books by native son Bruce Catton), and more.

A few steps away is **Arktos** (315 East Lake Street), a fine-arts studio and gallery that features charming and colorful art with an animal theme. More art by Michiganians is featured at **Made in Michigan** (311 East Lake), which has more than one hundred items by local craftspeople, including note cards by Gwen Frostic, porcupine quill boxes, Petoskey stone jewelry, and more.

Not a shopper? Downtown also holds charms for history buffs and Hemingway devotees, who will want to stop by one of the local stores and pick up a copy of the city's "Walking Tour" brochure, which includes background on the vintage storefronts as well as a history of former inhabitants and owners, both famous and otherwise. Shoppers, foodies, and just about everyone else appreciates **Symon's General Store** (401 East Lake Street, Petoskey, MI 49770; 231–347–2438), built in 1879. It ranks as one of the city's oldest buildings and today stocks fresh coffees and other gourmet goodies. The front steps are also a good resting place when you need a break.

More history (and more Hemingway) can be found at the city's charming **Little Traverse Historical Society and Museum** (100 Depot Court, Petoskey, MI 49770; 231–347–2620), housed in an 1892 railroad depot in Bayfront Park just steps from downtown. Within the museum's glass showcases are reminders of Ernest Hemingway's time in Northern Michigan (his family had a cottage at nearby Walloon Lake), including Christmas cards, rare first editions, family photos, and even the kerosene lamp he wrote by on dark country nights. Don't miss the informative forty-five-minute video that traces the Hemingway sites in the area. It's beautifully photographed and well worth watching as a primer and basic local history lesson. Many of the sites still remain—including the Staffords Perry Hotel, your base for the weekend. The museum is an interesting and worthwhile stop even if you're not a "Papa" fan.

Also worth a trip is the city's **Virginia McCune Arts Center** (461 East Mitchell Street, Petoskey, MI 49770; 231–347–4337), which has two exhibition galleries, works by local artists, and a tempting gift shop. The excellent Crooked Tree Arts Council has its offices and its annual juried show here. If you're looking for a break, the city's **Waterfront Park** has a pond, a 35-foot waterfall, and a public wheelway that links all the waterfront along Little Traverse Bay. It's a favorite of hikers, bikers, and Rollerbladers.

If you prefer to use a little horsepower instead of your own energy, consider a ride in one of the city's horse-drawn carriages. Tours are offered weekends from mid-June through Labor Day and take in the city's Gaslight District. Call (231) 347–7301 for a schedule and prices.

DINNER: Andante (321 Bay Street, Petoskey, MI 49770; 231–348–3321) is considered by many to be the city's best restaurant as well as one of the top eateries in all Northern Michigan. Classical music and Impressionist paintings fill the elegant dining room, in an unpretentious house at the edge of downtown. The fare is equally impressive, including dishes such as butternut squash bisque, whitefish baked in a potato crust and served with wasabi beurre blanc, and quail medallions marinated in chardonnay with junipers. It also has a great wine list. Expensive.

LODGING: Hemingway once stayed at the **Stafford's Perry Hotel** (Bay at Lewis, Petoskey, MI 49770; 231–347–4000) for 75 cents per night. Advertised as the only fireproof hotel at the turn of the century, it's the only original resort hotel still operating in town. Today the yellow brick structure (now called Stafford's Perry) is a little more expensive but still retains the charm that Hemingway enjoyed in the 1920s. The city's first brick hotel, it has been a landmark since 1899 and is known for its attentive service as well as its convenient downtown location. The eighty rooms and three suites are spacious and well-decorated with painted furniture (some original to the hotel), deep colors, and vintage wallpaper. Rates range from $80 to $200.

DAY 2

Morning

BREAKFAST: The **Flap Jack Shack** (314 West Mitchell Street, Petoskey, MI 49770; 231–347–1260) is a no-frills eatery (one of two in Northern Michigan) known for its amazing variety of pancakes—including buttermilk, silver dollar, blueberry, Alaskan sourdough, and buckwheat—as well as for other specialties such as multi-grain cinnamon cakes, pigs in a blanket, or a flapjack sandwich. Try the sampler plate (two pancakes of each variety), the blintzes, or the French rolled pecan cakes. Inexpensive.

After breakfast, jump on U.S. Highway 31 North to State Highway 119 into Harbor Springs. Along the way, stop at **Petoskey State Park** (800–543–2937) to hunt for Petoskey stones, the state stone. First-time visitors are often surprised to see people strolling the beach with heads bowed, hoping to find these prized pieces of fossilized coral. The stones are thought to be at least 350 million years old. (If you're out of luck, they're also sold as souvenirs and jewelry in town.) The park is blessedly peaceful, even in the heat of summer, and is a great place to wander the beach, enjoy an early picnic lunch, or take a dip in the bracing waters of Lake Michigan.

Afternoon

LUNCH: Juilleret's (131 State Street, Harbor Springs, Petoskey, MI 49740; 231–526–2821) has been in the Juilleret family for five generations and is the oldest family-run restaurant in the state. Originally an ice-cream parlor, it served briefly as a dance hall during Prohibition. Since 1960 it has been better known for its homemade ice cream than its hooch. Besides the ice cream, Juilleret's offers three meals daily. Specialties include the planked whitefish, homemade soups, and the famous "Velvet"—a silky concoction of ice cream, marshmallow, and bittersweet chocolate. Open in season only. Inexpensive.

Although close to Petoskey geographically, Harbor Springs seems like another world. Founded by the Jesuits and once called *L'Arbre Croche* (Crooked Tree), it thrived as a lumber town from 1880 to 1920. The **Ephraim Shay House** (396 East Main Street, Petoskey, MI 49740; 231–526–8966) dates from this period and is the former home of the inventor of the Shay locomotive. The 1891 house is sheathed entirely in embossed metal and is open only in summer.

Today's Harbor Springs caters to a decidedly affluent crowd, with its main draw being a Main Street full of antiques shops, art galleries, and exclusive boutiques filled with designer resort wear and home accessories. Redoing your decor? Pick up a few ideas along with some rustic-inspired furnishings at **Cedar Creek Interiors** (275 East Main Street, Petoskey, MI 49740; 231–526–9026). If you're looking for a more personal transformation, pick up something fun and funky at one of the many interesting clothing and accessories stores along Main Street.

If antiques are your thing, you'll be in heaven in Harbor Springs. **Elliot & Elliott** (292 East Third Street, Petoskey, MI 49740; 231–526–2040) is known for its jewelry, early boat models, and Native American art. **Joie de Vie** (154 East Main Street, Petoskey, MI 49740; 231–347–1400) specializes in French country. Or head for the strange-sounding **Pooter Ooloms** (339 State Street, Petoskey 49740; 231–526–6101), which imports antiques from

Scandinavia, Austria, and France, including creamy pine pieces, painted furniture, and antique quilts.

After shopping, you may need to relax awhile. The **Zoll Street Beach** west of the piers is a nice spot to soak your feet or let the kids loose for a while, with a small arc of sand and a few welcome picnic tables. From here you can see the grand "cottages" in the summer community known as Wequetonsing.

Wequetonsing is one of the few exclusive old colonies where you can catch a glimpse of how the other half lives—at least in summer. Although nearby Harbor Point is private, you can stroll or drive along the bay and enjoy Weque's (pronounced "wee-kwee") lavish summer homes. The resort was established by Presbyterians from Allegan, Michigan, and Elkhart, Indiana, so that "worn-out and sweltering humanity could repair to recover health and enjoy rational recreations."

The most impressive houses face Little Traverse Bay, and smaller cottages line back streets and pedestrian walkways. They range in size from small and simple to grand and glorious, complete with gingerbread, cupolas, and, of course, long, wide porches.

Finally, if the city's trendiness starts to be too much or if the kids are getting antsy, plan a stop at the charming **Deer Park** on the outskirts of town at Zoll and Main Streets. Watch for it closely—signs are few and you could easily miss it. Here you can watch the does cavort inside a pen area or buy a handful of feed for the wide-eyed babies, many of whom are orphans adopted from the surrounding woods.

DINNER: Head back to the Stafford's Perry Hotel for a dinner in the **H. O. Rose Room** (231–347–4000). It's famous for its elegantly rich atmosphere as well as for its excellent cuisine. Start with the Perry Salad (bibb lettuce, walnuts, mushrooms, and dried cherries with creamy cherry vinaigrette), followed by smoked whitefish sampler or baked oysters. For an entree, try the New Zealand lobster tails or the brace of quail in cherry bordelaise. There's piano music on Friday and Saturday evenings. It's expensive—but worth it.

DAY 3

Morning

BREAKFAST: Many consider the brunch at **Stafford's Bay View,** (2011 Woodland Avenue, U.S. Highway 31, Bay View, 49770; 231–347–2771) the best in

Northern Michigan (yes, it's owned by the same people who own Stafford's Perry). With a charming Victorian atmosphere and a friendly and knowledgeable waitstaff, it's hard to deny the claim. The brunch spread includes a gluttonous array of breakfast and lunch-style foodstuffs, including made-to-order omelettes and waffles, ham, turkey, eggs Benedict, great sweet rolls, a gourmet table of smoked fish and pâtés, and more. It's a bargain at just $16.95 per person; children ages seven to eleven are $7.95; ages four to six are $4.95; under three are free. Brunches are offered once a month in winter, weekly other seasons. Rooms start at $80.

Don't leave the area without a drive or walk through **Bay View,** the picturesque summer community founded in 1875 by the Methodist Church as a summer retreat for its members. The community has 430 homes on the National Historic Register and is the largest collection of historic homes in the country. Most are the product of Charles Caskey, a nineteenth-century architect who designed most of the gingerbread-trimmed confections, many of which are still occupied in summer by descendants of the original owners.

One-time guests include speakers such as William Jennings Bryan, Helen Keller, and Booker T. Washington. Attend a concert, lecture, or play; attend a class; or just wander through the beautifully preserved enclave. Activities today are much as they were in the nineteenth century and include lectures, concerts, recitals, and Sunday evening services. A fascinating archive and museum in the Encampment tell the Bay View story (231–348–2599).

THERE'S MORE

Camping. Petoskey State Park (800–543–2937) has a prime location and a sandy shore, both of which make it one of the state's most popular campgrounds.

Canoeing. Bear River Canoe Livery (2517 McDougall Road, Petoskey, MI 49740; 231–347–9038) rents canoes for excursions at all skill levels on local rivers.

Fall Foliage. Some say autumn is the best time to visit, when the surrounding countryside is transformed into a tapestry of scarlet and gold. If you're planning an autumn adventure, pick up a copy of the "Fall in Northwest Michigan" guide, which details five color tours, including the breathtaking and justly famous 20-mile road from Harbor Springs to Cross Village, known as the Tunnel of Trees.

Fishing and Boating. Walloon and Crooked Lakes, Lake Charlevoix, and Little Traverse Bay all offer superb fishing for trout, bass, panfish, and walleye as well as salmon and steelhead. Public fishing sites provide easy access. Stream fishers should try the Maple, Bear, Jordan, or Boyne Rivers for trout. The Bear River in downtown Petoskey is stocked yearly with brook trout and steelhead. Burt Lake and Indian River are excellent spots for walleye, bass, and pike. Crooked Lake is where you'll find walleye, smallmouth bass, pike, and perch. If you like the big water, steelhead, lake trout, and coho and chinook salmon can be found in Lake Michigan's cold waters. Boaters will also find unlimited access on the aforementioned lakes and bays as well as on the 38-mile inland waterway that winds from Crooked Lake to Lake Huron.

Hemingway Haunts. Except for a year in Italy during World War I, the famous author spent his summers on Walloon Lake and Horton Bay from the age of seven weeks until he was twenty-two. He married his first wife, Hadley Richardson, in Horton Bay in 1921 and immortalized many haunts and friends in "Up in Michigan," "The End of Something," "Torrents of Spring," and the Nick Adams series. Today, Petoskey is considered a pilgrimage for "Papa" fans from all over the world. For more on local Hemingway sites or the annual Hemingway weekend, contact the Little Traverse Historical Society, P.O. Box 162, Petoskey, MI 49770.

Herbs. Wintergreen Herbs & Potpourri (10970 Burnett Road, between Petoskey and Charlevoix; 231–347–7399) is on a scenic hillside in the midst of an old apple orchard and is known for its culinary and ornamental herbs as well as for its everlasting flowers. Pick up something sweet-smelling to take home or tour the more than thirty theme gardens.

Hiking and Biking. The Tunnel of Trees supplies bluff views of Lake Michigan and is especially scenic for hikers and bikers in the fall. The Bear River Trail is a 1.5-mile hiking route that follows the river through downtown Petoskey. There are good access points at Sheridan Street or Lake Street in front of City Hall.

Golf. Many people come here just to golf. The area sports a variety of courses, including the new Bay Harbor, 15 miles south of Petoskey, as well as Chestnut Valley, Crooked Tree, Little Traverse Bay Golf Club, Pine Hill, and Wilderness Golf Course. Boyne Mountain and Boyne Highlands alone offer six eighteen-hole championship courses; *Golf Digest* named Boyne's

Heather course and the Donald Ross Memorial among "America's 75 Best Resort Courses." For more information on which one suits your skills, contact the Boyne County Convention and Visitors Bureau at (800) 845–2828.

Kids. If you've brought the family, pick up a copy of *What Kids Like to Do in Harbor Springs and Petoskey* by two young local authors, Nathaniel Breighner and Todd Matelski. It's available at Between the Covers (152 East Main Street, Petoskey, MI 49740; 231–526–6658) in Harbor Springs and McLean and Eakin Books (307 Lake Street, Petoskey, MI 49770; 231–347–1180).

Nature Preserve. Thorne Swift Nature Preserve (State Highway 119, north of Harbor Springs, MI 49740; 231–347–0991) is one of the many properties owned and operated by the Little Traverse Conservancy. Here you'll find trails for cross-country skiing and great places for hiking as well as long stretches of wild and mostly deserted beach.

Skiing. Though summer is the peak season in the Petoskey area, winter is close behind. Boyne Mountain and Boyne Highlands (800–GO–BOYNE), as well as other resorts such as Nub's Nob (800–SKI–NUBS), attract thousands of downhill skiers each year and are probably the best-known runs in the state.

SPECIAL EVENTS

January. Winter Sports Festival, Petoskey

June. Concerts in the Park, Petoskey
  Home Tour, Petoskey

July. Little Traverse Historical Festival, Petoskey
  Art in the Park, Petoskey

August. PowWow, Harbor Springs
  Emmet County Fair, Petoskey

October. Annual Hemingway Weekend, Petoskey

November. Christmas Tree Lighting, Harbor Springs

December. Christmas Walk, Petoskey and Harbor Springs

OTHER RECOMMENDED RESTAURANTS

Harbor Springs

Harbor Springs Gourmet Take-Out (127 State Street, Harbor Springs, MI 49740; 231–526–9607) is a great resource for sandwiches, soups, and complete lunches that you can enjoy in the city's waterfront park. They also carry many Michigan-made products and gift baskets. Moderate.

The New York Restaurant (101 State Street, Harbor Springs, MI 49740; 231–526–1904) was established in 1904 and retains much of its turn-of-the-century charm. Bistro-style cuisine includes "Up North" classics such as broiled whitefish as well as more creative offerings such as Pasta Pollo (bow-tie pasta tossed with chicken breast, artichoke hearts, wild mushrooms, and fresh chive cream sauce) or a pâté plate with country-style pâté, cornichons, and whole-grain mustard served with vegetable slaw and fresh French bread. Moderate.

Petoskey

Jesperson's (312 Howard Street, Petoskey, MI 49770; 231–347–3601) has been family owned since 1903 and is well known as the home of the "cherry berry pie" as well as homemade soups, sandwiches, and classic desserts. Inexpensive.

The Terrace Inn (1949 Glendale Street, Petoskey, MI 49770; 231–347–2410) is an impressive 1911 Victorian-style hotel with an equally attractive dining room featuring classic country inn cuisine. Among the offerings: wild mushroom stew and Chicken Hemingway—a breast of chicken with basil cream sauce and dried Michigan cherries.

Walloon Lake

Walloon Lake Inn (4178 West Street, Walloon Lake, MI 49770; 231–535–2999 or 800–956–4665) is a one-hundred-year-old inn on the shores of Walloon Lake, with five guest rooms and an intimate dining room. Entrees range from regional specialties such as rainbow trout Hemingway to French-inspired cuisine such as salmon Normandy, all prepared with locally produced ingredients. Moderate.

OTHER RECOMMENDED LODGINGS

Harbor Springs

Kimberly Country Estate (2287 Bester Road, Harbor Springs, MI 49740; 231–526–9502) is the place to stay when you're splurging. The 8,000-square-foot home has just six guest rooms, each decorated in an elegant English country theme, with fresh flowers, oil paintings, and lots of chintz. Rates: $135–$225 per night; two-night minimum stay on weekends.

Petoskey

Bay Winds Inn (909 Spring Street, Petoskey, MI 49770; 231–347–4193 or 800–204–1748) offers attractive, Victorian-inspired rooms at an equally attractive price. Located on the strip of hotels off U.S. Highway 131, just minutes from downtown, it's a family favorite, with a cozy lobby with fireplace, a long front porch, and the area's largest indoor pool. Rates: $65–$125 per night.

Stafford's Bay View Inn (U.S. Highway 31, Petoskey, MI 49770; 231–357–2771) on the State Register of Historic Places, has twenty-five rooms, an unpretentious appeal, and a great view of Little Traverse Bay. The inn was founded in 1886 and is known for its Victorian parlor, sunroom, wide front porch, and period antiques. Lawn games and bikes are available for guests; Saturday night stays include the famous Sunday brunch. Rates: $79–$195 per night.

FOR MORE INFORMATION

Boyne County Convention & Visitors Bureau, 401 East Mitchell Street, Petoskey, MI 49770; (800) 845–2828.

Frankenmuth/Birch Run

SHOP 'TIL YOU DROP

1 NIGHT

Shopping • Christmas Wonderland • History • Sight-seeing

On their own, both Frankenmuth and Birch Run are popular and perennially appealing day trips for metro Detroiters. Together, however, they represent a great one-night getaway that offers excellent eating and super shopping close to home.

Though this is a good escape year-round, it's especially appropriate in November and December, when you can do all your Christmas shopping in one weekend as well as stock up on goodies for your holiday tree at nearby Bronner's Christmas Wonderland. Frankenmuth gets into the holiday mood further with an elaborate downtown display of sparkling lights, towering trees, and a full plate of holiday happenings. Throw in a relaxing night at one of Michigan's most elegant inns, and it all adds up to the quintessential "quick escape."

DAY 1

Morning

Plan on getting an early start so that you can enjoy two full days. From Detroit, the **Prime Outlets at Birch Run** (517–624–7467) are a straight, 125-mile shot northwest up Interstate 75. You can't miss the signs. If this is your first trip to an outlet mall, be prepared to be overwhelmed. Outlet fever has swept the country. Before 1986, Birch Run was an obscure village at the Frankenmuth exit off Interstate 75. Today it has grown into one of the largest

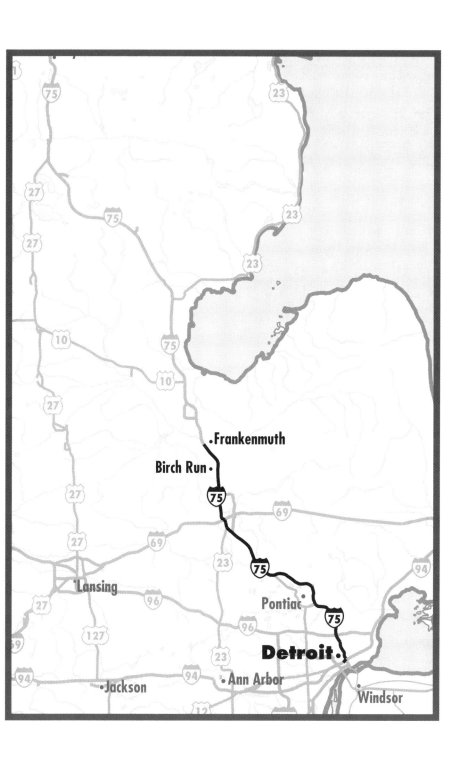

centers in the Midwest, with more than one hundred stores as well as a surrounding community of fast-food restaurants.

You may want to check a directory of stores ahead of time to plot your shopping strategy. As you'll soon discover, there's no way you can hit all the stores unless you devote an entire weekend to shopping (now that's not such a bad idea…). If you have only one full day, you'll have to be selective—come armed with a list and be prepared to check it twice.

Birch Run is divided into four main sections. The area closest to the freeway is the original and today includes stores such as **Carter's Childrenswear** (check the Oops! racks for great deals on irregulars and clothes with slight, mostly unnoticeable, flaws), **Pfaltzgraff Pottery,** charming party dresses by **Polly Flinders, Totes** umbrellas and rain gear, the **Kitchen Collection,** and more. Behind that is a small section with **Black & Decker** (tools), **Publisher's Outlet** (books), and **Bugle Boy** (clothes), among others.

Many dedicated die-hard shoppers, however, skip those sections altogether and concentrate on the newest addition to the mall: the designer and upscale area near the back. You can't miss it—you'll pass right by it as you enter the complex. Like anything else, outlet shopping can be a hit-or-miss proposition. But bargains are the rule rather than the exception at stores such as **Talbot's, Eddie Bauer, Ann Taylor, Polo/Ralph Lauren,** and **The Gap.** Other favorites include the fun and funky fashions by **Esprit** for both kids and adults; leftovers from the popular mail-order catalog at the **Spiegel** store, sports wares at **Nike,** and the warm and woolly outerwear at **London Fog,** all necessities for long midwestern winters.

Afternoon

LUNCH: If you're not a fast-food fan, check **Pizzeria Uno** (517–624–8667), a national chain that recently opened here, across from Polo/Ralph Lauren. Known for its deep-dish Chicago-style pizzas, its prices are inexpensive to moderate. Also a good choice is **Schlotzky's Deli,** near the entrance, which serves up fresh fare including salads, wood-smoked pizza, and sandwiches on their signature muffaleta-style bread. Inexpensive. Spend the afternoon hitting the stores you missed in the morning.

DINNER: Exhausted? If you're not in the mood for anything fancy and you just want to refuel, you won't go wrong at **Tony's** (517–624–5860) across from the mall. Descended from a famous Saginaw eatery, Tony's is known for its

MICHIGAN

huge portions of everything, from subs and salads to lasagna. It's also a great place for breakfast, with equally large portions. Inexpensive.

LODGING: If you've a mind to splurge on one night at someplace really special (you saved all that money on your shopping, after all), there's no better place than the **Montague Inn,** 1581 South Washington Street, Saginaw, MI 48601; (517–752–3939) in nearby Saginaw, just 16 miles north. It's housed in the former 12,000-square-foot mansion of civic leader Robert Montague, who made his fortune on an invention that used sugar beets to make hand creams and soaps, a process he later sold to the Jergens Company. The inn is in Saginaw's historic Grove District. Considered one of the best in the state, it sits on eight acres overlooking Lake Linton and is furnished with antiques and reproductions. The sixteen tastefully decorated guest rooms have four-poster beds and wing chairs. A favorite is the Montague Suite, which features a fireplace, green Pewabic tile, and great views of the landscaped grounds. Rates: $55–$170 per night, including continental breakfast.

DAY 2

Morning

BREAKFAST: Montague Inn. The room rate includes a continental breakfast of oatmeal, cereals, juice, and baked goods that you can enjoy in either of two dining rooms, one of which has a welcoming fire on cold mornings.

Set today aside for wandering the town of Frankenmuth, now the state's top tourist draw. It was settled in 1854, when pastors in Bavaria, concerned over the religious life of Lutheran immigrants and their American Indian neighbors, sent a colony of fifteen Franconians to the New World (*Frankenmuth* means "courage of the Franconians"). The Indians soon moved elsewhere, but the Bavarians remained, reinforced by later arrivals. The town became known as "Little Bavaria," with German remaining the principal language long after the turn of the century.

Today, that Bavarian heritage along the city's 2-mile strip is created and cultivated for increasingly large groups of tourists who travel here, attracted mostly by the notorious chicken dinners at Zehnder's and Bavarian Village. Much of the architecture, however, is still original, as is the town's genuine friendliness, known in German as *gemutlichkeit.*

On the way in to town, you'll pass **Bronner's Christmas Wonderland** (517–652–9931 or 800–255–9327). Check your skepticism at the door. Even the most die-hard Scrooges are enchanted by the more than 50,000 ornaments, tree toppers, lights, and decorations in this cavernous, 200,000-square-foot store (unbelievably, it's the size of four football fields). Nativity scenes range from minute hand-carved figures to life-size scenes. There are also more than 260 artistically decorated trees, a multi-image slide presentation, and a spectacular outdoor light display each night. Everything isn't commercial, however; Bronner's also includes a Silent Night memorial chapel, which is open daily, as well as Bibles in more than thirty languages. It also has a breathtaking collection of imported ornaments that are works of art in themselves. Bronner's also sells Precious Moments, Hummels, and other collectibles. Open 361 days a year. (It's closed New Year's Day, Easter, Thanksgiving, and Christmas.)

At the center of downtown's business district is **School Haus Square.** Originally the St. Lorenz Lutheran School, it's now a collection of twenty-five specialty shops, including the colorful Kite Kraft. Check out the wall murals along the corridors, which depict the state's educational system in the late 1800s.

Afternoon

LUNCH: Depending on your schedule, you may want to eat your main meal at midafternoon and catch a quick bite for dinner later on the way home. No visit to Frankenmuth is complete without a visit to the city's main claim to fame, **Zehnder's** (730 South Main Street, Frankenmuth, MI 48734; 517–652–9925) and **Bavarian Inn** (713 South Main Street, Frankenmuth, MI 48734; 517–652–9941 or 888–775–6343). Located across the street from each other, the two restaurants are operated by the Zehnder family. The meals are similar (both serve the trademark, all-you-can-eat chicken), but the atmosphere is different. Zehnder's is reminiscent of a southern plantation on the exterior, with white pillars and a huge, sweeping porch. Bavarian Village, on the other hand, is—not surprisingly—decorated in the Alpine style, complete with a thirty-five-bell automatic glockenspiel that plays three melodies followed by a presentation of carved wooden figures that depict the Pied Piper legend.

Whichever you choose, you're in for a family-style feast. For $15.50 per person you'll be served a multicourse meal that includes chicken, mashed potatoes and gravy, relishes, home-baked breads, even ice cream for dessert. If

you're not a chicken lover, you can also enjoy German specialties such as Wiener schnitzel, spicy sausages, sauerbraten, and *kasseler rippchen* (smoked pork loin). The lines can be long (they're generally shorter at lunch, another reason for visiting then), but they move quickly. Dining rooms are surprisingly intimate considering the number of people they serve each day. Moderate.

After lunch, walk off those calories with a tour through the rest of the village. **Frankenmuth Historical Museum** (613 South Main Street, Frankenmuth, MI 48734; 517–652–9701) recounts the area's history, starting with the Indian mission days. More history can be found at **St. Lorenz Church** and the **Log Cabin Church** (Tuscola at Mayer; 517–652–6141), which is the largest congregation east of the Mississippi River of the conservative Missouri Synod of the Lutheran Church. Here contemporary stained glass reveals the area's Lutheran history, from St. Paul to Frankenmuth's missionary ministers. The adjacent log church re-creates the original log church and pulpit.

A must-see attraction downtown is the enchanting **Zeesenagel Italian Alpine Village** (780 Mill Street, Frankenmuth, MI 48734; 517–652–2591) at the bottom of the hill south of Zehnder's. Interior designers David Zeese and Don Nagel were so inspired by an eighteenth-century nativity scene they saw in a Roman church that they decided to build one of their own. Today the scene comes alive with 500 realistic figures, including haughty dignitaries, fishmongers, lace makers, and fruit vendors. The eclectic gift shop next door is also worth a stop and sells an unusual mixture of merchandise, including Lladro Spanish porcelain and Greek icons.

If you're a wine fan, the **St. Julian Winery** (127 South Main Street, Frankenmuth, MI 48734; 517–652–3281) includes a room with free tastes (for those twenty-one and older) of the fruits of the state's largest vineyard as well as a small on-site winery. Free tours are offered weekends at 1:00 and 3:00 P.M.

Although much of Frankenmuth is oriented to the thousands of tourists who flock here annually, there are still places where the original German small town can be seen. Off the beaten path, these places give you the chance to experience the "real" town behind the Bavarian facades.

Satow's Drug Store (308 South Main Street, Frankenmuth, MI 48734; 517–652–8001) is a popular local hangout with homemade soups and great prices. Most of the regulars still speak German. Those who aren't at Satow's are probably over at the **Main Street Tavern** (310 South Main Street, Frankenmuth, MI 48734; 517–652–2222), a plain bar owned by an ex-baker at Zehnder's. All the breads and buns are made on the premises and filled with things such as local beef and cheese or tangy bratwurst. Finally, don't leave

Frankenmuth without a stop at **Willi's Sausage Haus** (316 South Main Street, Frankenmuth, MI 48734; 517–652–9041), where this master sausage maker cooks up sausages, hams, and bacon as well as some ninety-two other fragrant items. The beef jerky is famous. This is also the place to stop if you want to pack a picnic; Willi will grill your choice of meats to eat in the park across the street.

DINNER: If you find you're hungry again on the way home, a good place to stop is **Salvatore Scallopine's** just off the Miller Road exit on Interstate 75 (3227 Miller Road, Flint, MI 48507; 810–732–1070). If you're sick of chicken, you can indulge in a great Caesar salad and a plate of pasta covered with one of six signature sauces. Inexpensive.

THERE'S MORE

Art. Marshall Fredericks is one of the state's best-known sculptors. Saginaw Valley State University is home to Marshall M. Fredericks Sculpture Gallery (7400 Bay Road, University Center, Saginaw, MI 48601; 517–790–5667), the only gallery honoring the late sculptor's work. It's open Tuesday through Sunday from 1:00 to 5:00 P.M. and is free. This light-filled gallery includes models for more than 200 of Fredericks's most famous works, including the landmark *Spirit of Detroit*. An adjacent sculpture garden and fountain also feature works by Fredericks.

Golf. The Fortress (950 Flint Street, Frankenmuth, MI 48734; 517–652–9229) is considered one of lower Michigan's best courses. Call for tee times and more information.

Teahouse. Nearby Saginaw is a surprising place to find a Japanese Cultural Center and Tea House (Ezra Rust Drive and South Washington Avenue; 517–759–1648). It offers insights into Japanese culture and to the ritual and ceremony of tea service. The nearby Friendship Garden and many of the trees, bridges, and stones used in the garden came from Japan. The adjacent teahouse has tea and sweets and a full tea ceremony every second Sunday.

Wildlife. The Shiawassee National Refuge is one of only four refuges in Michigan and includes the Shiawassee Flats, known as "Michigan's Everglades." For more information, call (517) 777–5930.

SPECIAL EVENTS

January. Zehnder's Snowfest, Frankenmuth

March. Arts & Crafts Show, Frankenmuth

May. Cinco de Mayo, Saginaw

June. Bavarian Fest, Frankenmuth

July. Sidewalk Sales, Birch Run and Frankenmuth

August. Summer Music Fest, Frankenmuth

September. Oktoberfest, Frankenmuth

November. Holiday Lighting Ceremony, Frankenmuth

OTHER RECOMMENDED LODGINGS

Frankenmuth

Bavarian Inn Lodge (1 Covered Bridge Lane, Frankenmuth, MI 48734; 517–652–7200 or 888–775–6343) is just behind the Bavarian Village Restaurant and features 354 rooms decorated in—what else??—Bavarian style. There are also three pools, whirlpools, an exercise room, a family fun center, children's play village, eighteen-hole miniature golf, tennis courts, and nightly entertainment. Rates: $79–$160 per night.

Zehnder's Bavarian Haus (1365 South Main Street, Frankenmuth, MI 48734; 517–652–0470) has 137 rooms, as well as an indoor pool and game room. Rates range from $49 to $205 per night.

FOR MORE INFORMATION

Frankenmuth Convention and Visitors Bureau, 635 South Main Street, Frankenmuth, MI 48734; (800) 386-8696.

Ann Arbor

"GO BLUE" GETAWAY

2 NIGHTS

Galleries • Nightlife • Shopping • Restaurants

Sounds from a nearby gristmill allegedly inspired the local American Indians to name this area *kawgooshkawnick*. Luckily for modern tongues, later settlers preferred Ann Arbor, named for a local grape arbor and the first white pioneer wives, both named Ann. In 1837, not long after the town was settled, Ann Arbor bid for and was chosen as the new site for the University of Michigan, which was seeking to leave already bustling Detroit for greener pastures.

Today the well-known university is an integral part of the city's fabric—providing it with jobs, a young (and young-at-heart) population and a high quality of life. So high, in fact, that in 1996 *Money* magazine named Ann Arbor the fifth-best place to live in the United States.

From its original 40 acres, U of M has grown to cover more than 2,600 acres. The university has also spawned a wealth of museums, restaurants, shops, and nightlife. Here you'll find trendy Euro-style eateries as well as Old World German restaurants, tony art museums as well as the largest collegiate football stadium in the country, seating 104,000 Wolverine fans at a time. Many consider Ann Arbor the liveliest city in the state. It's been home to singers Bob Seger, Madonna, and Iggy Pop, Pulitzer prize–winning poet Robert Frost, President Gerald Ford, playwright Arthur Miller, director Lawrence Kasdan (of *Big Chill* fame), actor James Earl Jones, and comedienne Gilda Radner.

For those Detroiters who complain that Motown is comatose after hours, Ann Arbor is the perfect close-to-home getaway. You won't spend the week-

end driving; the State Street exit is just 45 minutes west of the Motor City on Interstate 94.

DAY 1

One charm of an Ann Arbor weekend is that Motown residents won't even have to leave work early to enjoy it. Ann Arbor is just 38 miles west of Detroit on Interstate 94. Plan to be in town early enough for dinner on the first night, however, because the city is known for its restaurants (more than 200) and offers some of the most diverse dining experiences in the state.

DINNER: Housed in a huge former theater, trattoria-style **Gratzi** (326 South Main Street, Ann Arbor, MI 48103; 734–663–5555) is considered the liveliest spot in town. It still stages spontaneous productions nightly, although today the emphasis is on people-watching. The surprisingly good Italian food runs the gamut from classic (veal saltimbocca, fried calamari) to nouvelle (smoked salmon pizza, butternut squash ravioli in walnut sauce). For dessert, don't miss the rich Chocolato Ultimato. There are strolling musicians Thursday through Saturday and crowded patio dining in season. Moderate to expensive.

LODGING: If you're traveling sans kids, the **Bell Tower Hotel** (300 South Thayer Street, Ann Arbor, MI 48104; 800–999–8693 or 734–769–3010) is an elegant, European-style inn in the heart of downtown. It's conveniently located across from the popular Hill Auditorium, the site of performances from pop to Puccini (most other hotels are clustered off the freeway). With a huge paneled fireplace in the lobby and sixty-six gracious guest rooms decorated in a clubby English style, the hotel offers a quiet retreat in the middle of campus. Nice touches include thick oversize towels, free valet parking, and a free continental breakfast. If you'd like a nightcap or a bite to eat, the hotel's Escoffier restaurant offers an extensive menu as well as a respected wine list. Rates: $135–$237 per night.

If you've brought the family (and there are plenty of reasons to do so), the best place to stay is the **Courtyard by Marriott** near Briarwood Mall (3205 Boardwalk, Ann Arbor, MI 48104; 800–321–2211 or 734–995–5900). Although not as centrally located as the Bell Tower, it's the best of the economy chains in the area, with 160 rooms, free coffee and newspaper, an indoor pool, hot tub, and even—a mixed blessing—free Nintendo in the guest rooms. There are also thirty-six two-bedroom units. Rates: $79–$130 per night.

DAY 2

Morning

BREAKFAST: The Bell Tower serves a nice complimentary continental spread in the conference room, including fruits, juices, coffee and tea, breads, bagels, and more. But if you want to try a local favorite, **Angelo's Restaurant** (1100 Catherine Street, Ann Arbor, MI 48103; 734–761–8996) is considered the city's best place for breakfast. College students and professional types queue up on weekends for the waffles and homemade breads and toasts (try the cinnamon raisin). Inexpensive.

You'll have to get up early, however, if you want to catch the real action at the **Farmers Market** on Fifth Street. The dealers come as early as 5:00 A.M. laden with fruits, flowers, crafts, and just about everything in between. The market is one of the highlights of historic **Kerrytown,** a restored nineteenth-century district of more than thirty shops and restaurants north of the campus. The area is lined with brick buildings and cobblestone streets with lovely courtyards, and is perfect for walking and wandering. It's named after County Kerry, Ireland, ancestral home of one of the original developers.

Kerrytown shops worth exploring include **The Kitchen Port** (734–665–9188), with an extensive array of goodies for foodies; **Mudpuddles,** with creative toys for kids, innovative **Workbench** furniture (734–668–4688), ("For Homes, Not Museums," the brochure claims); and **Vintage to Vogue** (734–665–9110), a chic clothing shop. If you need a snack, consider the **Moveable Feast Cafe** (326 West Liberty Street, Ann Arbor, MI 48103; 734–663–3278), which has a well-known bakery and—as the name implies—"totable" cuisine that's perfect for picnics or for enjoying while bench-sitting and watching the world go by.

Afternoon

LUNCH: Although Kerrytown has lots of tempting places for lunch, save them for another trip and head for **Zingerman's Deli** (422 Detroit Street, Ann Arbor, MI 48103; 734–663–3354), a city landmark and one of its best-known eateries. Zingerman's is the kind of deli that makes even New Yorkers jealous. This haven for foodies is jam-packed with gourmet foods for sale as well as an extremely popular counter business (although the staff is efficient, be prepared to wait in line). Ann Arborites line up around the clock for the more than one hundred sandwich varieties, including the Reuben, corned beef on rye, and others with more intriguing names such as Nate's Nosh, Pat & Dick's Honeymooner, Randy's Routine, and the Helen Have Trotter. Whatever your choice, you'll end up with a sandwich that's big enough for two. Zingerman's also serves Caesar and pasta salads, its own breads, and specialty coffees in the neighboring converted house known as "Zingerman's Next Door." Inexpensive.

Ann Arbor is divided into two distinct areas: downtown (the area along Main Street, west of the campus) and the central campus area. Both offer distinct shops and attractions. After lunch, head for Main Street to explore the rest of downtown. While you walk, pick up a cappuccino or Italian soda at **Espresso Royale** (734–668–1838), about halfway down the street. They have great biscotti, too.

Unlike other small downtowns, Ann Arbor thrives, with a mix of funky shops, art galleries, great bookstores (so great, in fact, that Ann Arbor is the number-one city in America in per-capita book buying), and restaurants. A few worthwhile stops include **AfterWords** (219 South Main Street, Ann Arbor, MI 48103; 734–996–2808), which features a wide selection of remaindered books; **FallingWater Books** (213 South Main Street, Ann Arbor, MI 48103; 734–747–9801), which appeals to the city's metaphysical community; the **Selo/Shevel Gallery** (335 South Main; 734–761–6263), a small space featuring hand-blown glass objects and fine contemporary American jewelry; and the **Peaceable Kingdom** (210 South Main Street, Ann Arbor, MI 48103; 734–668–7886), with folk art, crafts, and "fun stuff from here and far."

If you've brought the kids (or even if you haven't), be sure to stop at the **Ann Arbor Hands-On Museum** (219 East Huron Street, Ann Arbor, MI 48104; 734–995–5439), which is housed in a former fire station. A major expansion was completed in 1999. Spread out over four floors, it includes fascinating exhibits and displays such as "The Subject Is You," which teaches all about the human body, and "The Discovery Room," where kids can make waves, build an arch, even fly a hot-air balloon and get inside a soap bubble. The upper floors include "Crane's Roost," with holograms, strobes, and lights, and "How Things Work," which includes the opportunity to communicate via computer and play three-dimensional tic-tac-toe. The museum's Explore Store has lots of fun and educational stuff the kids can spend their allowance on. Admission is $6.00 for adults; $4.00 for kids ages three to twelve. The museum is closed Monday.

Not far away is another city landmark—the **Treasure Mart** (529 Detroit Street, Ann Arbor, MI 48103; 734–662–1363). The legendary resale store is

Ann Arbor's Hands-On Museum is popular with the young and the young at heart.

huge, with fast-moving and wide-ranging stock that includes a number of antiques at bargain prices. It's a favorite of students, city bargain hunters, and interior designers.

DINNER: Head back to Kerrytown for dinner at **Sweet Lorraine's** (303 Detroit Street, Ann Arbor, MI 48104; 734–665–0700). One of the newest restaurants in Ann Arbor, it's a friendly yet chic bistro (the original is in South-field, a Detroit suburb) that has quickly acquired a loyal clientele who will-ingly stand in line on weekends for the veggie burgers, salmon with maple syrup glaze, daily specials, and desserts such as Sinful Chocolate Decadence Cake. Moderate.

Afterward, if you're looking for music, you can't do better than the **Ark** (316 South Main Street, Ann Arbor, MI 48104; 734–761–1800), which has hosted both obscure and famous folk artists and other musicians for more than three decades.

DAY 3

Morning

BRUNCH: Few brunches compare with those at the **Gandy Dancer** (401 Depot Street, Ann Arbor, MI 48104; 734–769–0592) in fare or atmosphere. Housed in a restored train station on the outskirts of town, it's the flagship of the renowned Chuck Muer seafood chain. The extensive brunch spread includes made-to-order omelettes, great apple dumplings, fresh fruit, fish dishes, the restaurant's signature homemade rolls, and a separate table laden with rich desserts. The Gandy Dancer is also crowded at dinner, when diners feast on specialties such as bluefish pâté bouillabaisse, yellowfin tuna, and softshell crab. Reservations recommended for dinner on weekends; not taken for brunch. Moderate to expensive.

Afterward, walk off some of that meal with a tour of the U of M campus and the rest of downtown you missed yesterday. With one of the most picturesque campuses in the country, the university is famous for being a hotbed of liberalism (the annual Hash Bash is still well frequented by college students and others who favor legalizing marijuana) and for sites such as the Diag and the Union, where students congregate, and the Law Quad, which was modeled after Cambridge University in England.

State Street runs right through the heart of campus and is the anchor of the nearby shopping district. On State are the university's top attractions. The **University of Michigan Museum of Art** (525 South State Street, Ann Arbor, MI 48104; 734–764–0395) is among the top ten university art museums in the country, with more than twelve thousand works by Dürer, Delacroix, Rodin, Picasso, Rembrandt, Monet, and Miró. There's also an excellent Asian collection, including a fascinating display of snuff boxes. More than fifteen changing exhibits are featured annually. Then there's the **Kelsey Museum of Archaeology** (434 South State Street, Ann Arbor, MI 48104; 734–764–9304). Part of the Kelsey's attraction—besides the intriguing collection of art and artifacts that dates back almost to the beginning of time, all products of university-sponsored digs in the Mediterranean and Near East— is the 1891 fieldstone building that holds it. (Don't miss the large Tiffany window.) State Street is also the site of the famous Ann Arbor Art Fair, held each July, which encompasses twenty-two blocks, features 1,000 artists, and draws more than 400,000 people.

If you're out to exercise your credit cards, many of the city's best shops are found on State Street and the area surrounding it. One of the best is **Borders Books** (612 East Liberty Street, Ann Arbor, MI 48104; 734–668–7652), the new location of an Ann Arbor institution. Borders may have gone national, but it was born on State Street, where it became known as one of the country's best full-service bookstores long before it branched out around the country. Many prefer the old location, but the new East Liberty Street store, housed in a former Jacobson's, is still one of the city's best places to see and be seen. It has the same wide selection that made the original location famous, as well as a great coffee bar. Other shops and galleries in the neighborhood worth a stop include **Chris Triola** (5 Nickels Arcade, Ann Arbor, MI 48104; 734–996–9955), in the small arcade of worthwhile shops next to Espresso Royale. Known for bold and breathtaking (also expensive) knitwear, Triola's shop is a favorite of Ann Arbor's fashion conscious. **Middle Earth** (1209 South University Avenue, Ann Arbor, MI 48104; 734–769–1488) is an Ann Arbor institution, with everything from obscene greeting cards and more than 20,000 postcards to Elvis troll dolls and inflatable pink Cadillacs. If recordings are your thing, you won't want to miss **Schoolkids** (523 East Liberty Street; 734–994–8031), known for its wide array of alternative music and its great selection of imports.

THERE'S MORE

Antiques. The Ann Arbor Antiques Market is one of the premiere antiques events in the state. Now in its twenty-eighth season, it's held on the third Sunday in the month from April through November at the county fairgrounds (exit 175 off Interstate 94, then south for 3 miles). More than 300 high-quality dealers from all over the country bring every imaginable kind of antique to show and sell. It's also one of the few shows that guarantees its merchandise as represented. Admission costs $4.00.

Chelsea. The nearby town of Chelsea, about 10 miles west along Interstate 94, is known as home of both the Purple Rose Theater, owned and operated by actor Jeff Daniels, and the wonderful Common Grill (112 South Main Street, Ann Arbor, MI 48104; 734–475–0470), a great restaurant known for its innovative cuisine and casual atmosphere. Both are worth a side trip.

Dinosaurs and More. The Exhibit Museum of Natural History (1109 Geddes Avenue, Ann Arbor, MI 48104; 734–764–6085), also part of U of M, has more than 300 displays on four floors. Highlights include the Prehistory Life exhibits on the second floor (including the ever-popular dinosaurs), the Peruvian collection on the fourth floor, and the displays exploring the life of the Michigan timber wolf on the third floor.

Football. The Wolverines inspire some of the fiercest loyalty in the state, with hundreds of "Go Blue" fans converging on the stadium each fall. Many games are sold out far in advance, but tickets can often be had at the gate for surprisingly affordable prices. For information, call (734) 647–2583.

Gardens. When the concrete and the city get to be too much, urbanites retreat to Matthaei Botanical Gardens (1800 North Dixboro Street, Ann Arbor, MI 48104; 734–998–7060). Owned and operated by the university, it's a quiet and serene oasis of walking trails, display gardens, and a conservatory of exotic flora. The more than 600 acres include four nature trails, wetlands, a woodland wildflower garden showcasing Michigan and Great Lakes wildflowers, and a charming Herb Knot garden. The adjacent gift shop sells an unusual variety of gardening goodies as well as plants.

Golf. Golf enthusiasts can tee off at one of eight courses, including Stonebridge Golf Club (5315 Stonebridge Drive South, Ann Arbor, MI 48104; 734–429–8383), an eighteen-hole championship course by Arthur Hills; Leslie Park Golf Course (2120 Traver Road, Ann Arbor, MI 48104; 734–994–1163), rated one of the top ten municipal courses in Michigan, and the Eagle Crest Golf Club (1275 South Huron Street in Ypsilanti, MI 48197; 734–487–2441), one of the most challenging courses in Southeast Michigan.

Shopping. If you haven't had enough shopping, Ann Arbor's Briarwood Mall, at the State Street exit off Interstate 94, has more than 200 stores, including Jacobson's, Hudson's, Williams Sonoma, the Coach Store, Godiva, Banana Republic, the Disney Store, Gymboree, Gap and Gap Kids, and more.

SPECIAL EVENTS

January. Ann Arbor Folk Festival

March. Pow Wow

April. Flower and Garden Show

June. Summer Festival

July. Art Arbor Art Fairs

September. Blues & Jazz Festival

October. Winter Art Fair

November. Domino's Farms Christmas Lights Display

OTHER RECOMMENDED RESTAURANTS

Amadeus Cafe (122 East Washington Street, Ann Arbor, MI 48104; 734–665–8767) is one of the only places in the city where you can partake of Central European fare such as Hungarian goulash and pierogi with the background of nightly classical music. Moderate.

The Earle (121 West Washington Street, Ann Arbor, MI 48104; 734–994–0211) is one of the city's premiere dining spots. Appetizers include a tasty baked garlic and shrimp pesto pizza; poached salmon and breast of duck are popular entrees. Reservations recommended on weekends. Expensive.

Kerrytown Bistro (415 North Fifth Street, Ann Arbor, MI 48103; 734–994–6424) serves mostly country French cuisine in a casual setting accented with brick walls and wooden tables. Try the Cassoulet de Carcassonne, a house specialty. Reservations recommended Friday and Saturday nights. Moderate.

Moveable Feast (326 West Liberty Street, Ann Arbor, MI 48103; 734–663–3278) has spawned several take-out shops, but that doesn't dull the shine of the original location. The main eatery serves American specialties with a French accent, including chicken with walnuts and gorgonzola, poached salmon Hollandaise, and a bevy of delicious desserts, including chocolate pavé with raspberry sauce, Kahlua cheesecake, and more. Moderate to expensive.

Seva (314 East Liberty Street, Ann Arbor, MI 48104; 734–662–1111) is the city's best-known vegetarian restaurant and a favorite of students and health-conscious others. Menu highlights, most based on Mexican, Italian, and Oriental cuisines, include *tempeh* fajitas, meatless nachos, and more.

OTHER RECOMMENDED LODGINGS

Crowne Plaza Hotel (610 Briarwood Boulevard, Ann Arbor, MI 48108; 800–344–7829 or 734–761–7800) has 199 spacious rooms (all with irons and ironing boards, hair dryers, coffeemakers, and free Nintendo) as well as coffee and afternoon tea delivered to your door. Rates: $125–$175 per night.

Clarion Hotel & Conference Center (2900 Jackson Road, Ann Arbor, MI 48108; 734–665–4444) has 225 rooms (with free coffee) at reasonable rates. There are also Hampton Inns (734–996–4444 or 734–665–5000) north and south of the city.

FOR MORE INFORMATION

Ann Arbor Convention & Visitors Bureau, 120 West Huron Street, Ann Arbor, MI 48104–1318; (800) 888–9487.

MICHIGAN

Marshall

THE TOWN THAT TIME FORGOT

2 NIGHTS

Antiques • Architecture • Shopping • Museums • Magic

Tiny Marshall, Michigan, has had many claims to fame through the years. Early in the 1840s, this Calhoun County town was confident of being chosen to replace Detroit as the state's capital. Marshall, which sits almost dead center between Michigan's east and west coasts, lost out—incredibly, by just one vote—to Lansing, also centrally located but farther north (and today's home to Michigan State University).

In 1846, Marshall was once again in the news when Adam Crosswhite, an escaped slave living in the town, was taken by force by his former owner. Townspeople rose up and arrested the slave hunters, sending them back to Kentucky empty-handed and focusing national interest on the subject of fugitive slaves. (Some even say this incident fanned sentiments leading to the Civil War.) Later the town grew again, this time as an important shipping point and stop on the Michigan Central Railroad. Early in the 1900s, it also served as home to popular patent medicines such as "Lydia Pinkham's Pink Pills for Pale People."

Today's Marshall has once again reinvented itself. Ironically, it owes its current livelihood to its past—and, thanks to a forward-thinking mayor in the 1920s, to its reputation as one of America's best-preserved historic towns. Indeed, there are so many nineteenth-century homes and businesses (roughly 800) that the city was designated the country's largest National Historic District, the highest honor passed out by the National Park Service. The city's big event is the historic-homes tour, held each year on the weekend after Labor

Day. Townspeople pitch in to offer food, arts and crafts, and tours of more than a dozen local residences and structures. And though residents are proud of their past, Marshall is no ghost town. It's a charming mélange of young and old, antiques stores and new-wave cybercafes—a perfect getaway for architecture or antiques buffs or anyone who is looking to escape the modern world.

DAY 1

Afternoon

From Detroit, Marshall is about 100 miles west on Interstate 94. Worth a stop along the way is the **Common Grill** (112 South Main Street, Chelsea, MI 48118; 734–475–0470), a surprisingly cosmopolitan cafe lined with Edward Hopper–style murals that depict old town scenes. Seafood specialties, fresh pastas, and tasty signature rolls draw crowds from nearby Ann Arbor and beyond (for more on Chelsea, see Ann Arbor Escape, page 67).

LODGING: No visit to Marshall would be complete without a stay at the charming **National House Inn** (102 South Parkview Street, Marshall, MI 49068; 616–781–7374). The state's oldest inn, it was founded in 1835 as a stagecoach stop between Detroit and Chicago. In 1975, the inn was completely restored; it opened in 1976 as a bed-and-breakfast. Rooms are furnished with impressive wooden beds and comfortable country-style antiques. Rates: $68–$130 per night, including continental breakfast.

DAY 2

Morning

BREAKFAST: Your accommodations include a tasty breakfast of fresh breads and pastries, hot egg strata, cereals, and more. If you'd like something heartier or have a hankering for hash browns, head for the cozy **Coffee Pot** (228 West Michigan Avenue, Marshall, MI 49068; 616–781–7477), just across the square from the inn. This friendly diner-style eatery serves classic breakfast fare such as thick cinnamon French toast, golden brown pancakes, and fluffy "Good Ole Omelets"—from the plain-Jane variety to western. You can also get steak and eggs with American fries or toast for $8.00. At lunch or dinner, locals graze on favorites such as meatloaf sandwiches, chicken-fried steak, and homemade pie. Inexpensive.

Marshall's collection of vintage architecture is one of the country's finest.

So fortified, head out on a walking tour of the town's distinctive architecture. Before doing so, pick up a copy of the self-guided walking tour available at the hotel and at the town's shops or chamber of commerce. It lists more than 130 buildings, with short descriptions of style as well as notable architectural elements and former owners.

First stop: the fascinatingly eccentric **Honolulu House** (107 North Kalamazoo Street, Marshall, MI 49068; 616–781–8544), across from your hotel and the Brooks Memorial Fountain. The house was built in 1860 by Abner Pratt, a Marshall judge who became U.S. consul to the Sandwich Islands (now Hawaii). Forced to return to Michigan by an ill wife, he chose to bring the islands with him in the form of this unusual piece of architecture. Pratt topped his house with a pagoda-shaped tower and filled it with Polynesian souvenirs, but he died soon after returning to the mainland (it may have had something to do with his choosing to wear white linen suits even during frigid Michigan winters). Today the distinctive building functions as a museum and as home to the city's historical society. *The New York Times* called it "a tropical fantasy . . . the architectural equivalent of a four-rum cocktail served in a coconut." Highlights inside include tropical murals from 1885, with more than 120 paint colors, an elaborate made-in-Michigan dining-room suite from the 1876 Philadelphia Centennial Exposition, and the Marshall Folding Bathtub, a relic of the city's patent-medicine era. Be forewarned, however: The house is open daily only from mid-May through October from noon to 5:00 P.M.; from November to mid-May it's open weekends only from 1:00 to 4:00 P.M. Admission is $3.00.

After leaving the Honolulu House, wander Marshall's other streets and ogle the many fine homes. You'll get a lesson in nineteenth-century architecture—everything from Queen Anne to Italianate to Greek Revival. Even if you don't care about architecture, you'll go away impressed by the obvious love and care lavished on each of these historic structures.

The best houses are found spread out along the area known as **Prospect Hill**, 2 blocks north of Main Street. An easy hour or so walk gives you a good look at some thirty or more fine homes and gardens (be sure to peek behind the houses, too, for many sport fashionable carriage houses). Notable homes include the 1839 Greek Revival "Governor's Mansion" built by Governor James Wright Gordon before the capital was moved to Lansing; the 1857 Italianate Adams-Schuyler-Umphrey House, built on land that was once owned by James Fenimore Cooper; the 1907 Sears-Osborne House, ordered from the Sears catalog at the turn of the century for $1,995; the 1886 Queen Anne Cronin-LaPietra House, one of the city's most ornate, designed by the Detroit firm best known for the Michigan Central Railroad Terminal; and the 1843 Greek Revival Camp-Vernor-Riser House, once home to the founder of Vernor's Ginger Ale.

LUNCH: Malia (130 West Michigan Avenue, 49068; 616–781–2171), housed in a renovated storefront, is a recent addition to the city's restaurant scene. Open just four years, it features nouvelle Italian cuisine and delectable homemade pastas in a Tuscan-style setting with daily blackboard specials, glazed ocher walls, and an original tin ceiling. Try the grilled Portobello mushroom sandwich, the pesto linguine, or the refreshing *orchiette primavera*. Moderate.

Afternoon

Time for some shopping. The pineapple, the symbol of hospitality, flies on colorful flags all over downtown. That warm welcome is evident in many of the city's charming boutiques and antiques shops, where you'll find owners who are happy to chat, find out where you're from and what you're looking for, and linger over a little good-natured bargaining.

Fittingly, this historic enclave is also an antique-lover's dream. Along Michigan Avenue, the main drag, you'll find about a dozen antiques shops and mini-malls. Even the local dentist's office is full of antique dental equipment. It's sure to make you happy you live in the twenty-first century.

Downtown is full of terrific Italianate architecture and old-fashioned institutions such as a "variety" or dime store and a good hardware store. Other favorite stops include the **Kids' Place** (106 North Jefferson Street, Marshall, MI 49068; 616–781–3853), a small but choice children's bookstore that also stocks a number of books on Marshall.

The **J. H. Cronin Antique Center** (101 West Michigan Avenue, Marshall, MI 49068; 616–789–0077) features the offerings of more than twenty-five local dealers. If you've got kids in tow, head for **Tunes & Toons** (102 South Eagle Street, Marshall, MI 49068; 616–789–1000), where Paul Braggeman buys and sells classic comics, discs, and more, and **Pineapple Lane** (209 West Michigan Avenue, Marshall, MI 49068), which has a staggering selection of heirloom teddy bears as well as a wide array of general antiques. Nearby, **McAuliffe's** (203 West Michigan Avenue, Marshall, MI 49068) has locally made ice creams that are a bargain at 50 cents for a mini dip, $1.25 for a sundae. Go ahead—indulge.

Marshall is also home to one of the country's unique and little-publicized museums. The **American Museum of Magic** (107 East Michigan Avenue, Marshall, MI 49068; next to the chamber of commerce; 616–781–7674) is a passionate fan's tribute to the world of professional magic and magicians. It's a mecca for modern masters such as David Copperfield, who has called it "one of my favorite places on earth." Founder Robert Lund was a longtime fan of the "conjuring culture." Even if you're not interested in magic, you'll be won over by this intriguing museum housed in an 1868 building with a handsome cast-iron front, once a saloon, billiard hall, and bakery. The Lunds restored the building themselves and opened it in 1978. The memorabilia inside date to 1584 and include "notional whimsies, cabalistic surprises, phantasmagorical bewilderments, and unparalleled splendors." Roughly translated, that means anything and everything remotely related to the practice of magic. The extensive collection spans four centuries and six continents and includes advertising and promotional posters, beautiful antique props, a carrying case once used by Harry Blackstone, even posters celebrating Marjorie Waddell, one of the few successful woman magicians. Although Bob passed away not long ago, his wife Elaine carries on in his memory and keeps the museum open only by appointment. Admission is $4.00 for adults, $2.00 for kids ages eight to twelve. If you're unable to arrange for a tour, you can catch a glimpse of the collection through the front window.

If you haven't seen enough museums, check out the **Postal Museum** (616–781–2859) inside the town's small post office (202 East Michigan Avenue, Marshall, MI 49068). Built of locally quarried sandstone, it includes interesting artifacts such as the old post office boxes that once graced general stores as well as unusual see-through glass mailboxes and canceled stamps. Tours by appointment or by chance.

DINNER: By now, you should be ready to eat. No visit to Marshall would be complete without a stop at **Schuler's** (115 South Eagle Street, Marshall, MI 49068; 616–781–0600), a local institution. Signs in the Centennial Dining Room include one that reads: THE DIFFERENCE BETWEEN GOOD AND GREAT IS A LITTLE EXTRA EFFORT. Extra effort is a specialty here, where the Schuler family has been serving up comforting fare such as Swiss onion soup, barbecued meatballs, and prime rib for more than eighty-five years. The first Schuler's opened in Marshall in 1909 as a combination cigar store and restaurant. Not long ago, the restaurant added lighter cuisine to its menu, including Sicilian grilled chicken pizza, Calico Bay scallops with angel hair pasta, Caesar steak salad, wood-grilled Texas bay shrimp with black bean quesadilla, and almond-crusted orange roughy. Moderate.

The clubby **Winston's** is a great place for a post-dinner drink. Afterward, you might take in a movie at the old-fashioned **Bogar Theater** (223 East Michigan Avenue, Marshall, MI 49068), which features first-run films in a vintage movie house.

DAY 3

Morning

Linger over breakfast at the National House Inn. After a leisurely start, you might choose to head to the Calhoun County Fairgrounds south of downtown, where the **Marshall Antiques Market** is a popular hunting ground for enthusiasts from all over the Midwest. Held weekends from May through October, the market includes more than one hundred high-quality dealers. All merchandise is guaranteed. Admission is $4.00; if you're obsessive enough to want to be there first, you can pay $20 and get in Friday night. There has been talk of discontinuing the market, however, except for selected weekends, and so be sure to call ahead. For more information, call (616) 789–0990.

Before heading back onto Interstate 94, fuel up with a stop at the **Hi-Lite Drive In** (1005 East Michigan Avenue, Marshall, MI 49068; 616–781–6571). Home of local Elvis sightings (remember, he supposedly hides out in nearby Kalamazoo) and super-thick shakes, it's a popular hangout for all ages on the eastern city limits. Inexpensive.

THERE'S MORE

Albion

Just 11 miles east of Marshall, Albion is the birthplace of Albion College, one of the state's best private institutions. The classic tune "Sweetheart of Sigma Chi" was penned and first sung here. The town's downtown is one of the last all-brick main streets; Victory Park is considered one of the most picturesque sights in the state and has good fishing to boot. Nearby Riverside Cemetery has an unusual mixture of monuments, from simple Russian crosses to ornate Victorian tributes. A walking-tour guide is available at the office. Hiking fans flock to the 135 acres at the Whitehouse Nature Center (517–629–0582), which, unlike many other attractions, is open year-round. For information write the Albion Chamber of Commerce, 416 South Superior, Albion MI 49224; (517) 629–0582.

Battle Creek

Famous as the "Cereal City," Battle Creek is just 15 miles west of Marshall. The city's sanitarium made Battle Creek famous as the "health city" (it was also featured in the film *The Road to Wellville*). Today the city's industries are more diverse, with a minor-league class A baseball team, a fine-arts center with a unique Michigan artworks shop, a respected zoo, the Kellogg Bird Sanctuary, McCamley Place mall, a new indoor water park, and much more. For information call or write the Greater Battle Creek/Calhoun County Visitors and Convention Bureau, 77 East Michigan Avenue, Battle Creek, MI 49017; (616) 962–2240 or (800) 397–2240.

SPECIAL EVENTS

February. Moonlight Madness

March. Quilter's Weekend

July. Old-Fashioned Fourth

August. Calhoun County Fair

September. Marshall Historic Home Tour

November. Annual Christmas Parade

December. Christmas Candlelight Walk

OTHER RECOMMENDED RESTAURANTS

Cornwell's Turkeyville U.S.A. (18935 15½ Mile Road, Marshall, MI 49068; 616–781–4293) is a campy, country-style restaurant just north of downtown Marshall. Wayne and Marjorie Cornwell introduced their first turkey sandwich at a county fair thirty years ago; today their restaurant has become a 180-acre turkey farm and a complex of buildings known as "Turkeyville." The menu includes everything from a classic buttered turkey sandwich and turkey hot plate to a piled-high Reuben sandwich or turkey stir fry. An adjacent 170-seat dinner theater gives afternoon and evening performances accompanied by a carved-roast-turkey buffet. The Coffee Coop serves cappuccino and other specialty drinks. Open seven days a week; inexpensive to moderate.

Dug Out (107 West Michigan Avenue, Marshall, MI 49068; 616–781–8373) has been a local favorite since 1928 (many residents have been making daily stops for years). Recently renovated, it still specializes in family dining, with classics such as egg salad sandwich and a side of macaroni salad or new additions such as turkey croissants and Irish-style omelettes (Swiss cheese and corned beef hash). Inexpensive.

Espresso Yourself (301 East Michigan Avenue, Marshall, MI 49068; 616–789–1136) is a European-style coffeehouse on the outskirts of downtown. It serves light meals including low-fat pitas, bagels, and croissants as well as specialty coffee drinks. It's also a cybercafe, with access to the Internet. Inexpensive.

OTHER RECOMMENDED LODGINGS

Amerihost Inn (204 Winston Street, Marshall, MI 49068; 616–789–7890) is a newer, sixty-room chain motel with in-room coffee, sauna, and pool. Rates: $74–$91 per night, including continental breakfast.

Arbor Inn (15435 West Michigan Street, Marshall, MI 49068; 616–781–7772) is a budget-minded chain hotel located along a strip of fast-food restaurants outside the historic downtown. It features forty-eight well-kept units with air-conditioning and an outdoor pool. Rates: $52–$64 per night.

McCarthy's Bear Creek Inn (15230 C Drive North, Marshall, MI 49068; 616–781–8383) once was the home of a wealthy agricultural inventor (his claim to fame was the automatic milking machine). Just 1 mile from downtown, it's now an elegant bed-and-breakfast, with seven rooms in the original house and seven in a renovated dairy barn. The property overlooks charming Bear Creek and is ringed by fieldstone fences. Rates: $65–$125 per night, including breakfast.

FOR MORE INFORMATION

Marshall Area Chamber of Commerce, 424 East Michigan Avenue, Marshall, MI 49068; (800) 877–5163 or (616) 781–5763.

MICHIGAN

Saugatuck

MICHIGAN'S ART COAST

2 NIGHTS

Art Galleries • Shopping • Sand and Sun • Fishing • Golf

There are two sides to Saugatuck. The city is the home of world-famous Broward Marine, where multimillion-dollar yachts are assembled for well-heeled clients around the world. It's also home to the Saugatuck Drug Store, with a soda fountain that has served up cream sodas, phosphates, and malted milks for more than seventy years. That contrast is seen downtown, where quiet city parks coexist with sophisticated urban restaurants and where midwestern families share the picturesque streets with members of Chicago and Detroit's gay elite.

The city is nestled near the shore of Lake Michigan and defined by steep, rolling dunes to the west and lush, green orchards to the east. Saugatuck ("river's mouth," in the parlance of the American Indians who originally lived in the region) was settled in the mid-1800s by lumber interests, which produced a thriving mixture of sawmills, factories, and enough people to support them. Saugatuck, in fact, produced the majority of the lumber used to rebuild the Windy City (Chicago) after the Great Fire of 1871.

When the trees disappeared, however, so did much of the city. The lack of trees proved especially fateful to a neighboring village known as Singapore. Without the windbreak the trees provided, blowing sand eventually buried the village. Today this "ghost town" lives on in local lore and in stories told by tour guides and is a popular stop on the free-wheeling dune rides.

Saugatuck, however, survived and found new life as an art colony. In 1914, the Art Institute of Chicago, less than 130 miles away, began sponsoring a sum-

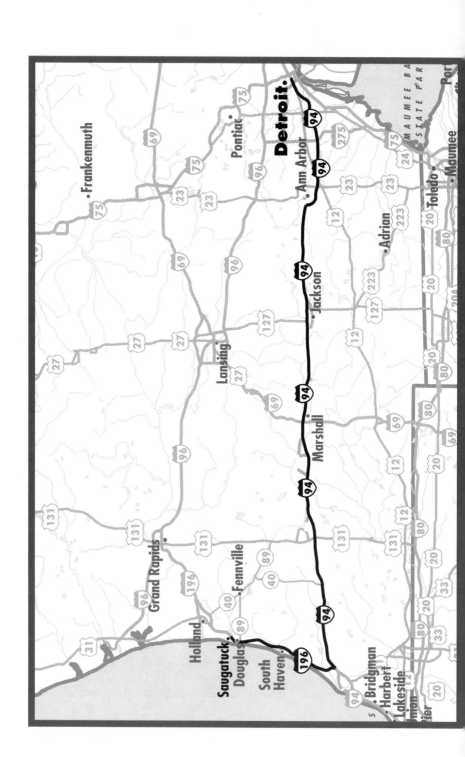

mer camp at nearby Ox-Bow. Lured by the warm breezes and picturesque location, other creative types and eventually tourists soon followed, earning Saugatuck a reputation as Michigan's "art coast." (Ox-Bow is still open to the public from mid-June through mid-August with galleries, demonstrations, and changing exhibitions in one of the most scenic spots in the area.)

Today Saugatuck is one of Michigan's most popular resort towns. Art still has a major role and is one of the main draws. (In Saugatuck, even the public restrooms are artistic—they're painted with scenes from Impressionist painter Georges Seurat's *Sunday Afternoon on the Island of La Grande Jatte*.) Art is so popular, in fact, that in summer the streets of Saugatuck become overwhelmingly crowded. If you do go in summer, try midweek. Otherwise, consider visiting during the off-season, when prices are lower and crowds are smaller. Or consider combining a few days in Saugatuck with a few in Holland (Michigan Escape Nine) or Southwestern Michigan (Michigan Escape Ten) for a longer vacation.

DAY 1

Saugatuck is 190 miles west of Detroit. (It's also just 127 miles from Chicago, which explains the proliferation of Illinois license plates in the town's parking lots.) To get there, take Interstate 94 west from Detroit to Interstate 196 north into the city. Plan on arriving in time for lunch.

Afternoon

LUNCH: The **Loaf & Mug** (236 Culver Street, Saugatuck, MI 49453; 616–857–2974) is a comfortable, casual eatery, winery, and bakery that serves breakfast and lunch daily. The airy backyard terrace has garden furniture where you can rest a while and partake of fresh salads, hearty muffins, or the restaurant's signature hollowed-out round loaf of bread filled with steaming soup du jour. Inexpensive to moderate.

Saugatuck has some of the best shopping in West Michigan. An eclectic blend of more than fifty stores and twenty-five art galleries—most housed in picturesque nineteenth-century storefronts—hawk stylish twentieth-century merchandise. Stores range from highbrow antiques and a year-round Christmas store to a campy boutique that lures browsers and buyers with a pair of female mannequin legs dangling from a second-story window. Depending on your interests, you can easily spend a weekend exploring the town's varied offerings.

Most of the shops and boutiques are clustered along Butler Street, the main drag. Here you'll find everything from funky jewelry to fine art. A few highlights are **American Spoon Foods** (308 Butler Street, Saugatuck, MI 49453; 616–347–3084), for gourmet made-in-Michigan treats; **Now and Then** (136 Butler Street, Saugatuck, MI 49453; 616–857–3036), with eclectic home wares; the **Singapore Bank Bookstore** (317 Butler Street, Saugatuck, MI 49453; 616–857–3785), saved from the sands when it was moved here; and **East of the Sun** (252 Butler Street, Saugatuck, MI 49453; 616–857–2640), a large and eclectic gift shop. **Bentley's** (616–857–4692) features English art and antiques. If trendiness threatens to overwhelm you, however, duck into the town's old-time hardware store, **Wilkins** (439 Butler Street, Saugatuck, MI 49453; 616–857–7501), where you'll find reassuring necessities such as fertilizer, mailboxes, and garden gloves as well as wicker and wind socks. It's been in business since 1864.

It was the area's reputation as an art coast that initially attracted galleries here. And they're still coming—between 1994 and 1996 the number jumped from fourteen to twenty-five. Strolling the city's galleries is a pleasant pastime, whether you're a browser or a buyer. Highlights include the **Button Gallery** (955 Center Street, Saugatuck, MI 49453; 616–857–2175), with its spectacular outdoor sculpture garden; the **Cain Gallery** (322 Butler Street; Saugatuck, MI 49453; 616–857–4353), specializing in midwestern artists; and **Good Goods** (106 Mason Street, Saugatuck, MI 49453; 616–857–1557), in a restored Victorian boardinghouse. Good Goods is also the only place in town where you can pick up a one-of-a-kind piece by one of the area's founding artists, Sylvia Randolph Bekker, still prolific at age 93.

Three other galleries in nearby Douglas (½ mile east of Saugatuck) are worth a special trip. The **Joyce Petter Gallery** (161 Blue Star Highway, Douglas, MI 49406; 616–857–7861) has been West Michigan's largest marketplace for fine art for more than twenty years and is housed in a landmark building. Not far away, the **Out of Hand Gallery** (147 Center Street, Douglas, MI 49406; 616–857–1420) showcases regional artists in all media, and **Australian Galleries** in Douglas (95 Blue Star Highway, Douglas, MI 49406; 616–857–6022) imports aboriginal art, landscapes, and wearables.

For a midafternoon snack, don't miss **Saugatuck Drug Store Soda Fountain** (201 Butler Street; Saugatuck, MI 49453; 616–857–2300). Here visitors take a trip back in time at the 1913 counter tucked in back of more modern necessities such as video games and a souvenir shop. (With movie rentals, an arcade, and more, this is a also a good place to remember for rainy days.)

DINNER: Friday nights are generally less crowded than Saturday at Saugatuck's many restaurants. A good one to try is **Toulouse** (248 Culver Street, Saugatuck, MI 49453; 616–857–1561), which features French country cuisine in a relaxed Provençal setting. If you're lucky, you'll get a table for two by one of the cozy fireplaces. Specialties include classic cassoulet, rack of lamb, veal scallopini, and a sinful chocolate fondue for dessert. Moderate.

If you're looking for something more casual, consider **Chequers** (220 Culver Street, Saugatuck, MI 49453; 616–857–1868) down the street. It's a comfy, English-style pub with a classic British menu that includes fish and chips and a famous shepherd's pie as well as a wide selection of beers and ales. Be forewarned, however: Reservations aren't accepted, and lines can be long on weekends. Moderate.

LODGING: Saugatuck, with thirty bed-and-breakfasts, is fast becoming the B&B capital of the Midwest. It would be a shame not to enjoy one while in town.

Where you'll be most comfortable depends on whether you're traveling with or without children. If you've got kids in tow, head for the **Twin Oaks Inn** (227 Griffith Street, Saugatuck, MI 49453; 616–857–1600). Jerry and Nancy Horney, who have owned Twin Oaks since 1989, welcome children with wide smiles and open arms. Spacious rooms in the 1860 English-style inn have portable cribs and pull-out beds. A large basket in the common room is full of well-loved and well-used toys. There's even a resident "grandma"— Nancy's mother, Kay, who oversees the property. Rates: $75–$100 per night.

If romance is your goal, few places compare to the **Fairchild House** (606 Butler Street, Saugatuck, MI 49453; 616–857–5985). Felicia Fairchild—who also happens to run the Saugatuck/Douglas Area Convention & Visitors Bureau—has furnished the three bedrooms in her white, two-story 1919 inn with European feather beds, Battenburg lace linens, down comforters, and on-request bathrobes. Fairchild is as well known for its elegant champagne break-fasts (with great crab eggs Benedict and raspberry nut bread) as for its elegant accommodations. Rates: $125 per night, double occupancy. The inn is closed in winter.

Unlike many other resort towns, Saugatuck has a lively nightlife scene. If you're in the mood for a nightcap, head for one of the popular late-night spots such as **Coral Gables** (220 Water Street, Saugatuck, MI 49453; 616–857–2162), which has four different bars under one roof. If ice cream's more your style, you won't do better than a lick at **Round the Corner** ice-cream parlor (134 Mason Street, Saugatuck, MI 49453; 616–857–8851), a town landmark that boasts more than fifty delicious flavors.

DAY 2

Morning

BREAKFAST: Enjoy the complimentary breakfast at your B&B or head for **Ida Red's Cottage** (645 Water Street, Saugatuck, MI 49453; 616–857–5803), considered by many locals to have the best breakfasts in town. Breakfasts are served all day; specialties include entrees with a Greek or Italian flair, such as the Italian sausage omelet. Inexpensive.

Morning is the best time to head to 1,100-acre **Saugatuck Dunes State Park**, one of the best-kept secrets in West Michigan. Just 3.5 miles north of downtown, it boasts a remote location and an early-morning serenity that's hard to beat. Families appreciate the 2 miles of Lake Michigan beachfront and 14 miles of hiking trails with breathtaking dune-top views. Uncrowded even in the heat of summer, it's also a great place for a picnic. Stop at one of the grocery stores and pack your own, or pick up the fixin's at the Loaf & Mug or at **Pumpernickel's Eatery** (210 Butler Street, Saugatuck, MI 49453; 616–857–1196), known for its sandwiches, its hearty daily specials served with homemade bread, and its gooey sticky buns; inexpensive. Be sure to bring along a bottle of local Michigan-made wine.

Afternoon

If you've had a taste of the dunes and want to see more, hop aboard one of the sixteen-seat open-air "schooners" (actually, a converted pickup) for a traditional half-hour thrill, the **Saugatuck Dune Ride** (6495 Washington Road, Saugatuck, MI 49453; 616–857–2253). You'll travel over shifting sands and take in a number of the attractions. Along the way, the driver is likely to suddenly yell, "We've lost the brakes!" But don't worry, it's all a planned part of the adventure.

The 1907 **S. S. *Kewatin*** (P.O. Box 638, Saugatuck, MI 49453; 616–857–2464) is an easy landmark to spot and another local favorite. Docked near the bridge that separates Saugatuck from neighboring Douglas, it had to be cut in half to fit through the narrow channel linking Lake Michigan and the Kalamazoo River. Now reassembled, it's the last of the classic Great Lakes steamships and a fascinating maritime museum that recaptures a lost era.

If you're looking to use your sea legs, the ***Star of Saugatuck*** (716 Water Street, Saugatuck, MI 49453; 616–857–4261) is a two-level stern-wheeler that offers cruises along the Kalamazoo River. Along the way, it passes beautiful homes (including one that once belonged to Al Capone) as well as the city's famous boatyard and other points of interest. Price: $10.00 per ride; $6.00 ages 3–12.

DINNER: The **Global Bar & Grill** (215 Butler Street, Saugatuck, MI 49453; 616–857–1555) is a rustic bistro that's one of those rare restaurants that are popular with both families and singles. It has brown-papered tables with crayons and an avant-garde menu that features many southern specials such as grilled shrimp with mango salsa. Moderate.

Afterward, you may want to check out what's on stage at the **Red Barn Playhouse** (3657 Sixty-third Street, Saugatuck, MI 49453; 616–857–7707), Saugatuck's popular summer-stock venue and the third-largest playhouse in the state. Performances such as "Ain't Misbehavin" and "Born Yesterday" are offered May through October. Next door is the **Belvedere Inn and Restaurant** (3656 Sixty-third Street, Saugatuck, MI 49453; 616–857–5501), which has a restaurant as well as a wonderful new dessert and cappuccino bar. It's the perfect place to top off your day with a creamy cafe latte.

DAY 3

Morning

BREAKFAST: Depending on your appetite, you have two choices. You might grab a bite at your B&B. But if you have something heartier in mind and don't feel like stopping for lunch (or dinner!) on the way home, head for the brunch at the **Clearbrook Golf Club & Restaurant** (6494 Clearbrook Drive, Saugatuck, MI 49453; 616–857–2000), just a few minutes outside of town. Many residents consider this the city's best restaurant. The brunch features the well-known 1912 breakfast (just $8.50), which includes a frittata, redskin potatoes, fruit, and your choice of French toast or pancakes.

Afterward, check out any shops or attractions you may have missed earlier, or head to neighboring Fennville, about 6 miles away. Here you'll find one of West Michigan's landmarks, also known as the **Crane Orchards and Pie Pantry Restaurant** (6054 124th Avenue, Fennville, MI 49408; 616–561–2297).

This is one of the best orchards in the state, with a cider mill, great-tasting pies to take home, and U-pick fruit orchards. It's also the site of the Crane House, the 1872 family homestead that's now a charming five-bedroom bed-and-breakfast. If you're here at lunch or dinnertime, don't miss the chance to sample the old-fashioned cooking in the adjacent farm-style restaurant. Inexpensive.

THERE'S MORE

Amusements. Blue Star Playland (6069 Blue Star Highway, Saugatuck, MI 49453; 616–857–1044) has go-kart rides, bumper boats, miniature golf, a driving range, moon walk, and more.

Antiques. If the prices in the downtown antiques shops are a bit steep for your budget, try to snag a bargain at the Allegan Antique Market (616–453–8780), about 30 miles away. The market is held at the Allegan County Fairgrounds and features more than 300 dealers on the last Sunday in each month from April through September.

Blueberries. Krupka's (2647 Sixty-eighth Street, Douglas, MI 49406; 616–857–4278) was the first blueberry farm in Michigan. It's been offering U-pick fun since the 1930s. If you're here during harvest time—traditionally between July 4 and Labor Day—this is great, if messy, fun for the whole family.

Canoe Rental. Old Allegan Canoe Rental (2722 Old Allegan Road, Fennville, MI 49408; 616–561–5481) offers three- and five-hour canoe trips through the scenic Allegan State Forest.

Fishing. Looking to bag the big one? From April through November a number of charters will take sport fishers out after chinook and coho salmon and lake, brook, and steelhead trout. Popular charter operators include Can't Miss Charters (616–857–6007) and Best Chance Charters (616–857–4762). A few even clean your catch and provide a box lunch.

Golf. West Shore Golf Club (14 Ferry Street, Douglas, MI 49406; 616–857–2500) was founded in 1917 and is the second-oldest golf course in the state. Mi-Ro (Blue Star Highway and 130th Street, Douglas; MI 49406; 616–857–6161) has a nine-hole course and a driving range.

Wineries. The Fenn Valley Winery (6130 122nd Avenue, Fennville, MI 49408; 616–561–2396) offers free tastings, direct discounts on products, and a picnic area. Tabor Hill, another local award-winning vineyard, maintains a wine-tasting room in downtown Saugatuck (214 Butler Street, Saugatuck, MI 49453; 616–857–4859).

SPECIAL EVENTS

February. Midweek Winterfest, Saugatuck
Mardi Gras Celebration, Douglas

May. Memorial Day Parade, Saugatuck
Sauga-Duck Festival, Saugatuck

July. Fourth of July Celebration, Saugatuck
Harbor Days/Venetian Night, Saugatuck

August. Sidewalk Sale, Saugatuck
Taste of Saugatuck/Douglas

September. Allegan County Fair, Allegan
Clown Festival, Saugatuck

October. Gallery Stroll Weekend, Saugatuck
Halloween Harvest, Fennville

November. Moonlight Madness Sale, Saugatuck
Holiday Lights of Saugatuck

OTHER RECOMMENDED RESTAURANTS

Douglas

Auction House (8 Center Street, Douglas, MI 49406; 616–857–4292) is known for its huge breakfasts and low prices (you can get pancakes smothered in strawberries for less than $4.00). The homemade biscuits and gravy are also a big draw. Inexpensive.

Fennville

Restaurant SuCasa (306 West Main Street, Fennville, MI 49408; 616–561–5493) has surprisingly authentic Mexican eats and atmosphere for a West Michigan town and has been written up in both the *Detroit Free Press* and the *Chicago Tribune*. Moderate.

Saugatuck

Douglas Dinette (11 Center Street, Saugatuck, MI 49453; 616–857–4240) features low-fat and vegetarian meals as well as weekend breakfast specials in a smoke-free setting. Inexpensive to moderate.

OTHER RECOMMENDED LODGINGS

Fennville

Kingsley House (626 West Main Street, Fennville, MI; 616–561–6425) features six rooms in an 1886 mansion built by the man who introduced fruit trees to the area. Spacious, Victorian-inspired rooms are named after a variety of apple. Rates: $75–$145.

Saugatuck

Maplewood Hotel (428 Butler Street, Saugatuck, MI 49453; 616–857–1771) has fifteen antique-filled bedrooms in the heart of Saugatuck's shops, galleries, and restaurants. The 1860s Greek Revival inn was a former home; breakfast is served in the Burr Tillstrom Dining Room, named for the former Saugatuck resident and creator of the TV puppet show *Kukla, Fran, and Ollie*. Rates: $85–$155 per night.

Seymour House (1248 Blue Star Highway, Glen, MI 49407; 616–227–3918) is an eleven-acre estate near Saugatuck. The 1862 inn has five spacious guest rooms, a log cabin, and gourmet breakfasts. Rates: $120–$180.

Wickwood Inn (510 Butler Street, Saugatuck, MI 49453; 616–857–1465) is probably Saugatuck's best-known (and most-expensive) bed-and-breakfast. It's owned and run by Julee Rosso-Miller, a New York expatriate and a coauthor of the *Silver Palate Cookbook*. The eleven-room European-style inn is filled with French and English antiques, overstuffed chairs, fresh flowers, and original art. Guest rooms are equally attractive. Rates: $140–$190 per night.

FOR MORE INFORMATION

Saugatuck/Douglas Area Convention and Visitors Bureau, 303 Culver Street, P.O. Box 28, Saugatuck, MI 49453; (616) 857–1701 or www. saugatuck.com..

Holland

DUTCH TREAT

2 NIGHTS

Flowers • Dutch Village • Discount Shopping • Museums

If a trip to the Netherlands is beyond your travel budget this year, you can still enjoy a touch of Dutch in Holland, Michigan. Nestled in the state's tulip country, the village is full of nostalgia for the Old World, with wooden-shoe dancers, authentic windmills, and other Dutch treats.

For years, people of Dutch ancestry dominated the city. Holland, in fact, remained 90 percent Dutch for more than a century. The ethnic makeup is a bit more varied today (the area is also home to the state's largest Hispanic community), but it still has local families who can trace their roots back to the 1840s, when Dutch separatists settled in this part of the Midwest. Whatever their original heritage, Holland residents know that it's the city's Dutch traditions that attract thousands each year, and all are pleased to roll out the *welkom* mat for visitors.

Many people head for Holland in May (reason enough, for some, to go at other times), when the annual Tulip Time Festival is in full bloom. At that time, downtown's scrubbed streets are full of flowers, costumed *klompen* dancers, local bands, parades, and thousands of tourists. There's even an inspector—called the *burgemeister*—to make sure everything is in top shape. If Holland's amusement-park quality wears thin or you start longing for all-American attractions, head for Grand Haven, about 20 miles north, which has a great lakefront and a new 3-mile boardwalk. Together, the two cities make a great quick getaway.

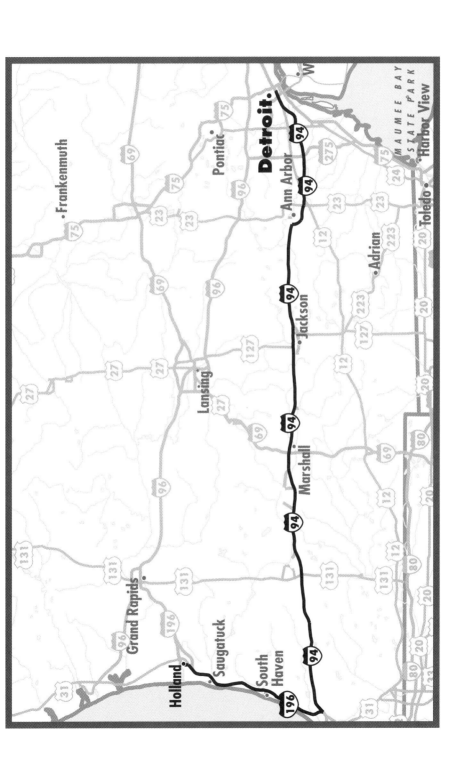

DAY 1

Afternoon

From Detroit, Holland is about 172 miles. To get there, take Interstate 94 west to Interstate 196 north into Holland. Plan to leave in midafternoon and arrive in time for dinner.

DINNER: After the three-hour ride from Detroit, you should be ready to eat. To get into the Holland spirit, head for **Queen's Inn** (12350 James Street, Holland, MI 49423; 616–393–0310), which claims to be the only town eatery serving authentic Dutch fare. A top choice is the Pigs in a Blanket, the thick pea soup, and a helping of Dutch apple pie. Reservations recommended for dinner on weekends. Moderate.

LODGING: Bonnie's Parsonage 1908 (6 East Twenty-fourth Street, Holland, MI 49423; 616–396–1316) was the area's first bed-and-breakfast, and it's still one of the best. It offers three spacious rooms in a former 1908 parsonage (hence the name) near Hope College and features a full breakfast of freshly baked breads, muffins, and egg specialties served in the formal dining room. The finely landscaped backyard has a croquet set; in summer, guests choose to enjoy the view with breakfast on the outdoor patio. Rates: $85–$135 per night. *Note:* Children are allowed, but adults are preferred. Most families go to the Holiday Inn (see "Other Recommended Lodgings").

DAY 2

Morning

BREAKFAST: Parsonage 1908 will fill you up for a busy day. If it's April or May, you'll be overwhelmed by the spectacle at **Veldheer Tulip Gardens** (12755 Quincy Street at U.S. Highway 31, Holland, MI 49423; 616–399–1900). Veldheer's is Holland's only tulip farm and perennial gardens. Tulips take center stage in spring, followed by perennials, such as lilies and peonies, and annuals from June through October. Green thumbs are in their glory; you can also pick up bulbs and flowering plants for your at-home garden. Beds are numbered to correspond with mail-order catalogs so that you can place orders for bulbs after seeing the real thing. Admission: $5.00. *Tip:* Locals recommend visiting at dusk, when the tour buses are gone and the sunset casts a warm glow on the thousands of beautiful blooms.

Adjacent to the tulip gardens is **DeKlomp Wooden Shoe & Delftware Factory**, the only production Delft factory in the United States. You can watch the crisp blue-and-white china made by hand. Artisans carve wooden shoes on authentic Dutch machinery, and you can try on a pair to take home.

Just 2 miles from downtown is **"De Zwaan"** (The Swan), a 230-year-old working Dutch windmill. It's part of the **Windmill Island Municipal Park** (Seventh Street and Lincoln Avenue, Holland, MI 49423; 616–355–1030). Shipped to Holland in 1964, it's the last windmill the Dutch government allowed to leave the Netherlands. At 12 stories high, its steel beams and sails span 80 feet and crank out a fine graham flour, which is available for purchase within the park. Costumed guides escort visitors through the mill. Other park highlights include the **Posthouse Museum,** a charming replica of a 200-year-old Dutch country inn, with an interesting collection of Dutch furniture, free rides for kids on an authentic Dutch carousel, a miniature display of Dutch life in the "Little Netherlands," and the ubiquitous gift shop. Admission is $5.50 for adults and $2.50 for children ages five to twelve.

Afternoon

If you're ready for some all-American shopping, downtown Holland has both small boutiques and a large outlet mall. Wander along the restored nineteenth-century storefronts in the central business district, where shops range from the whimsical **Sand Castle Toys** (2 East Eighth Street, Holland, MI 49423) to the literary-minded **Center Aisle Books** (77 East Eighth Street). Downtown's **Centennial Park** is an old-fashioned shady downtown square with a canopy of century-old trees. It's a good starting point for walking tours of downtown, nearby Hope College, and the historic district. Good walking-tour brochures are available at the Herrick Public Library on River and Twelfth Streets.

Also worth a stop is the gallery shop of the **Holland Area Arts Council** (25 West Eighth Street, Holland, MI 49423), which has an eclectic collection of interesting stuff, including jewelry, games, and art by local artists and craftspeople. If you're looking for bargains, the **Holland Outlet Center** (800–866–5900) has more than thirty-five stores, including Carter's Childrenswear, Barbizon Lingerie, Eddie Bauer, and Royal Doulton in a—what else?—re-created Dutch village.

DINNER: Piper (2225 South Shore Drive, Holland, MI 49423; 616–335–5866) in nearby Macatawa (ten minutes from downtown Holland), was

named the best restaurant in southwestern Michigan by *Grand Rapids* magazine. It overlooks Lake Macatawa and features a menu of nouvelle cuisine, including a sixteen-ounce pork chop topped with arugula, roma tomatoes, and goat cheese; oregano-seared Atlantic salmon; and for dessert the rum-vanilla-caramel flan or chocolate Chambord cake. Moderate to expensive.

If it's summer, you might want to take in a performance at the **Hope Summer Repertory Theater** (141 East Twelfth Street, Holland, MI 49423; 616–395–7895). Besides staging three musicals and two plays in a rotating repertory from mid-June through mid-August, the group mounts an annual Christmas celebration. Plays are held at DeWitt Center, part of Hope College.

DAY 3

Morning

BREAKFAST: On Sunday, **Calypso's** in the Holiday Inn (U.S. Highway 31 at Twentieth Street, Holland, MI 49423; 616–394–0111) is the place to be. From 10:00 A.M. to 2:00 P.M., the hotel serves the area's largest Sunday brunch, with more than 70 feet of breakfast and lunch entrees, including chicken, fish, roast beef, eggs, baked goods, and more for just $12.95 per person. Moderate.

Today's the day to hit the beach and relax before heading home. Sun and sand can be found at Holland State Park or at one of the many spots in nearby Grand Haven. **Holland State Park** (2215 Ottawa Beach Road, Holland, MI 49423; 616–399–9390) is one of the state's most popular parks, with Victorian gingerbread cottages (part of a beach development that dates back to the 1880s), 1,800 feet of sugary sand, and a full gamut of water sports, from boating and pier and charter fishing to jet skis and windsurfing. There are also a number of picnic tables that face the channel, good spots to relax and watch the world go by.

Before heading home, be sure to stop at the **Crane's Orchards Pie Pantry and Restaurant** (6054 124th Avenue, Fennville, MI 49408; 616–561–2297) , an attraction in its own right and a West Michigan institution. Crane's U-pick farms are popular with families, as are the famous pies and the adjacent inexpensive country-style restaurant. There's even a B&B in the original mid-nineteenth-century homestead.

THERE'S MORE

Academia. Serene Hope College (141 East Twelfth Street, Holland, MI 49423; 616–395–7000) is a great area in which to wander. The institution traces its roots to the same Dutch expatriates who founded the town. Today, Hope is a nationally recognized liberal-arts college affiliated with the Reformed Church in America. Guided tours are available by appointment, but you can easily take in the campus on foot.

Antiques. The Tulip City Antique Mall (3500 U.S. Highway 31, Holland, MI 49423; 616–786–4424) has more than eighty dealers with collectibles that range from oak furniture and imported Dutch wares to old advertising and maritime paraphernalia.

Bicycling. Holland State Park (2215 Ottawa Beach Road, Holland, MI 49423; 616–399–9390) has more than 100 miles of scenic paths. Bring your own wheels or rent some at Papa Donn's (2250 Ottawa Beach Road, Holland, MI 49423). They're open seven days a week from Memorial Day through Labor Day.

History. City residents are justly proud of two local museums, the Holland Museum (31 West Tenth Street, Holland, MI 49423; 616–392–9084) and the Cappon House (228 West Ninth Street, Holland, MI 49423, 616–392–6740). Together they hold more than 400 years of Dutch and American heritage, with displays that cover Holland's 150-year history. Interesting exhibits include an 1866 Amsterdam dollhouse, a display of items from the 1939 New York World's Fair, a section on the area's Great Resort era in the nineteenth century, and a display on Lake Michigan's maritime lore.

Water Sports. Holland Water Sports (2212 Ottawa Beach Road, Holland, MI 49423; 616–786–2628) rents jet skis, parasailing paraphernalia, and other watery family fun.

SPECIAL EVENTS

February. Valentine's Day Gallery Stroll

April. Cambodian New Year's Celebration

May. Cinco de Mayo Fiesta
Tulip Time Festival

June. Celebration of the Arts

July. Ottawa County Fair
Fourth of July Fireworks

August. Art in the Park

September. Fall Color Tours

November. Gallery Stroll

December. Dutch Winter Festival
Vietnamese New Year's Bash

OTHER RECOMMENDED RESTAURANTS

The Hatch (1870 Ottawa Beach Road, Holland, MI 49423; 616–399–9120) has steak, seafood, and a popular brunch. Moderate.

OTHER RECOMMENDED LODGINGS

Country Inn by Carlson (12260 James Street, Holland, MI 49424; 616–396–6677) has 116 rooms near the outlet center. Rates: $79–$99.

Dutch Colonial Inn (560 Central Avenue, Holland, MI 49423; 616–396–3664) has five elegant guest rooms in a 1928 colonial home best suited to adult guests. All have private baths; some have whirlpools. Rates: $80–$150 per night.

Holiday Inn and Conference Center (650 East Twenty-fourth Street, Holland, MI 49423; 616–394–0111 or 800–465–4329) is the place for you if you don't like B&Bs or if you've brought the kids along. It has 168 rooms, an indoor pool, exercise and game rooms, as well as a restaurant and nightclub. Rates: $89–$129 per night.

FOR MORE INFORMATION

Holland Area Convention and Visitors Bureau, 76 East Eighth Street, Holland, MI 49423; (800) 506–1299.

MICHIGAN

Southwestern Michigan

HARBOR HOLIDAY

3 NIGHTS

Antiques • Shopping • Sun and Fun • Nature • Wineries

A weekend visit to West Michigan's Harbor Country reveals as many Chicago natives as Detroiters. Just an hour from the Loop, this has become the chosen summer community for Windy City expatriates such as movie critic Roger Ebert, novelist Andrew Greeley, and scores of others who build and inhabit the pricey condos and glass-fronted luxury homes that line Lake Michigan.

Located along the lakefront in the most southwestern corner of the state, Harbor Country (a Chamber of Commerce nickname) includes eight communities that form the gateway to Michigan: Michiana, Grand Beach, New Buffalo, Union Pier, Lakeside, Harbert, Sawyer, and Three Oaks. As a destination, the area is sometimes called (most often by its Convention and Visitors Bureau and local public-relations efforts) the "Riviera on Lake Michigan" and the "Hamptons of the Midwest." The area also encompasses nearby towns such as Baroda, Buchanan, Bridgman, and Berrien Springs.

Behind its silver-spoon facade, however, much of the area's sleepy old charm remains. Tony shops may line the main streets, but the sand, surf, and sunsets are still famous—and still free. Hotels cover all price ranges, as do restaurants. You can easily drop $100 for dinner for two at one of the city's tony restaurants, but you can also easily enjoy a huge breakfast of thick French toast slices, two eggs, and two slices of bacon for just $3.00 at Rosie's in downtown New Buffalo. And there are plenty of things to keep you busy, whether you're a solo sojourner, a curious couple, a fun-loving family, or any other type of traveler.

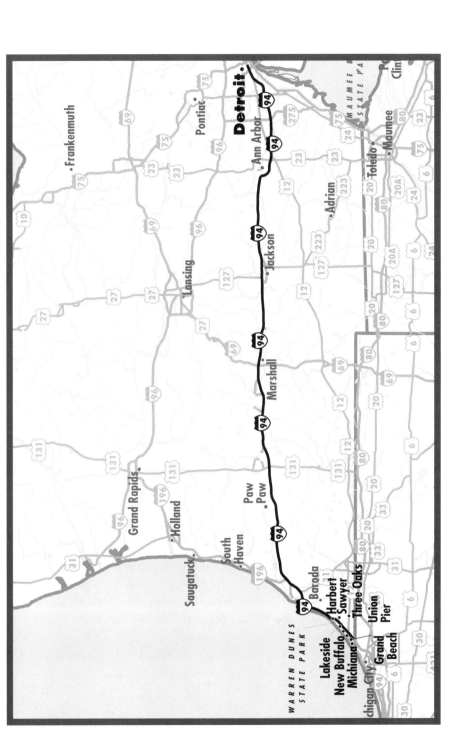

DAY 1

Afternoon

Harbor Country is about 200 miles from Detroit, roughly a three-hour trip west along Interstate 94. Plan to leave early enough to arrive in time for dinner.

DINNER: The **Red Arrow Roadhouse** (15710 Red Arrow Highway, Sawyer, MI 49129; 616–469–3939) is a quintessential Harbor Country eatery. Located in Union Pier, it's a laid-back place with fresh fish, pastas, and salads that won't break your budget, along with more than thirty varieties of beer. Good people-watching too, colorfully combining locals and landed gentry.

LODGING: Harbor Country is a haven for bed-and-breakfast fans. One of the best and most popular is the **Pebble House** (15093 Lake Shore, Lakeside, MI 49116; 616–469–1416). Unlike many B&Bs, the Pebble House is appropriate for children as well as adults. Travelers without kids may choose one of the rooms in the 1912 main house, and families often opt for the three-bedroom Coach House or the two-bedroom Blueberry House. The main house has seven rooms and suites in three guest buildings connected by wooden walkways and pergolas. Guests are encouraged to use the tennis courts and the nearby beach. Everyone enjoys the public areas filled with arts-and-crafts-style antiques and Mission furniture, as well as a hearty breakfast. Rates: $110–$170 per night, including breakfast.

DAY 2

Morning

BREAKFAST: The Pebble House will fortify you for the day ahead. Now it's time for a little exploring. Harbor Country's towns offer widely varying personalities, from simple to sophisticated. Your first stop will probably be New Buffalo, the area's historic hub. Now a seaside boomtown, it's been almost overrun with development that threatens to obliterate its small-town charm. Tiny summer cottages that once sold for almost nothing now command six-figure prices. The town's the chosen outpost of choice for most wealthy Windy City residents, as well as the center for most shopping. Nonetheless, the town still maintains vestiges of its former self, including the hundred-year-old **Barbie's Department Store** and a number of friendly neighborhood taverns that serve up simple fare such as fresh fish and fries.

Wander New Buffalo's Whittaker Street and you'll find wares that run from small collectibles to major home furnishings. You'll also find the most sophisticated clothing stores this side of the Magnificent Mile, with favorites including **Trillium** (30 North Whittaker Street, New Buffalo, MI 49129; 616–469–1400), and ready-to-wear from classic to trendy at **La Grande Trunk** (447 South Whittaker Street, New Buffalo, MI 49129; 616–469–2122). If you want to update your house instead of your wardrobe, ideas and inspiration can be found at **Le Panâche** (122 North Whittaker Street, New Buffalo, MI 49129; 616–469–4610) and **By Design** (427 South Whittaker, New Buffalo, MI 49129; 616–469–1930), both run by local designers, and **Hearthwoods at Home** (110 North Whittaker Street, New Buffalo, MI 49129; 616–469–5551), which specializes in hand-crafted furniture made from Michigan logs and twigs as well as a wide selection of rustic accessories, including candlesticks, frames, mirrors, and whimsical wares. Other shops worth a stop include **The Shop Across the Street** (126 South Whittaker Street, New Buffalo, MI 49129; 616–469–0669), with an eclectic collection of antique pillows, furniture, robes, jewelry, and other goodies; **Michigan Thyme** (107 North Whittaker Street, New Buffalo, MI 49129), a foodie's fantasy; the **Clipper Ship Gallery** (116 North Whittaker Street, New Buffalo, MI 49129), the place for marine-inspired art; and the **Art Barn Gallery North** (419 South Whittaker Street, New Buffalo, MI 49129), which sells fine art, jewelry, sculpture, and pottery and features an open-air art market each third weekend in summer, when you can watch artists at work under sunny skies.

More sunny skies can be enjoyed at the **New Buffalo Lakefront Park and Beach,** at the north end of Whittaker Street across the bridge. It can be crowded on a really hot day, but families enjoy the dune climb and resulting panoramic views as well as feeding the ducks, geese, and gulls. Another popular place is the **Warren Dunes State Park** (616–426–4013), where the massive dunes encourage climbing and, later, resting along the beautiful sandy beach. On a clear day you can see the Sears Tower and other Chicago landmarks across the way.

Afternoon

LUNCH: Redamak's (616 East Buffalo Street, New Buffalo, MI 49129; 616–469–4522) is known as the home of "the hamburger that made New Buffalo famous." This casual eatery with a range of food is perfect for the whole family—and has two game rooms if the kids (or you) get restless. Try the "workingman's special" during the week, when burger and fries are just $3.25. In good weather, there's dining on the open-air patio. Inexpensive.

Had enough shopping? If not, more can be found along the Red Arrow Highway. If antiques are your passion, you'll be in heaven here. Harbor Country is one of the state's major antiques centers, with an assortment of shops and malls spread out across the picturesque countryside. Wandering through the shops, schmoozing with dealers, and browsing and buying is a great way to spend an afternoon—or longer.

Most shops are spread out along the Red Arrow Highway. If you prefer the wide selection at antiques malls, Harbor Country has those as well. **Dunes Antique Center** (12825 Red Arrow Highway, Sawyer, MI 49129; 616–426–4043) is the newest. With more than 20,000 square feet and ninety dealers, it presents a broad selection of antiques and collectibles, from heirloom quality through funky 1950s furniture and more. In Harbert you'll find the **Harbert Antique Mall** (13887 Red Arrow Highway, Sawyer, MI 49129; 616–469–0977), with more than fifty dealers with a constantly changing inventory of goods. But the most unusual antiques mall in the state—possibly in all the Midwest—is the **Antique Mall and Village** (9300 Union Pier Road, Union Pier, MI 49129; 616–469–2555). In addition to a main building housing varied dealers, it has a chapel with a (surprisingly good) copy of the ceiling of the Sistine Chapel, a diner, a pottery emporium, and a log cabin full of Native American artifacts.

DINNER: Rest your feet over a meal at **Miller's Country House,** not far from the antiques malls, at 16409 Red Arrow Highway, Union Pier, MI 49129; (616–469–5950). Depending on your mood, you can choose to eat in the rustic dining room and watch chefs prepare food in the exhibition kitchen or opt for the more formal dining rooms that overlook a beautiful woodland garden (wherever you choose, dress is strictly casual). Entrees range from gourmet pizzas and steakburgers to more creative cuisine such as grilled Portobello mushrooms and New Zealand Rack of Lamb with Mango Chutney, the house specialty. Moderate.

DAY 3

Morning

BREAKFAST: If you're opting to eat out, consider a stop for an impromptu breakfast at **Harbert Swedish Bakery** (Red Arrow Highway, Harbert, MI 49115; 616–469–1777). Traditional Swedish breads and cakes are the draw; tables inside and out are usually crowded. Inexpensive.

Not far from the Red Arrow Highway is the area's other big attraction—rolling hills covered with lush grapevines that yield award-winning wines. Talented local winemakers attribute their success to the sandy, well-drained, fertile soil; the hilly terrain; and Lake Michigan's weather-tempering influence. Whatever the cause, you'll enjoy the results. Wineries offer free tasting and tours as well as fine dining and specialty food items. Depending on the time of day when you visit, you can enjoy picturesque picnic sites and scenic lookouts as well as great gift shops. One winery—Tabor Hill—is also home to a gourmet restaurant, the only such eatery of its kind in the state.

Start your vineyard tour at **Heart of the Vineyard Winery** (10981 Hills Road, Baroda, MI; 800–716–9463). The winery is housed in a restored 1881 post-and-beam plank barn, and sampling is done inside at the hand-hewn bar or outside on an open-air veranda. The Moersch family take pride in their product and are happy to share their secrets. After a tour and tasting, you can opt to stay longer in the vineyard's adjacent bed and breakfast. Heart of the Vineyard also has a tasting room and gift store at exit 6 on I–94.

St. Julian Winery (716 South Kalamazoo Street, Paw Paw, MI 49129; 616–469–3150) is the state's oldest and largest-selling winery. It has a wine-tasting center near Interstate 94 in Union Pier, where oenophiles can stock up on more than thirty-five varieties of wine, nonalcoholic juices, and the vineyard's famous Italian dressing. The vineyard has won a number of national and international awards.

Top off your day with a tour of **Tabor Hill Winery** (185 Mt. Tabor Road, 49129; 800–283–3363). A vineyard visit takes guests through the rows of huge vats and small oak casks that hold the aging wines. Afterward, enjoy the wines at the winery on Mt. Tabor Road in Buchanan or at the Tabor Hill Champagne Cellar on the Red Arrow Highway in Bridgman.

LUNCH: Tabor Hill Winery & Restaurant (800–283–3363) is the perfect place to end your Harbor Country weekend. Lunch and dinner are served

Wednesday through Sunday from April through November. From December through March, it's open only on weekends. Entrees include specialties such as mesquite-grilled shrimp, Maryland soft-shell crab, and raspberry chicken. Not surprisingly, the dining room overlooks the surrounding vineyards and breathtaking countryside. Moderate.

THERE'S MORE

Family Fun. Pee-Wee golf, go-karts, bumper boats, and batting cages are just a few of the thrills for small fries found at Captain Mike's Fun Park on Red Arrow Highway in Sawyer (616–465–5747). Open on weekends only.

Flora and Fauna. Fernwood, not far away between Berrien Springs and Buchanan (13988 Range Line Road, Niles, MI 49120; 616–683–8653) is a relaxing, six-acre botanical garden and nature facility. A pleasant sidetrip, it includes a lilac garden, a boxwood garden, a fern trail, a perennial garden, and a rock garden. There's also a nice Visitors Center, with a tea room that's a great place to take a break before hitting the interstate.

Golf. The Harbor Country area is home to fine courses, including Pebblewood (9794 South Jericho Road, Bridgman, MI 49106; 616–465–5611).

Orchards. Tree–Mendus Fruit Farm (East Eureka Road, Berrien Springs, MI 49103; 616–782–7101) is one of the largest orchards in the Midwest, with a delightful one-hour harvest tour, 560 acres of U-pick orchards, a nature park with hiking trails and swings for the kids, even a picnic area and chapel in the woods.

SPECIAL EVENTS

March. Other Side of the Lake Art Exhibition, New Buffalo

April. Art Attack, areawide

June. Flag Day, Three Oaks

July. Lakeside Arts and Crafts Festival, Lakeside

August. Ship and Shore Festival, New Buffalo
Berrien County Youth Fair, Berrien Springs

September. Apple Cider Century Bike Tour, areawide

November. Antique Trek, areawide

OTHER RECOMMENDED RESTAURANTS

New Buffalo

Hannah's Restaurant (115 South Whittaker Street, New Buffalo, MI 49117; 616–469–1440) serves lunch and dinner daily, with an extensive menu that features everything from pot roast to an award-winning apple-brandied pork chop. There's also a children's menu. Reservations recommended. Moderate.

Union Pier

Jenny's (16220 Lakeshore Road, Union Pier, MI 49129; 616–469–6545) is regarded by many as the best restaurant in the area. On weekends, it's also incredibly crowded, with reservations a necessity. Specialties include Cornish hens with raisins and almonds, anything with Portobello mushrooms, and the profiteroles for dessert. Housed in a restored 1920s inn, it's also open for lunch. Expensive.

Skip's Other Place (Red Arrow Highway between New Buffalo and Union Pier, Union Pier, MI 49129; 616–469–3330) is Harbor Country's oldest fine-dining restaurant and is known for its prime rib and steaks. There's also a children's menu. Reservations are suggested. Moderate to expensive.

OTHER RECOMMENDED LODGINGS

Lakeside

Lakeside Inn (15281 Lake Shore, Lakeside, MI 49129; 616–469–0600) is reminiscent of another era, with a 100-foot-long front porch lined with rockers. There's also a private beach. Breakfast is included in the rates for the thirty rooms, and children are welcome. Rates: $75–$150 per night.

Harbor Grand Hotel & Suites (111 West Water Street; New Buffalo, MI 49117; 616–469–7700) is the newest addition to New Buffalo and the only larger hotel in Harbor Country. Just steps from the marina, beach, shops, and restaurants, its architecture and fifty-seven guest rooms were inspired by

Frank Lloyd Wright. There are also an indoor pool and spa with sundeck, gym, and harbor and lake views. Rates: $165–$205 per night.

Union Pier

The Inn at Union Pier (9708 Berrien, Union Pier, MI 49129; 616–469–4700) has sixteen spacious guest rooms that are just 200 steps from the beach and Lake Michigan. The charming inn also has the largest private collection of *kakelugns*—antique Swedish ceramic fireplaces—in the country. Rates: $125–$195.

The Pine Garth Inn & Cottages (15790 Lakeshore Road, Union Pier, MI 49129; 616–469–1642) was built in 1905 as a summer home. There are seven bedrooms and five romantic cottage suites with private hot tubs that are surrounded by wooden fences. Located on a high bluff, six of the seven rooms and all the suites offer vistas of Lake Michigan. The inn also has a private beach. Rates: $130 per night.

FOR MORE INFORMATION

Harbor Country Chamber of Commerce, 3 West Buffalo Street, New Buffalo, MI 49117; (616) 469–5409.

Southwest Michigan Tourist Council, 2300 Pipestone Road, Benton Harbor, MI 49022; (616) 925–6301.

Grand Rapids

GRAND TIMES IN GRAND RAPIDS

2 NIGHTS

Restaurants • Nightlife • Museums • Gardens

Grand Rapids is Michigan's second city, in both size and in psyche. Quieter and more reserved than Detroit, it is still a surprisingly vibrant urban area, with lots of appeal for weekend visitors. The city owes its development to the hydropower provided by the nearby Grand River and to the abundant lumber in nearby forests. By 1900, Grand Rapids was legendary for its high-quality furniture, a reputation it maintains. (For years, it was known as the Furniture City.) Two Grand Rapids giants—Steelcase and Herman Miller—are responsible for most of the office furniture used across the United States.

There is, however, much more to Grand Rapids than furniture. Today's city is an eclectic blend of old and new, liberal and conservative. The renovated downtown boasts a burgeoning entertainment district with a full plate of new restaurants, a second high-rise hotel, a riverwalk park, Museum Row, and a skywalk that links downtown landmarks.

It all adds up to a city that has become one of Michigan's fastest-growing travel destinations, no longer just a pit stop on the way to the Lake Michigan shoreline.

DAY 1

Grand Rapids is about three and one-half hours west of Detroit via Interstate 96. Plan on leaving town a little early on Friday to beat the rush-hour traffic and to leave you enough time to arrive in Grand Rapids in time for a late dinner.

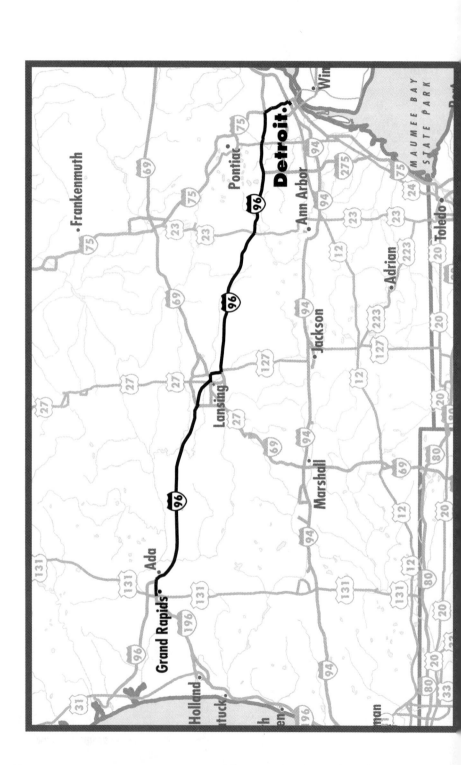

Afternoon

DINNER: To get yourself in the mood for some weekend fun, check out the **Rhythm Kitchen Cafe** (Monroe Center 49503; 616–774–4199), which features big-name bands and blues singers in a cafe-style setting. Talent from around the country shows up for jams every night, but Thursdays through Saturdays are the best. The music is accompanied by a full menu of spicy Cajun and Creole-style entrees and lots of great people-watching. Moderate.

After dinner, check out one of the city's newest entertainment venues. The **B.O.B. (Big Old Building)** has become Grand Rapids' hottest new hangout. Located at the corner of Fulton and Monroe, this former grocery warehouse is home to seven new restaurants and nightclubs, including Sharkey's Pool Room, Dr. Grins Comedy Club, a microbrewery, coffeehouse, wine room, and movie house. It's worth checking out if only for the people-watching, best on Friday and Saturday nights.

LODGING: **The Amway Grand Plaza Hotel** (187 Monroe Street NW, Grand Rapids, MI 49503; 616–774–2000 or 800–253–3590) is the best hotel in the city, with 682 rooms in a renovated 1913 building. It was restored by the Amway Corporation in nearby Ada, hence the name. Chandeliers, period furnishings, and lots of antiques help set an elegant mood. Rooms are spacious and traditionally decorated. There are six well-regarded restaurants and an indoor pool and sauna as well as racquetball and squash courts. Rates start at $95.

DAY 2

Morning

BREAKFAST: **Arnie's Bakery** (3561 Twenty-Eighth Street SE, Grand Rapids, MI 49503; 616–956–7901) is a good place to head for homemade baked goods and other tempting treats. Inexpensive.

For a better understanding of the city and its history, start your day with a few hours at the **Van Andel Museum Center of the Public Museum of Grand Rapids** (272 Pearl Street NW, Grand Rapids, MI 49503; 616–456–3977). Despite the ponderous name (a political move to please an influential patron), the museum is a mostly lighthearted look at the city's fascinating and diverse history. Here, in bright and informative displays, the area's past is literally laid out at your feet.

Walk through a re-creation of a downtown street from the 1890s, peek in the windows of a vintage department store, theater, and other shops. Curious about how your sofa is made? Wander through the twentieth-century furniture factory, where you can turn cranks and learn about the once-arduous chore of making a chair. Don't miss "Ashinabek: The People of This Place," one of the best exhibits on Native Americans of the Great Lakes found in any American museum. Kids of all ages (that means adults, too!) love taking a spin or two on the restored nineteenth-century Spillman carousel on the first floor. If you're a science buff or if you have small kids, be sure to check out the fine museum shop, which stocks everything from rubber snakes to educational videos, along with reproduction vintage jewelry, and lots more.

LUNCH: Resist the temptation to grab lunch in the museum cafe—you'll be disappointed. A number of fast-food places are near the museum, in case you're starving. If you want something a little more original, head over to **J. Gardella's Tavern** (11 Ionia Avenue SW, Grand Rapids, MI 49503; 616–459–8824). It features a painted tin ceiling and an enormous wooden bar, where friendly bartenders serve up an extensive list of beers, wines, and mixed drinks. Homemade tavern entrees range from brie and fresh fruit to gourmet burgers and chicken gyros, served with potato chips baked on the premises. Inexpensive.

Afternoon

Back downtown, you may want to check the rest of the city's fine museums. The **Grand Rapids Children's Museum** (616–235–4726) opened in mid-1997 after an ambitious $4 million fund-raising campaign. Housed in a loft-like downtown space just east of the Van Andel Arena (there's that name again), it has two floors of kid-pleasing displays, including a covered bridge and sand tables, giant bubbles, and a "Wee Discover" toddler area. Even grandparents seem to get caught up in the fun, as they navigate a boat in the water area or try to pilot a make-believe plane.

If you like your entertainment a little more sophisticated, check the recently renovated **Gerald R. Ford Museum** (303 Pearl Street NW, Grand Rapids, MI 49503; 616–451–9263). The city's native son and Michigan's only president is honored inside this triangular building with a glass wall overlooking the west bank of the Grand River,

The museum sank $5 million into its ten galleries in 1997, and it shows. Displays explore both Ford's public career and his private life, including a re-creation of the Ford Paint & Varnish Company, where the future president worked as a boy. Visitors can also take a holographic tour of the White House, wander through a surprisingly interesting section on First Lady Betty Ford, watch a multiscreen video account of the Watergate scandal, and even boogie along with a lighthearted re-creation of 1970s pop music. The museum also hosts a variety of traveling exhibits.

Not far away, on Division Street, the **Grand Rapids Art Museum** (155 North Division Street, Grand Rapids, MI 49503; 616–831–1000) is housed in a renovated 1903 federal building that once served as the city's post office and courthouse. Far-ranging permanent collections include nineteenth- and twentieth-century prints, paintings, sculpture, and decorative arts emphasizing —surprise!—furniture. Highlights include works by Impressionist Childe Hassam and modernist Alexander Calder. There's also a fine children's gallery with colorful hands-on displays. Be sure to ask if any special exhibitions are on view: The museum recently was the only American museum to feature a traveling exhibition on the art of the Italian master Perugino.

DINNER: Head back to the hotel and dress up for a splurge in the hotel's **Cygnus Restaurant** (616–776–6425). Here you can dance the night away under the stars or feast on continental cuisine in this rooftop dining room, which many consider Grand Rapids's most romantic eatery. Expensive, but worth it.

Up for a little excitement after dinner? Check the impressive **Van Andel Arena**, a quick walk from the Amway. It serves as home for the IHL Grand Rapids Griffins and the CBA's Grand Rapids Hoops, with screaming fans who rival those of the Red Wings and Pistons. Taps Sports Bar (8 Ionia Avenue, Grand Rapids, MI 49503; 616–774–3388) offers an upstairs cigar bar and a pool room. If you don't feel like leaving the hotel, you can enjoy dueling pianos and a Hollywood-themed atmosphere at Tinseltown (616–776–6495).

DAY 3

Morning

BRUNCH: Start Sunday in style with brunch at the **1913 Room** (616–774–2000) in the Amway Grand. This succulent spread features a great variety of hot and cold entrees and a lush, Victorian-inspired decor that harkens back to the city's early days. Moderate.

After hitting the city's major attractions on Saturday, you may want to spend a more leisurely Sunday. One good place to do it is up on **Heritage Hill,** where the majority of the city's vintage Victorian architecture can be found. At the turn of the century, wealthy industrialists and furniture makers built their homes here, overlooking the city. Today, it's still a popular residential area, and some of the homes are open to the public.

One of the most interesting is the **Meyer May House** (450 Madison SE, Grand Rapids, MI 49503; 616–246–4821). It was designed in 1908 by Frank Lloyd Wright for a local clothier and has been restored to Wright's original concept: a building, its furnishings, and its natural setting working in harmony. Most of what you'll see was designed by Wright and his associates, including the linens, carpet, color scheme, light fixtures, exterior art glass, and terraces. At the other extreme is the opulent Voigt House. Built late in the nineteenth century, the Victorian-style mansion retains much of its heavy drapery, ornate furniture, and original family furnishings. Between the two architectural styles are more than sixty others, from Eastlake to Greek Revival, all of which can be seen on a self-guided walking tour.

If it's a nice day and you'd rather spend it outside, consider a trip to either the **John Ball Zoo** (I–196 and State Road 45, Grand Rapids, MI 49503; 616–336–4300) or the **Frederik Meijer Gardens** (1000 East Beltline Avenue, Grand Rapids, MI 49503; 616–957–1580). The zoo is one of the state's largest and houses 1,000 animals from many parts of the world. Check out the special exhibit on nocturnal animals, the new Living Shores aquarium, and the popular children's zoo.

The impressive $20-million Meijer Gardens opened in 1995 and were built by the Meijer grocery-store family. Exhibits include the Lena Meijer Conservatory—the state's largest—a five-story glass structure housing exotic plants from around the world. Outside, the landscaped grounds feature nature trails, a desert garden, and more than fifty bronze sculptures by international artists, including the well-known Michigan sculptor Marshall Fredericks. Among the newest features is a 24-foot-tall horse designed by Leonardo da Vinci. If you need a break, try the Victorian garden, where a popular afternoon tea is served on weekends.

THERE'S MORE

Bridges. The Grand Rapids area has two of the state's remaining covered bridges, in Ada and Fallasburg. The Ada Covered Bridge is a reconstruction of an 1867 span and straddles the Tornapple River. The Fallasburg Covered Bridge crosses the Flat River just north of Lowell in Fallasburg County Park.

Culture. Broadway-style shows are presented at the Broadway Theatre Guild (50 Monroe Place, Grand Rapids, MI 49503; 616–940–9009); community theater stars at the Grand Rapids Civic Theater (30 North Division Street, Grand Rapids, MI 49503; 616–456–8886); and *grands jetés* (leaps) and pirouettes can be found at the Grand Rapids Ballet (233 East Fulton). Opera Grand Rapids (207 Waters Building, Grand Rapids, MI 49503; 616–451–2741) and Grand Rapids Symphony (220 Lyon Street NW, Grand Rapids, MI 49503; 616–454–9451) provide a variety of classical music.

Skiing. Cannonsburg (6800 Cannonsburg Road, Grand Rapids, MI 49503; 616–874–6711) has two T-bars, eight rope tows, and more. Pando (8076 Belding Road, Grand Rapids, MI 49503; 616–456–3977) has six rope tows, seven lighted runs, and a cafeteria.

Water Park. A.J.'s Action Territory (4441 Twenty-eighth Street, SE, Grand Rapids, MI 49503; 616–940–0400) features water slides, a lazy river tube ride, kids' wave pool, eighteen-hole mini golf, bumper boats, go-karts, and more.

OTHER RECOMMENDED RESTAURANTS

Bistro Bella Vita (44 Grandville Avenue SW, Grand Rapids, MI 49503; 616–222–4600) is north of DeVos Concert Hall and the Grand Center. Inside this 1940s-style bistro you'll find polished woods and colorful murals and an open kitchen, where selections change almost daily. Try the gnocchi, the Colorado lamb chops, or the smoked-salmon filet. The Bistro also offers the city's largest martini bar. Moderate to expensive.

Celtic Fields (3305 Three Mile Road, Grand Rapids, MI 49503; 616–364–5640) is a tea room, gift cottage, and Irish-themed eatery that has been featured in *TEA* magazine. It's a great place to take a break after museum hopping. Inexpensive.

One Trick Pony (136 Fulton Street, Grand Rapids, MI 49503; 616–235–7669) is next to the well-loved Cottage Bar and under the same ownership. Inside the oldest commercial building in the city, it features a variety of pizzas (the Chicken Pesto with Roasted Onions and Pine Nuts is a favorite). There's also a good number of Cajun and Caribbean-style entrees. Moderate.

San Chez—A Tapas Bistro (Fulton Street, Grand Rapids, MI 49503; 616–774–8272) has a fine wine list as well as an excellent menu of Cuban- and Spanish-style tapas. Moderate.

OTHER RECOMMENDED LODGINGS

Courtyard by Marriott (11 Monroe Avenue, NW, Grand Rapids, MI 49503; 616–242–6000) is a 214-room, centrally located hotel, that opened in 1997. Rates start at $82.

Days Inn Downtown (310 Pearl Street, Grand Rapids, MI 49504; 616–235–7611) is another good budget-minded choice. Close to the Ford Museum and the city's riverfront parks, it has 175 rooms, a restaurant, pool, and more. Rates start at just $65.

FOR MORE INFORMATION

Grand Rapids/Kent County Convention and Visitors Bureau, 140 Monroe Center NW, Grand Rapids, MI 49503; (800) 678–9859 or (616) 459–8287.

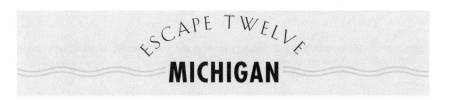

Garland Resort

WONDERFUL WINTER WEEKEND IN

NORTHERN MICHIGAN

1 TO 2 NIGHTS

Sleigh Ride • Cross-Country Skiing • Romantic Dinners

The resorts on the western side of the state may be more famous, but Michigan's northeast corner has some special places, too. Quieter, less built up, and certainly less crowded, the area is washed by gentle Lake Huron tides and has become a favorite of golfers looking for challenging tees and winter weather lovers looking for a great getaway.

Top of the list of northeast resorts is Garland, the Midwest's only AAA four-diamond resort. The largest log cabin resort this side of the Mississippi, it has 3,500 acres. Summer means golf, and winter brings a variety of outdoor activities, including cross-country skiing, ice skating, and the very popular Gourmet Glides and Zhivago night weekends.

DAY 1

Evening

Garland Resort is about a 3½-hour drive from Detroit. Take I-75 north to exit 254 (Grayling); go right at M-72 East for 23 miles to Luzerne. Garland is 14 miles north.

So much for romance, I thought as our horse-drawn sleigh pulled away from **Garland Resort** in Lewiston, Michigan (HCR–1, Box 364 M, Country Road 489, MI 49756; 800–968–0042), about 45 minutes southeast of

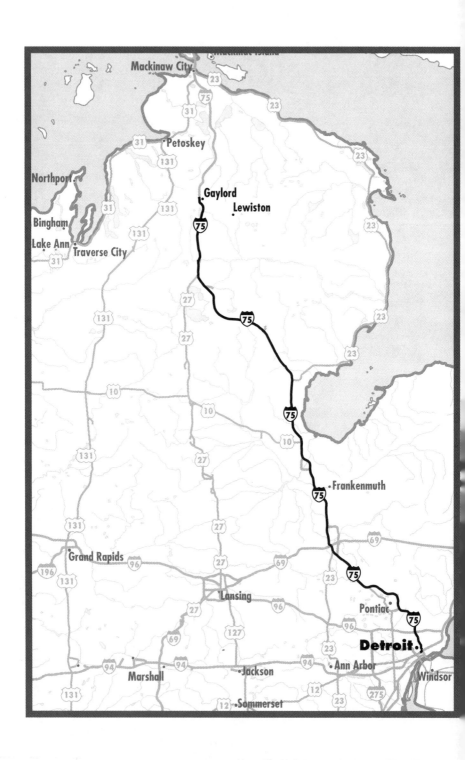

Gaylord. I was in town to try the famous Zhivago Night, a winter weekend favorite, but I hadn't counted on the low temperatures. It was c-c-c-cold, with temperatures hovering right around zero. Even my nose hairs were frozen, making it hard to breathe. Thank God for body heat, I thought as I pulled the heavy woolen blanket around me and snuggled closer to my husband as the twelve other couples in the sleigh did the same.

Well, maybe this was a *little* romantic; the cuddling was nice. And the stars seemed close enough to touch, long-lost friends we vaguely remembered from our pre-city days.

We soon arrived at our destination: Garland's little cabin in the big woods, the setting for the resort's popular Zhivago Night dinners. Once resort owner Ron Otto's hunting lodge, the small log structure is now used for romantic getaways that include a gourmet dinner, sleigh ride through the woods and more.

After the frosty trip, the cabin's roaring fire and glowing candlelight was especially welcome. We shrugged off our many layers, blew hot breath on numb fingers, and took our places around a large table set for 24. In the background, "Lara's Theme" from *Dr. Zhivago* was being played on the mandolin.

During the five-hour meal, the wine and conversation flowed. We started as strangers from across the Midwest—the majority, of course, from Michigan and Ohio—but we soon felt like an extended family sharing a celebration.

Some five hours later, we buckled, snapped, zipped, and wrapped back up, once again preparing to face the almost-record cold outside. As if on cue, snow the size of cotton balls began to fall softly as we headed back (this is Northern Michigan, after all). This time we fell silent, lulled by full stomachs, jangling sleigh bells, and the velvet blackness of night that quickly enveloped us.

Once back, each couple went its own way—some back to more private romance in their cozy rooms; others to the lounge for a nightcap or for a spin on the small dance floor. We chose a warming glass of brandy and a spot by the fire in the lounge, where we discussed the evening and our plans for the day ahead.

LODGING: Garland Resort, Lewiston

DAY 2

Morning

BREAKFAST: Garland Resort, Lewiston

The next morning, options included sleeping in, indulging in the resort's Sunday brunch, twirling on the skating pond, or skiing the winter Gourmet Glide, available weekends through March.

We chose the glide, in part to work off some of the calories from the night-before meal. The program includes 5 miles of easy cross-country skiing on the resort's trails (lessons and rentals available), punctuated by pit stops. Five trailside buffets offer plenty of opportunities for sustenance (and those all-important bathroom breaks).

We started out at the Herman Grill, where muffins, granola, and mimosas fueled us for the trek ahead. A mile later, the Hard Wax Cafe (and golf club watering hole) offered artichoke and goat cheese fondue, smoked salmon, cheese, and beverages. You could perch inside at one of a few tables or warm your hands with a seat outside around a huge bonfire.

The next leg in the trip took us into the woods behind the resort, part of which cross a wildlife preserve. Before we knew it, it was time to eat again. This time, however, we had to supply our own meal from Garland's well-stocked lakes and ponds.

LUNCH/DINNER: A wooden fishing shack offered skiers and would-be anglers the chance to catch a fish, have it filleted and fried on an outdoor grill and then enjoy it at one of three picnic tables set up in the window. Those who didn't feel lucky (myself included) could ladle up a big bowl of thick veggie soup from a huge cauldron over an open fire or sample the fresh trout pre-caught and precooked by Garland's staff.

Two stops to go. At the rustic Buckhorn Lodge, tables were laden with a buffet of lamb and tasty white-bean chili. The last stop back at the lodge (about 1 and one-half miles later) lets you fill up on wild-game ravioli, egg-plant, salads, and varied desserts, including a delicious berry cobbler.

After skiing for 5 miles, you'll be surprised at the appetite you've worked up. Later that night, we worked out a few kinks in the resort's indoor pool and hot tub and slept like babies in our two-bedroom cabin across from the lodge, where we relaxed and rested until it was time to head home the next morning.

THERE'S MORE

Camping. Leave civilization behind at one of six campgrounds. Some, such as Pigeon River County State Forest, are rustic, and others, such as Otsego Lake County Park (517–731–6448), have electrical hookups and access to nearby stores. Ostego Lake State Park (517–732–5485), 6 miles south of Gaylord, has 203 campsites and modern restrooms.

Elkwatching. Thunder Bay Resort in Hillman (27800 M 32 East, Hillman, MI 49746) offers its own version of Zhivago Night in fall and winter. A horse-drawn carriage or sleigh takes you deep into the forests around Hillman searching for the resort's main claim to fame, a 120-member herd of Rocky Mountain elk. For more information, call (800) 729–9375 or visit thunderbaygolf.com. Otsego County is filled with natural wonders, including the elk herd found in the 95,000-acre Pigeon River County State Forest. Call (800) 345–8621.

Family Fun. If you brought the kids along, check out the nearby Jimmy Jukebox Family Center (610 South Wisconsin Avenue, Gaylord, MI; 517–732–5099). It has an arcade, video games, and a pool table as well as pizza and other fast-food favorites. Another family-friendly spot is Bavarian Falls Golf/Go Cart Track (850 South Wisconsin Avenue, Gaylord, MI; 517–732–4087), an eighteen-hole adventure golf course and a quarter-mile go-kart track open April through October.

Golf: Garland Resort is known as one of the state's—and the Midwest's—premier golf resorts, with a number of challenging courses and a beautiful North Country setting. For more golf information, call the resort (877–4GARLAND).

Hiking. Two good choices near Gaylord include the Pine Baron Trail, which winds through the woods on a 6-mile loop, and Spring Brook Pathway, with two challenging loops. Or try the nearby Pigeon River County State Forest, east of Vanderbilt. For more information, call the state Department of Natural Resources office at (517) 732–3541.

Horseback Riding. If you're looking for a change of pace, El Rancho Stevens (Box 495, Gaylord, MI 49735; 517–732–5090) is a family-style ranch on Dixon Lake some 5 miles south of Gaylord. You'll find twenty-two rooms, a heated pool, boating, horses, and a well-run children's program. Open May through September only.

Lumber Lore. The Hartwick Pines Lumbering Museum (State Highway 93 south of Frederic; 517–348–7068) is in a state park that preserves one of the largest remaining stands of virgin white pine. Get a taste of the lumbering life through its nineteenth-century logging camp and interpretive center, guided tours, camping, and fishing. While there, don't miss the charming Chapel in the Woods.

Snowmobiling: Snowmobile fans have recently discovered Garland's trail network, long a favorite with cross-country skiers. It stretches over an eight-county area between Gaylord and Alpena.

Winter Sports. Fans of figure eights and doggie paddlin' have a home away from home at the $4.5 million Sportsplex (1250 Gornick Avenue, Gaylord, MI 49735; 517–731–4REC), with a huge rink, walk-around track, and an Olympic-size pool. It even has a junior hockey team, the Gaylord Grizzlies (for tickets, call 517–732–4447).

SPECIAL EVENTS

June. Otsego Lake Fly-In

Gus Macker Basketball Tournament

July. Alpenfest

August. Otsego County Fair

Michaywe Arts & Crafts Fair

Alpine Cup Snowmobile Drag Races

OTHER RECOMMENDED RESTAURANTS AND LODGINGS

There's not much else in Garland's immediate vicinity and most Zhivago guests stay at the resort. Gaylord, about 45 minutes away, has plenty of other options and activities. For additional information other than the recommendations listed here, contact the Gaylord Convention & Tourism Bureau (see number below).

The Blue Goose (900 Charles Brink Road, Gaylord, MI 49735; 517–732–8254) has eclectic cuisine and fine dining in a lakeside home. Moderate.

Diana's Delights (143 West Main Street, Gaylord, MI 49735; 517–732–6564) is a good spot for homemade breakfasts and lunches. Inexpensive.

Hidden Valley Resort & Golf Club (696 M–32 East, Gaylord, MI 49735; 517–732–5181) has 132 rooms, including condos and chalets, in a wide price range. Open May through October only. Rates: $60–$99 per night.

Holiday Inn of Gaylord (833 West Main Street, Gaylord, MI 49735; 517–732–2431) is a good budget–minded choice or a good spot if you've brought kids along. It has 140 newly renovated rooms and a Holidome with a heated indoor pool, whirlpool, and sauna. Rates: $70–$91 per night.

Michaywe Resort (1535 Opal Lake Road, Gaylord, MI 49735; 517–939–8914) is just 5 miles south of the city, with more than fifty condos, chalets, and lodges on or near the golf course. There are also tennis courts, a driving range, two private beaches, a lakeside clubhouse, and miles of cross-country and snowmobile trails to use in winter. Rates: $110 and up per night.

Schlang's Bavarian Inn (3917 Old U.S. 27 South, Gaylord, MI 49735; 517–732–9288) is the kind of place you'd expect to find in this Bavarian-inspired city, with German and American fare. Inexpensive to moderate.

FOR MORE INFORMATION

Zhivago Nights and Gourmet Glides are scheduled December through March. Prices start at approximately $125 per person; accommodations are extra. Lodging options include in-lodge rooms with four-poster beds, gas fireplaces and whirlpool tubs, or one- and two-bedroom golf cabins with galley kitchens and private decks. For more information, call (517) 786–2211.

Rates at Thunder Bay start at $105 per person, midweek. For more information, call (800) 729–9375 or log on to www.thunderbaygolf.com.

For more information on nearby attractions, contact the Gaylord Area Convention & Tourism Bureau (800–345–8621) or visit their Web site at www.gaylord-mich.com.

Gaylord Area Convention and Tourism Bureau, 101 West Main Street, Gaylord, MI 49735; (517) 732–6333 or (800) 345–8621.

ILLINOIS
ESCAPES

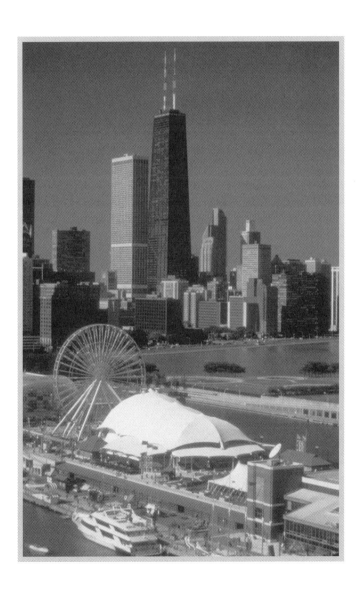

Chicago

WINDY-CITY WEEKEND

3 NIGHTS

Shopping • Restaurants • Museums • Sports • Theater

Chicago has so many things to do, the famed "City of Big Shoulders" could easily be called the "City of Big Decisions." Like to shop? Head for the Magnificent Mile or Oak Street. Into architecture? Sign on for one of the tours offered by the city's renowned Architecture Foundation. How 'bout sports? You won't find more loyal fans than those who cheer for the Bulls, the Bears, the Cubs, and the White Sox.

Chicago is all Detroit aspires to—a big midwestern city that's both friendly and sophisticated, mixing elegance and economics. Known for its hard-working mentality, it's also incredibly beautiful, with the blue infinity of Lake Michigan edged by curling swaths of parks and beaches. Downtown's gleaming towers meld gracefully with the high-rises on the Gold Coast and the flatter surrounding prairie. When summer finally arrives, all the city moves outdoors, where you'll find residents enjoying the legendary 29 miles of lakeshore and twenty-nine beaches.

There is no way to do the city justice in a weekend, and entire guidebooks are dedicated to exploring its many facets. Two worth picking up before you go are Marilyn J. Appleberg's *I Love Chicago* guide and Paul Engleman's *Chicago Access*. Both offer great ideas for putting together your own Chicago adventure; consider the following itinerary just a starting point for a lifetime of weekends spent exploring the Windy City.

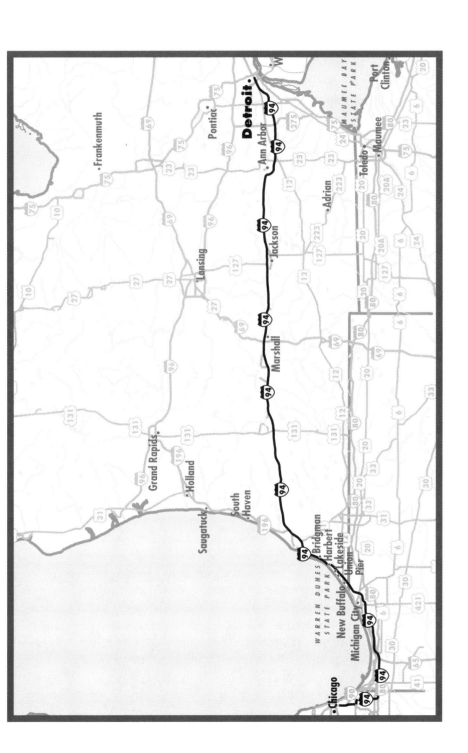

DAY 1

Chicago is roughly a six-hour drive along Interstate 94 west. To squeeze the most into your trip, plan to skip work on Friday so that you can hit the road early. Chicago is known for its variety of great restaurants—try to arrive in time for dinner.

Afternoon

DINNER: Need something meaty after the long drive? **Morton's of Chicago** (1050 North State Street, Chicago, IL 60611; 312–266–4820) is famed for catering to carnivores, with huge porterhouse steaks and a wide variety of beef entrees. There are also veal and chicken dishes, as well as wonderful dessert soufflés. Moderate to expensive.

LODGING: The Windy City has dozens and dozens of hotels to choose from, many catering to the convention crowd. If you're looking for something a little more personal, the **Whitehall** (105 East Delaware Place, Chicago, IL 60611; 312–944–6300 or 800–323–7500) is an intimate hotel with 221 English-style rooms. Just a block from the Magnificent Mile, the stretch of tony shops along Michigan Avenue, it's surprisingly quiet and makes a welcome retreat at the end of a hectic day of sight-seeing and shopping. From it, you can "toddle" anywhere quite easily. Room rates for two people start at $195 per night, but ask about regular weekend specials.

DAY 2

Morning

BREAKFAST: Lou Mitchell's (565 West Jackson Boulevard, Chicago, IL 60611; 312–939–3111) has been a city institution for more than seventy years. It's the kind of place that attracts diners who range from chauffeur-driven CEOs to tourists. The restaurant is famous for its double-yolked fried eggs, served in skillets, along with huge glasses of freshly squeezed orange juice. If you're not into eggs, try the malted-milk Belgian waffles. Inexpensive.

Saturday is the best day to shop the Magnificent Mile, when the stores have extended hours (some are closed on Sunday) and the people-watching is prime. This high-rent district between the Chicago River and the Drake Hotel is home to **Saks Fifth Avenue** (700 North Michigan Avenue, Chicago, IL 60611; 312–944–6500), **Neiman Marcus** (737 North Michigan Avenue,

Chicago, IL 60611; 312–642–5900), and **Bloomingdale's** (900 North Michigan Avenue, Chicago, IL 60611; 312–440–4460), as well as the limestone **Water Tower,** one of the few major buildings to escape the Great Chicago Fire of 1871. Just about every designer boutique and upscale store in the country has a presence here. But there are also stores for more everyday budgets, including **Banana Republic** (835 North Michigan Avenue, Chicago, IL 60611; 312–642–7667) and a huge, sparkling glass-sided **Crate & Barrel** store (646 North Michigan Avenue, Chicago, IL 60611; 312–787–5900).

Shopping the "Mag" Mile can take up the better part of the day if you let it. If, however, you're looking for an alternative to Michigan Avenue's crowds, take your credit cards to Oak Street, a quiet street of tony boutiques housed in vintage brownstones, or State Street, the city's old retail center, where you'll find institutions such as beautifully renovated and huge **Marshall Field's** (111 North State Street, Chicago, IL 60611; 312–781–1000) and the classic **Carson Pirie Scott** (1 South State Street, Chicago, IL 60611; 312–641–7000). State has been a famous urban thoroughfare for more than a century, and people continue to meet under Marshall Field's landmark corner clock, as they have since the late 1800s.

South of the river is the **Loop,** the old heart of the city, where the world's first skyscraper (the nine-story Home Insurance Building, long since demolished) was erected in 1885. Today the Loop boasts the nation's tallest building, the 110-story **Sears Tower** (233 South Wacker Drive, Chicago, IL 60611; 312–875–9696) as well as a host of other famous buildings by architects such as Louis Sullivan, Ludwig Mies Van der Rohe, and Helmut Jahn.

Afternoon

LUNCH: You've been looking up all morning, now look down on the city from the Signature Room on the ninety-fifth floor of the **John Hancock Center** (875 North Michigan Avenue, Chicago, IL 60611; 312–787–9596 or 888–875–VIEW). Huge, floor-to-ceiling windows offer an amazing view of the Chicago cityscape and the Lake Michigan shore. On a really clear day you can see all the way across the lake to Michigan. The lunch buffet is a pleasing array of salads and pastas—all at just $8.95 per person. When you consider that admission to the observatory deck is about $5.00, it's also an incredible deal. The tower is open 9:00 A.M. to midnight 365 days a year.

If you'd prefer not to navigate the city on your own, sign on for one of the walking tours offered by the excellent **Chicago Architecture Foundation** (312–922–8687). Stops along the way include the turn-of-the-century mansions along the Gold Coast, the Frank Lloyd Wright home in suburban Oak Park, the Gothic towers of the University of Chicago, native son Louis Sullivan's cast-iron classic, the Carson Pirie Scott department store at the corner of State and Madison, and more.

If you'd rather rest your feet, the foundation also offers the **Chicago from the Lake** cruise, a 90-minute ride on the river that highlights some of the city's glittering gems. Cruises leave at 10:00 A.M. and noon Wednesday through Sunday; 10:00 A.M., noon, and 6:00 P.M. Monday and Tuesday. Admission is $15 per person. You can also stow away on one of the sight-seeing tours offered by boats. **Wendella Sightseeing Boats** (312–337–1446) ply the Chicago River and Lake Michigan several times each day and depart from the Chicago River from the lower level of Michigan Avenue at Wacker Drive. Cruising season runs from mid-April through mid-October. If you're looking for something a little different, check out **Black Coutours** (773–233–8907), which takes visitors to the city's notable African-American sites; **Supernatural Tours** (708–785–2530), offered by professional ghost hunter Richard Crowe; or **Untouchable Tours** (773–881–1185), a two-hour guided trek through the city's infamous gangster haunts.

DINNER: Looking to splurge? The five-star **Everest** (440 South LaSalle Street, Chicago, IL 60611; 630–663–8920) is on everyone's list of the city's best restaurants. On the fortieth floor of the Chicago Stock Exchange, it has dramatic city views and light-as-a-whisper French cuisine, created by the Alsatian chef Jean Joho. Entrees include dishes such as a salmon soufflé or sautéed elk with wild mushrooms. Try to get one of the few tables at or near a window for an incredible view of downtown. Closed Sunday and Monday. Very expensive.

DAY 3

Morning

BREAKFAST: Enjoy breakfast in bed or head for the **Oak Tree** (900 North Michigan, Chicago, IL 60611; 312–751–1988), where you can join other diners in the Sunday morning ritual of noshing a bagel and perusing a copy of the thick weekend edition of the *Chicago Tribune*. Inexpensive.

Sunday is a great day to explore the city's museums. The **Art Institute of Chicago** (111 South Michigan Avenue, Chicago, IL 60611; 312–443–3600) is the city's answer to New York's Metropolitan Museum of Art and one of the

Don't miss the stunning Museum of Contemporary Art.

finest institutions in the world. Inside these hallowed halls are masterpieces that range from the earliest civilizations to modern times. Among the most famous are works by the always popular French Impressionists, including Monet's haystacks and water-lilies series, Renoir's *Two Sisters (On the Terrace),* and Seurat's pointillist canvas known as *Sunday Afternoon on the Island of La Grande Jatte,* which later inspired the successful Broadway play *Sunday in the Park with George.* Other works of note include Grant Wood's pioneer father and daughter in *American Gothic,* Picasso's *Old Guitarist*, and important works by more modern masters. You can easily spend the entire day here. When museum feet hit, however, be sure to take a break in the cafe or the cavernous gift shop, where you can pick up a few reprinted masterpieces for your walls at home as well as books, note cards, jewelry, and more.

The stunning **Museum of Contemporary Art** (MCA) debuted in 1996 in new lakefront digs (220 East Chicago Avenue, Chicago, IL 60611; 312–280–2660). You won't want to miss the lake views from the terraced sculpture garden or the mind-bending exhibitions of contemporary culture. If you've brought the family, there's no better place to spend the day than **Navy Pier** (600 East Grand Avenue, Chicago, IL 60611; 312–595–7437), a renovated festival marketplace of shops, parks, restaurants, and entertainment on Lake Michigan. Reopened to great fanfare in 1995, the huge lakefront playground features a 150-foot-tall Ferris wheel, a musical carousel, and the **Chicago Children's Museum** (700 East Grand, Chicago, IL 60611; 312–527–1000), an exciting collection of hands-on exhibits for the young and young at heart.

Afternoon

LUNCH: The **Berghoff** (17 West Adams Street, Chicago, IL 60603; 312–427–6781) has been a city institution for more than a century. This crusty, oak-paneled beer hall has served up some of the most authentic German food in the city along with foamy steins of home-brewed, Dortmunder-style beers. The specialties are the huge platters of sausage, succulent Wiener schnitzel, crisp potato pancakes, and bowls of smooth creamed spinach. Be sure to leave room for the strudel. Moderate.

Walk off your lunch with an afternoon visit to **River North,** the heart of Chicago's art district. To get there, head north 4 blocks on either Clark or Adams Streets. Along the way you'll pass the controversial **James R. Thompson Center,** named after a former longtime Illinois governor and also known as the State of Illinois Center (100 West Randolph Street, Chicago, IL 60610; 312–814–6660). An ultramodern glass and steel structure, it was designed by modernist architect Helmut Jahn. Inside is a tempting artisan center with quilts, carvings, textiles, and other works by the state's best artists. As for the building, locals either love it or hate it. You decide.

If you were inspired by the works at the Art Institute, you can take a few River North paintings and other goodies home and support local artists at the same time. Dozens of River North galleries showcase painting, sculpture, and the decorative arts. Some of the best are **Ann Nathan Gallery** (218 West Superior Street, Chicago, IL 60610; 312–664–6622) and the southwestern-style **Mongerson Wunderlich** (702 North Wells Street, Chicago, IL 60610; 312–943–2354). If you prefer, you can do some power shopping at the **June Blaker** boutique (200 West Superior Street, Chicago, IL 60610; 312–751–9220), **Mig & Tig** (549 North Wells Street, Chicago, IL 60610; 312–644–8277), and **Sawbridge Studios** (406 North Clark Street, Chicago, IL 60610; 312–828–0055).

DINNER: Kiki's Bistro (900 North Franklin, Chicago, IL 60610; 312–335–5454) is a cozy, French-style bistro with great onion soup and a stylish, unpretentious atmosphere. Other specialties include the steak and *frites* and the silky custard *crème caramel,* the perfect ending to a memorable meal. Moderate.

Looking for some late-night action? **Gordon** (500 North Clark Street, Chicago, IL 60610; 312–467–9780) is an eclectic restaurant that serves innovative American cuisine and has dancing on weekends. Jackets required. Or you can head for the Loop, where you'll find **Yvette Wintergarden** (311 South Wacker Drive, Chicago, IL 60611; 312–408–1242). This is where pianist Harry Connick Jr. heads to tickle the ivories when he's in the Windy City. The mood is decidedly 1940s—diners even get up and take a few dips and twirls on the dance floor between courses.

Other good options include the legendary **Pump Room** (1301 North State Street, Chicago, IL 60610; 312–266–0360), **Jazz Showcase** (59 West Grand Avenue, Chicago, IL 60610; 312–670–2473), or **Buddy Guy's Legends** (754 South Wabash Avenue, Chicago, IL 60610; 312–427–0333). Guy plays only in January, but he drops in often and jams through the rest of the year.

Fans of alternative rock head for the **Empty Bottle** (1035 North Western Avenue, Chicago, IL 60614; 773–276–3600), a funky club in the Ukrainian Village neighborhood that features cutting-edge music on weekends and experimental jazz on Wednesdays. You're a blues fan? **Willie Dixon's Blues Heaven Foundation** (2120 South Michigan, Chicago, IL 60614; 312–808–1286) was founded by the late blues legend and honors artists such as Chuck Berry, Bo Diddly, and Muddy Waters. Tours are offered weekdays at noon and 2:00 P.M.

The ninety-fourth-floor observatory at the **John Hancock Center** (875 North Michigan Avenue, Chicago, IL 60611; 312–751–3681) offers a spectacular nighttime view of the city, including a look down on the four glowing towers of the Bloomies building at 900 North Michigan Avenue.

DAY 4

Morning

BREAKFAST: Because this is your last day, have something special sent up from room service and eat it in bed. If you want to go out, a good choice is the **Park Avenue Cafe** in the Doubletree Guest Suites (198 East Delaware Place, Chicago, IL 60611; 312–944–4414). This New York import made an initial sensation because of trademarked entrees such as Pastrami Salmon and Sword-fish Chop. It's also known for its American dim sum Sunday brunch, which features a full array of appetizers and entrees for $33 per person. Don't plan to eat for the rest of the day.

Try to squeeze anything you missed into your last day here. You might choose to experience the Great Chicago Fire or let the kids climb on the city's first locomotive at the **Chicago Historical Society** (Clark Street and North Avenue, Chicago, IL 60611; 312–642–4600), or take in a manageable museum such as the **Terra Museum of American Art** (666 North Michigan Avenue, Chicago, IL 60611; 312–664–3939), where works by Sargent, Chase, and Wyeth are exhibited in a soothing, dove-gray interior. The museum is a great antidote to the teeming crowds outside.

End your Windy City weekend with a bit of Great Britain. Indulge in a "veddy" English-style tea at one of the city's exclusive hotels. They all have one, but the scones, sandwiches, cakes, and pastries at the **Drake** (Michigan at Lake Shore Drive, Chicago, IL 60611; 312–787–2200) are closest to the real thing. If they're crowded, your next best choice is the **Four Seasons** (120 East Delaware Place, Chicago, IL 60611; 312–280–8800), where you can sink into a plush couch by the fire.

THERE'S MORE

Cycling. Zoom along the lakefront on rented bikes or Rollerblades from Bike Chicago (800–915–2453), which has six locations, including Buckingham Fountain, Navy Pier, and Oak Street Beach. Rates start at $7.00 an hour, protective gear included.

Natural History. The Field Museum of Natural History (Roosevelt Road at Lake Shore Drive, Chicago, IL 60611; 312–922–9410) is a hands-on, science-oriented museum that has succeeded admirably in transforming itself from a dusty institution into an innovative learning center for all ages. The stuffed animals and dinosaurs are perennially popular; special exhibitions aim at expanding visitors' knowledge of critters from bats to spiders. You'll pay about $5.00 admission for adults, $3.00 for students and seniors; free on Wednesday.

Science. The Museum of Science and Industry (Fifty-seventh Street and Lake Shore Drive, Chicago, IL 60611; 773–684–1414) is a longtime city favorite, with everything from a German submarine to a re-created coal mine. Though the old favorites are still popular, the museum has reached the twenty-first century with the Crown Space Center, a state-of-the-art approach to space exploration. There's also an awe-inspiring Omnimax theater with a 76-foot screen, "Curiosity Place" for kids up to age sixteen, and a Transportation Gallery, where you can engineer virtual car wrecks and view antique cars in the "Auto Gallery." Admission is $6.00 per person, $2.50 for kids; free on Thursdays. The Omnimax costs extra, even on Thursdays.

Sky Shows. Adler Planetarium (1300 South Lake Shore Drive, Chicago, IL 60611; 312–922–7827) gives you the chance to look up at one of the planetarium's sky shows and look down at the lake as well as all around at the panoramic view of the city skyline.

Sports. Chicago is a big sports town, with the Cubs playing on the North Side at Wrigley Field (312–404–2827) and the White Sox on the South Side at Comiskey Park (312–924–1000) in summer as well as the Bulls (312–455–4000), the Bears (708–615–2327), and the Blackhawks (312–455–7000) when the legendary Chicago winter winds blow.

Television. One of the city's most unusual—and probably most fun—museums is the Museum of Broadcast Communications in the Chicago Cultural Center (78 East Washington Street, Chicago, IL 60610; 312–629–6000). Here you'll find everything from classic commercials to the infamous Nixon-Kennedy debate.

Water World. The John G. Shedd Aquarium (1200 South Lake Shore Drive, Chicago, IL 60611; 312–939–2438) has a wonderful Oceanarium, where families can watch the antics of dolphins, beluga whales, and perky penguins. Admission to the aquarium costs $11.00 for adults; $9.00 for children; free on Thursday. Oceanarium admission costs extra.

SPECIAL EVENTS

January. Skate on State

February. African-American History Celebration
Navy Pier County Fair

March. Chicago Flower and Garden Show, Navy Pier

April. Chicago Latino Film Festival

May. Asian Heritage Month Celebration
    Cinco de Mayo, Navy Pier
    Viva! Chicago Latin Music Festival

June. Gospel Fest, Grant Park
    Blues Festival, Grant Park
    Taste of Chicago, Grant Park

July. Chicago Air and Water Show

August. Gold Coast Art Fair

September. Jazz Festival, Grant Park

OTHER RECOMMENDED RESTAURANTS

Ambria (2300 North Lincoln Park West, Chicago, IL 60614; 773–472–5959) is the place to go when you've won the lottery. Prices are expensive (entrees start at $24 a la carte) but worth every penny. Housed in a turn-of-the-century hotel, the restaurant is the dream of chef Gambino Satelino, who specializes in fresh seafood and changes the menu seasonally. Prix fixe dinners are available and often offer a good deal. Note: The dining room is nonsmoking only. Very expensive.

Billy Goat Tavern (430 North Michigan Avenue, Chicago, IL 60611; 312–222–1525) is famous for its role in *Saturday Night Live*'s "cheezburgah, cheezburgah" skit. The walls are papered with articles by the city's hard-nosed journalists, who still pack this famous lower-level bar after work. Moderate.

Bistro 110 (110 East Pearson Street, Chicago, IL 60611; 312–266–3110) is a bustling restaurant with wood-roasted meats, chicken, and fish and staples such as baked onion soup, crusty baguettes, and *steak frites.* Don't miss the oven-roasted whole garlic served with crusty French bread. Expect waits at peak periods. Moderate.

Brasserie Jo (59 West Hubbard Street, Chicago, IL 60611; 312–595–0800) is one of the hottest restaurants to open in recent years and is run by Jean Joho, of Everest fame. The food has a number of Alsatian specialties as well as good baguettes and cheeses, affordable wines, and house-brewed beer. Try the Shrimp Bag—a phyllo purse filled with shrimp, wild mushrooms, and leeks in a lobster sauce—or the classic coq au vin. Moderate to expensive.

Charlie Trotter's (816 West Armitage Avenue, Chicago, IL 60614; 312–248–6228) is one of the most unusual restaurants in the city and a must for serious food lovers. Housed in a tastefully renovated townhouse, it features food that is both appetizing and artfully arranged. Patrons order from two tasting menus for either $65 or $85 per person; each includes six to eight courses. The table in the kitchen reserves years in advance. Dinner only. Expensive.

Ed Debevic's (640 North Wells, Chicago, IL 60610; 312–664–1707) is a fun and funky version of a classic '50s diner, with costumed waitresses and blue plate specials. Moderate.

Gino's East (160 East Superior Street, Chicago, IL 60611; 312–943–1124) is a city deep-dish pizza institution, although many people prefer Bacino's (75 East Wacker, Chicago, IL 60611; 312–263–0700 or 2204 North Lincoln, Chicago, IL 60611; 773–472–7400), especially for its heart-healthy spinach pies. Inexpensive to moderate.

Prairie (500 South Dearborn Street, Chicago, IL 60605; 312–663–1143), in the Hyatt on Printer's Row, evokes the midwestern landscape in an atmosphere inspired by Chicago native Frank Lloyd Wright. Regional cuisine with fresh heartland ingredients and creative presentation is featured; try the chilled tomato soup, sturgeon with horseradish crust, or the buffalo steak in shallot sauce. Expensive.

OTHER RECOMMENDED LODGINGS

Days Inn (644 North Lake Shore Drive, Chicago, IL 60611; 312–943–9200) is the best choice when you're on a budget. It has 578 rooms and an excellent location on the lakefront within walking distance of Michigan Avenue. Rates: $149–$234 per night.

The Drake (140 East Walton Place, Chicago, IL 60611; 312–787–2200) is the favorite of kings, queens, and presidents, with 535 rooms. It's famous for its turn-of-the-century charm and for its marble lobby and lavish tea rooms. Guest accommodations are equally plush, and go for $275 to $365 per night, although weekend packages are sometimes available for less. Ask for a room that faces north; those have the best views.

Renaissance Chicago (1 West Wacker Drive, Chicago, IL 60601; 312–372–7200) has 553 rooms and forty suites in a hotel that evokes the ambience of the nineteenth century. It has multiple fountains, crystal chandeliers, lots of marble, and a grand staircase. Rooms can be small, but all have sitting rooms and many offer dramatic river views. Rates start at $149 per night.

Ritz Carlton Chicago (160 East Pearson Street, Chicago, IL 60611; 312–266–1000) is an elegant and understated inn with magnificent flower arrangements in the public rooms and a two–story greenhouse lobby on the twelfth floor with a fountain, wicker, and palms. The 429 guest rooms are spacious, furnished with mahogany armoires and wing chairs. The dining room has a French-inspired menu and rates four Mobil stars. Water Tower Place shopping is just across the street. Rates: $260 and up per night.

FOR MORE INFORMATION

Chicago Office of Tourism, 78 East Washington Avenue, Chicago, IL 60602; (800) 487–2446 or (312) 744–2400.

Chicago Convention and Tourism Bureau, 2301 South Lake Shore Drive, Chicago, IL 60616; (312) 567–8500.

OHIO
ESCAPES

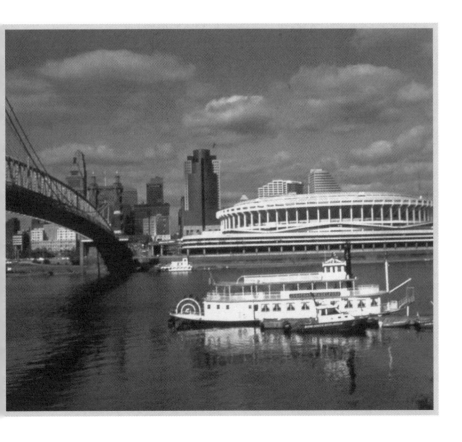

Maumee Bay State Park

BEAUTY BY THE BAY

1 NIGHT

Beaches • Birds • Winter and Water Sports

You need to get away but don't have a full weekend free until who knows when. Is there someplace nearby—no more than an hour away—that offers a relaxing one-day respite from the city's fast pace and frantic lifestyle? Stop looking—and start driving. Just across the Ohio border is Maumee Bay State Park, a dream of scenery and serenity on Lake Erie. It's just one of seventy-two great parks—eight with deluxe resorts—in the Buckeye State.

Ohio boasts what many consider the best park system in the country. From the sandy shores of Lake Erie to the wooded banks around the Ohio River, the 207 acres of parkland offer many activities and experiences. More than 70 million visitors pass through the parks' gates each year, making Ohio's the most-used park system in the United States.

Unlike some other states, entrance to all Ohio's parks is free. And each park has its own distinct personality. You'll find flatlands and forests, wilderness and wildlife, waterfalls and wetlands, pristine streams and prairies as well as lakes both big and small. You can visit a working farm, see a canal lock in operation, rough it in a primitive camp, or pamper yourself in a deluxe resort cabin with all the comforts of home. Along with all that scenic splendor and the welcome chance to chill out for a while, you'll also find opportunities for dozens of outdoor adventures, including backpacking, bicycling, horseback riding, swimming, boating, canoeing, skiing (both water and cross-country), and more.

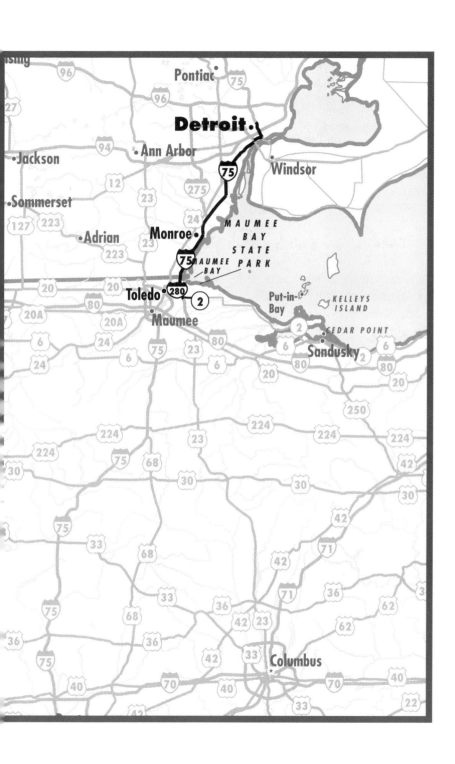

DAY 1

Afternoon

Although all eight Ohio parks with resort-style accommodations are within driving distance for Michiganders, only Maumee Bay is within an hour's drive from Detroit. Luckily for us, it's also the most luxurious of the state's parks, with a classy Cape Cod lodge, a challenging Scottish links golf course, and cozy yet elegant cabins.

To get there, take Interstate 75 from Detroit. Along the way, you may want to stop and shop at the **Monroe Outlet Mall** (exit 11 on I–75; 734–241–4804) in nearby Monroe, Michigan, with some three dozen stores offering discounts and deals on everything from kitchen gadgets to children's wear. Once in Toledo, follow Interstate 280 south to State Highway 2 east for 6 miles to North Curtice Road. Watch for signs from there. Try to get to the park in time to watch the sun set over Lake Erie; it's a sight you won't soon forget.

LODGING: Depending on your taste (and family size, if you've brought the kids), Maumee Bay has two options. You may choose to stay in the showpiece **Quilter Lodge** (Maumee Bay State Park; 419–836–1466 or 800–282–7275 for reservations and other information), named for state Representative Barney Quilter. Overlooking Maumee Bay, it has 120 guest rooms, all with modern conveniences such as coffeemakers and blow-dryers. Lodge rooms also allow easy access to the facility's racquetball courts, game room, saunas, exercise rooms, whirlpool, indoor and outdoor pools, snack bar, and restaurants. *Tip:* Ask for a room at the end of the north wing—they're more isolated and have the best views. Loft rooms with a refrigerator are also available. High-season rates in the lodge start at $135 per night.

If you're lucky, however, you'll be able to book one of the twenty modern beach-house–style cottages, known to park employees simply as "the cabins." There's nothing simple about them, however. Forget your experiences at state-park cabins as a Boy or Girl Scout—these are nothing short of luxurious by those standards. Each is equipped with a gas fireplace, central heat and air-conditioning, television, telephones, even a microwave. Two- or four-bedroom units are available, all with views of either the surrounding swamp woods or the resort's golf course. Two bedrooms will accommodate six people; up to eleven friends or family members can stay in one of the four-bedroom units. Favorites include No. 16, a two-bedroom unit that sits on a picturesque pond; No. 12, a four-bedroom unit near a small peninsula; Nos. 13, 14, and 15, set

Maumee Bay State Park is just an hour from Detroit.

against the woods; or Nos. 3, 7, 17, and 19, all opposite the golf course. Cottage guests, of course, have use of all resort facilities. Notice, however, that cottages are rented by the week only from Memorial Day through Labor Day. They're available nightly for the remainder of the year. High-season rates are $225 per night for the two-bedroom cabins, $275 for the four-bedroom.

DINNER: The lodge's full-service dining room has a varied menu, featuring soups, salads, steaks, lighter fare, and kid cuisine. If you're looking for something a little spicier, however, head into downtown Toledo, just a ten-minute drive away. In one of the older neighborhoods near the river you'll find **Tony Packo's** (1902 Front Street, Toledo, OH 43602; 419–691–6054), an area institution. Native son Jamie Farr, better known as the quirky, cross-dressing Corporal Klinger on the TV series *M★A★S★H,* grew up in this neighborhood bordering the river and brought this Hungarian-style eatery to national attention when he starred in the long-running hit series in the 1970s and early in the 1980s. The cafe had been a local favorite for decades before it was "discovered" by the sitcom's audiences. Despite recent additions to the menu, visitors of all ages still opt for the house specialties: stuffed cabbage smothered with tomato sauce, tangy chicken paprikash, or the signature chili dog, made with sausage and Packo's famous chili. While there, don't miss the chance to peruse the hot dog buns signed by past visitors—from avant-garde musician Frank Zappa to President Bill Clinton—framed throughout the inside. Inexpensive to moderate.

DAY 2

Morning

BREAKFAST: Linger over toast and coffee in your cottage kitchen or head for the moderately priced dining room for something heartier. You have a full day ahead of you, so be sure to fuel up.

Maumee Bay has 1,850 acres in a section of the state once known as the corn capital of the world. It was once dominated by huge coastal marshes and by an area known as the Great Black Swamp, a once-impenetrable barrier and one of America's most forbidding forests. These marshes once teemed with waterfowl and other wildlife—even wild rice. The Black Swamp was also among the state's last strongholds for elk, bison, wolf, black bear, and mountain lion. You'll find evidence of that swampy past throughout the park, where wildlife and flora and fauna are still found in abundance.

Today's the day to enjoy all the park has to offer. Like to fish? Many anglers opt to fish from the park's sandy shore for largemouth bass, bluegill, and catfish. As a result of a connection to the bay, small walleye can also be found in Inland and Canoe Lakes. If you're a hiker or horseback rider, easy trails are available off Cedar Point Road west of the park entrance. For walkers, joggers, or cyclists, a 6-mile asphalt walkway connects park facilities. There's also a 7-mile system of grass paths and two other popular trails, a 2.8-mile loop known as **Mouse Trail** (a great place to observe owls in winter) and the 1.9-mile **Boardwalk Trail,** which starts by the Nature Center and traverses both marsh and swamp forest along the way. Bikes—from toddler-size to tandem—are available at the boat rental or the lodge or you can bring your own.

Afternoon

LUNCH: The **Surfside Snack Bar** near the amphitheater serves up all-American burgers, fries, and hot dogs during summer. If it's off-season or you're not into fast food, pack a picnic lunch. The nearby city of Oregon and State Highway 2 offer plenty of places to stock up for some al fresco adventure. Picnic areas are concentrated around the beach and at the base of Big Hill. Or hike up the paved walkway to the small shelter above the amphitheater, where you'll find a small open area with a fine view of the bay.

Resist the urge to stretch out on the picnic blanket afterward and take an afternoon siesta. There's a lot more to do after lunch. You might want to soak up some sun on the 2,000-foot beach, where guests are entertained by free performances—from solo artists to symphonies—on summer weekends. Or you might peruse the displays at **Trautman Nature Center,** where interactive exhibits concentrate on local nature, history, research, and wildlife. If it's winter, the park also boasts a network of cross-country trails, with skis available for rent at the lodge, as well as some breathtaking (literally!) sledding on Big Hill. Big Hill is also a great lookout point in summer.

If you're a nature lover or bird-watcher, you won't want to miss the park's 2-mile elevated walkway. It wends its way through the freshwater marshes, punctuated by 20-foot-high scanning towers and lovely seating areas. The marshes are teeming with life, from muskrat and red fox to more than a dozen species of ducks, including mallards.

If you visit in fall, nothing beats the tundra swan migration for sheer drama. This is Ohio's greatest expanse of coastal marsh and a favorite staging area for birds traveling south on the Great Lakes flyway. If you're really lucky, you'll be rewarded with the sight of a bald eagle nesting nearby.

If you're a golfer, **Maumee Bay Golf Course** is well worth playing. The 18-hole par 72 championship course was designed by Arthur Hill, who has attempted to re-create a Scottish course with moors, low, rolling, grass–covered mounds, bent-grass fairways, banks of sand bunkers, lots of water, and, in the true Scottish style, no trees. Tee times are available by calling the pro shop at (419) 836–9009.

Enjoy a leisurely dinner in the **Dining Room** before heading home. Or hit the road in time for a stop and an early meal at the **Toledo Museum of Art** (2445 Monroe Street, Toledo, OH 43697; 419–255–8000), which has an airy and art-filled cafe that serves appetizing entrees such as Caesar salads, fresh deli sandwiches, and daily specials. Afterward, wander through the many excellent galleries. Local residents are justifiably proud of this small but choice collection, which includes works by all the big names: El Greco, Rubens, Van Gogh, Picasso, Monet, Matisse, and more. If you've brought the kids, skip the museum and top off your escape with a trip to the respected **Toledo Zoo** (Route 25, Toledo, OH 43609; 419–385–5721). A few miles from downtown, the zoo houses more than 3,000 animals representing 525 species on fifty-one acres. Highlights include the world's only "Hippoquarium," where you'll come nose-to-nose with a hippo, the "Diversity of Life" exhibit, winner of a Significant Achievement Award from the American Zoological Association, and the Carnivore Cafe, once home to the zoo's primates and large cats, where *you're* the species behind bars as you nosh on hamburgers, hot dogs, and deli-style snacks. Another worthwhile stop is the new Toledo branch of the **Center of Science and Industry,** affectionately known as COSI (1 Discovery Way, Toledo, OH 43602; 419–255–COSI). Kids (and their parents) love the hands-on exhibits, including WaterWorks, a giant treehouse, a real tornado, even a high-wire bike.

OTHER RECOMMENDED RESTAURANTS AND LODGINGS

Ohio State Park Resorts are located throughout the state. If you're looking for something more rustic and are willing to travel a little farther afield, consider one of the seven other parks with resorts.

Burr Oak State Park Resort & Conference Center (Route 2, Box 159, Glouster, OH 45732; 614–767–2112) is northeast of Athens in the southern part of the state. Not far from picturesque Athens University, it borders part of the huge Wayne National Forest and the Sunday Creek Wildlife Area. The sixty-room Burr Oak Lodge is one of the older state-park lodges, but its modern glass-and-beam construction keeps it comfortably up to date. The cathedral-ceilinged sitting area is a great place to relax by the fire. The park is also known for its Cardinal Dining Room, with great views and a warm country atmosphere. It's a popular eating place for local residents as well as hotel guests. All rooms have great views, but no balconies as in other state parks. There are also thirty family-style two-bedroom cabins, many of which are booked up to a year in advance, and a number of theme weekends. Rates start at $90 per night.

Deer Creek Resort & Conference Center (22300 State Park Road, Mt. Sterling, OH 43143; 614–869–2020 or 877–678–3337) is just a 30-minute drive from Columbus. It's the second-newest facility in the state-park system, with 110 luxurious guest rooms, including lofts, king-size beds, and suites. Cradled by the main section of the lodge is an outdoor recreation area that includes a pool, shuffleboard, children's area, basketball, and practice putting green. There are also twenty-five two-bedroom cabins, an eighteen-hole championship golf course, indoor and outdoor pools, and more. For something really different, try the Harding Cabin, a rustic one-and-a-half-story cabin built in 1918 that overlooks the lake. It was built by William Daugherty, attorney general in the Harding administration, and was once used by President Warren Harding. It sleeps up to nine people in three upstairs bedrooms and also has a screened-in porch, dishwasher, and private dock. Rates start at $125 per night. All reservations can also be made through 800–AT-A-Park (Ohio State Parks Reservation Center).

Hueston Woods State Park (Rural Route 1, College Corner, OH 45003; 513–523–6381) is 5 miles north of Oxford, Ohio, and north of Cincinnati. It's one of the oldest parks in the Ohio system and dates back to 1797 and Matthew Hueston, the state's first conservationist, who held the land until 1941. It has varied amenities, including hiking, horseback riding, a historical museum, and a wildlife rehabilitation center. The lodge is on Acton Lake in an unusual building that was originally a council site for the Western Ohio Indian tribes. Today that theme is carried through the resort in the 110-foot-tall sandstone fireplace and ninety-four guest rooms. There are also sixty one- or two-bedroom cabins as well as an 18-hole golf course, sauna, hiking trails, and cross-country skiing. Rates start at $109 per night.

Mohican State Park Resort & Conference Center (Rural Route 2, Perrysville, OH 44864; 419–938–5411) is in southern Ashland County, about halfway between Cleveland and Columbus. Its main focus is the Mohican, a rare "reversed stream" that was formed as a result of glacial activity 12,000 years ago. The lodge has ninety-six guest rooms with private balcony as well as twenty-five cabins and a dining room with a sparkling lake view. There are also an Olympic-size pool, a sauna, and a charming fireplace in the round—a great place to relax with a glass of wine or cup of hot cocoa on chilly fall and winter weekends. Rates start at $110 per night.

Punderson Manor Resort & Conference Center (11755 Kinsman Road, Newbury, OH 44065; 216–564–9144) is just 30 miles east of Cleveland and 15 minutes from Sea World and Geauga Lake Amusement Park.

Located on one of the few natural lakes in the state, it has a charming English Tudor lodge that was completely renovated in 1982. The 31 rooms share an Old English decor, including some suites with fireplaces and large windows overlooking the lake. It also has an eighteen-hole golf course, twenty-six cabins perched at the south end of the lake, and an outdoor pool, tennis and basketball courts, and a popular sledding hill. Rates start at $115 per night.

Salt Fork Resort & Conference Center (Route 22 East, Box 7, Cambridge, OH 43725; 614–439–2751) is a pleasantly hilly surprise with great golf and wonderful wildlife viewing. It has fifty-four modern cabins along the shore of Salt Fork Lake (try No. 20, by itself at the north end of the beach) as well as the Salt Fork Lodge and Conference Center, largest in the park system. Guests in its 148 rooms have access to a number of recreation and dining options, including pools, tennis, volleyball, indoor and outdoor shuffleboard, and exercise and playground equipment. The modern resort is softened by huge wood-beamed ceilings, stone fireplaces, and paneled guest rooms. Ask about the special rates and theme packages. Rates start at $118 per night.

Shawnee State Park (P.O. Box 189, Friendship, OH 45630; 614–858–6621) is in the Appalachian foothills on the banks of the meandering Ohio River and is surrounded by the 60,000–acre Shawnee State Park. It's a dramatically hilly wilderness known affectionately as the Little Smokies of Ohio because of the foggy haze that sometimes descends on the forest. You can enjoy the forest on foot, on horseback, with a backpack, or from a car and, afterward, stay the night at the fifty-room Shawnee Lodge or one of twenty-five two-bedroom cabins. Built in 1973, the lodge has a rustic flavor that's complemented by the Native American motif throughout. Big stone fireplaces, timber framing, and a full-size birchbark canoe enhance the setting; even the menu in the dining room is full of Shawnee lore and legends. Rates start at $95 per night.

FOR MORE INFORMATION

Ohio State Park Information Center, 1952 Belcher Drive, Building C–3, Columbus, OH 43224–1386; (800) 282–7275. Information on the individual parks and surrounding attractions is also available directly from each park or lodge or www.atapark.com.

Kerr House Spa

OASIS IN OHIO

2 NIGHTS

Health • Fitness • Pampering • Self-indulgence

It's hard to believe that a spa with the high quality of the Kerr House could lie just over an hour from Detroit. It has no desert sun, mineral springs, or hot-shot aerobics instructors. The Kerr House does, however, have Laurie Hostetler. A determined dynamo, it was her dream to buy a rundown Victorian mansion in Grand Rapids, Ohio, and transform it into one of the Midwest's most exclusive health retreats.

Some say the Kerr House is the best spa in the country. It consistently ranks up there with more famous sun-filled getaways such as Canyon Ranch and the Golden Door. The touch that makes a weekend at the Kerr House so special, however, is the personal attention each guest receives. Hostetler takes no more than eight guests at a time for a weekend full of personal pampering. This getaway is designed for adults.

DAY 1

Afternoon

The Kerr House is a 20-minute drive southwest of Toledo. To get there from Detroit, take Interstate 75 south and then Interstate 475 west; then follow U.S. Highway 24 into Grand Rapids. From Ann Arbor, take U.S. Highway 23 to Highway 24 and on into Grand Rapids.

Plan to leave late on Friday afternoon. The Kerr House requests that guests arrive between 6:30 and 7:30 P.M., and so eat at home or grab some-

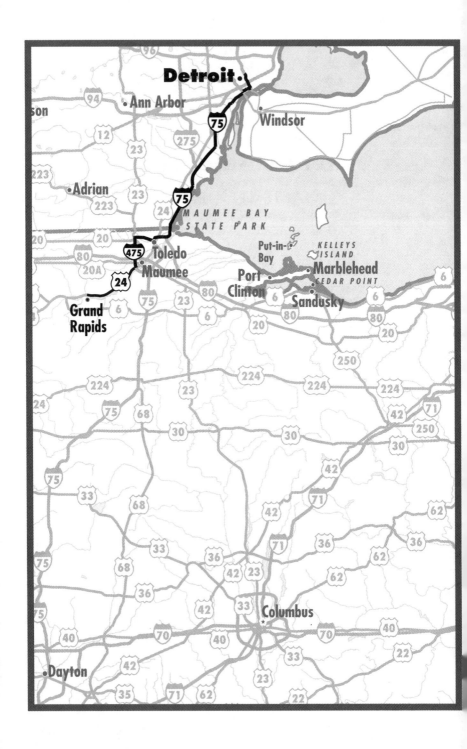

thing quick along the way. Just about every exit between Detroit and Grand Rapids has restaurants, if only for fast-food. Later arrivals are okay too; just let the staff know in advance. You'll be tempted along the way to stop and shop in nearby Waterville and downtown Grand Rapids, both charming river towns, but save that for Sunday afternoon. There's also some free time for wandering on Saturday.

Whenever you arrive, you'll be given a warm welcome by Hostetler and her staff, who will show you to your room. All rooms are spacious and decorated, like the house, in high Victorian style. Filled with antiques and items from Laurie's vast collections, they manage to be both elegant and cozy, with imposing wooden beds covered with crisp cotton sheets and homey quilts. After a chance to relax, guests are invited downstairs to meet other guests, some of whom come from as far away as Australia and Saudi Arabia, says Hostetler. The majority, however, are from the United States, with a number from Detroit, Chicago, and the East Coast.

Friday night is casual. You can relax in your room and recover from the drive or enjoy the whirlpool and sauna in the whitewashed basement. Everything is flexible, but recommended lights-out time is 11:00 P.M. Bring a good book if you're a night owl; there is no television.

DAY 2

Morning

BREAKFAST: If you've never been served breakfast in bed, you're in for a treat. Anywhere from 7:30 to 8:30 A.M. (depending on the number of guests and the day's schedule), a gentle knock rouses you before a staff member enters with a tray full of homemade granola, fresh fruit, juice, and (if you want it) coffee or tea. (Hostetler insists that although she will try to teach you healthy habits during your stay, she's not a fanatic.)

After breakfast, a full day of pampering awaits. During the day you'll enjoy three "treatments"—generally a herbal wrap, a one-hour massage, and a finger facial. Between sessions (all are given in the treatment rooms in the house's former basement, now a whitewashed space full of chintz and wicker), guests are encouraged to use the whirlpool or sauna. Two of the treatments precede lunch.

The Victorian Kerr House offers an atmosphere unmatched by any other U.S. spa.

Afternoon

LUNCH: Served in the cheerful basement cafe, lunch consists of healthy yet satisfying vegetable soup and a crunchy salad made from Amish-grown chicken, celery, nuts, and Dijon mustard. You may come expecting only carrot sticks, but food here is surprisingly flavorful and ample. Hostetler makes a point of telling you it's more important that you relax during the weekend than reform. If you really want a pizza from the in-town pizzeria during your stay, she'll deliver.

There's a third treatment after lunch, then guests are free to relax, nap, read, or wander into Grand Rapids's one-block downtown, just a block from the Kerr House. First settled in 1833, the town is perched on the scenic banks of the Maumee River and is full of shops that carry antiques and collectibles. Highlights include the **Olde Gilead Country Store** (24139 Front Street, 43522; 419–832–7651), a 100-year-old mercantile establishment with a sophisticated collection of gifts, books, toys, and more than 100 varieties of old-fashioned candy; and **Angelwood Gallery** (419–832–0625), a recent addition to the townscape, with abstract and avant-garde works by local artists.

Downtown is small, giving you plenty of time to explore and still be back in time for the 4:00 P.M. yoga class in the house's renovated attic, now an airy, light-filled exercise studio. Don't miss the framed blueprints of the house that line the walls—a lucky find during renovation.

Another thing that sets the Kerr House apart from more regimented spas is its attitude toward exercise. You won't be bombarded with strenuous step classes or power aerobics. In fact, on weekends, you'll attend just two classes, both of them yoga—and even those are optional. The first is a 2-hour beginning class. During the class, Hostetler teaches breathing, philosophy, and proper movement—you'll be surprisingly winded afterward. She also gives fascinating demonstrations of the mind–body connection that'll be enough to turn you off French fries forever—or at least for a few weeks. The second class comes tomorrow.

DINNER: Served in the elegant, high-ceilinged dining room, dinner is a more formal affair, served with silver and glowing candlesticks and accompanied by a harpist. An appetizer of meatless minestrone soup is followed by an Amish chicken breast, crunchy brown rice pilaf, and freshly steamed broccoli. Dessert is a fabulous frozen whipped banana that tastes remarkably like ice cream, topped with plump raspberries and blueberries. Afterward, teas (herbal or otherwise) are served in the parlor, where guests can chat and further enjoy the elegant strains of the harp.

DAY 3

Morning

BREAKFAST: Breakfast in bed again? After a few days of being waited on, you'll find it hard to go back to the bagel-and-coffee-on-the-run way of life. Today breakfast is yogurt and bananas topped with chewy granola, sliced apples, juice, and (because I'm a wimp) coffee.

So fortified, it's time for your second yoga class. This one is for just for an hour and gives more of the same from the day before as well as more discussion on nutrition, body performance, and Hostetler's general philosophy of health and life. Depending on how much you want to learn (or reform), Hostetler also sells related books in the small basement gift shop.

Time is quickly running out. After class, it's time to don the white robe again and head to the basement for (sigh), one last full-body massage. Afterward, there's time to soak in the hot tub or heat up in the sauna before joining Hostetler and the other guests for a farewell lunch in the cafe.

Afternoon

LUNCH: After eating here for a few days, you'll be requesting Hostetler's recipes. She recently published a cookbook, but is also happy to share her secrets with interested guests. Sunday lunch includes a tasty couscous with chopped-up vegetables and a creamy veggie-based soup. Most guests leave after lunch (if you're flying here, the limo will pick you up and take you back to the airport), although there is no set checkout time. Either way, you'll want to say good-bye to the staff and your newfound friends and promise to keep in touch.

THERE'S MORE

Canals. The Maumee River is very scenic and a great place for a stroll. The Isaac Ludwig Mill (419–535–3050) on Highway 65 and 278 gives you an idea of a working mill, with free tours Wednesday through Sunday as well as Sunday afternoon milling demonstrations. Canal rides are offered Wednesday to Friday, 10:00 A.M.–4:00 P.M., Saturday and Sunday 11:00 A.M.–5:00 P.M. from May 20 to October. Cost: $4.00.

History. The Wolcott House Museum Complex (1031 River Road, 43522; 419–893–9602) centers on the Federal-era home of James and Mary Wolcott and includes both American Indian artifacts and period antiques. There's also a mid-1800s saltbox farmhouse, a railroad depot, and a charming nineteenth-century church.

Train. On weekends in season, the Bluebird takes passengers on scenic routes from Grand Rapids through the surrounding countryside. For tickets and schedules, call (419) 878–2177.

SPECIAL EVENTS

You may want to time your visit to coincide with one of the Grand Rapids events and enjoy it during or after your Kerr House stay.

April. Spring Fling

May. Colonial Lost Arts Festival

July. Rapids Rally Days

August. Community Garage Sale

September. Canal Days

October. Applebutter Fest

November. Christmas Open House

FOR MORE INFORMATION

Rates at the Kerr House range from $695 (semiprivate) for a weekend to more than $2,750 for a week-long stay. For more information, contact the Kerr House, P.O. Box 363, 1777 Beaver Street, Grand Rapids, OH 43522; (419) 832–1733.

Cedar Point

FAMILY FUN

1 NIGHT

Roller-Coasters • Rides • Water Park • Historic Hotel

When I was a kid, summer didn't start until the day we went to Cedar Point. Thirty years later, the annual trek to this amusement park east of Detroit is still one of the highlights in my summer, although more now because of my children's excitement than my own. The weather is barely above 50 degrees when they start badgering me about setting a date. And they don't let up until we're in the car and heading east.

Now in its 130th year, Cedar Point has changed since the days when its biggest attraction was a dance hall. Today it's best known for its twelve scream machines, including the 205-foot-tall Magnum XL-200, the soaring Raptor, the wicked thirteen-story Demon Drop, the new Mantis, and fifty-six more down-to-earth rides spread out over more than 364 acres.

Amusement Today magazine recently named Cedar Point the best amusement park in the country. New in 2000 was the awe-inspiring Millennium Force, the highest roller-coaster in the United States, with a scream-inducing drop of more than 70 feet.

Although much larger than it was when I was a child, the park still holds much of the thrill that drew us all those years ago—snow cones, sun, and fun. If you're not the type for roller-coasters, you have many alternatives to being spun, twisted, dropped, or turned upside down. Check out the IMAX film in the cinema. Come nose-to-nose with performing sea creatures at the Oceana Stadium. Wander the Lake Erie beach and boardwalk. Dance to live stage shows. Record your kids' fleeting childhoods with a $10 crayon sketch.

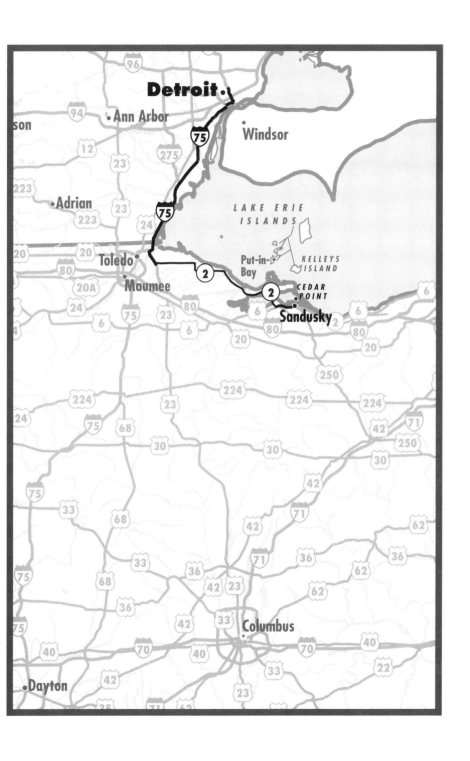

Many metro Detroiters choose to make this a one-day pilgrimage (exhausing for both parents and offspring), but smart families stay over at least one night, which lets you add the watery fun in the adjacent Soak City and maybe some of the family-style attractions in nearby Sandusky. Either way, adding time to your trip means you can pack as much pleasure as possible into a visit to the park and make the trip a mini-vacation for the whole family. *Tip:* The park is less crowded early and late in the season. Plan to visit anytime in June or late in August and September if you tend toward claustrophobia (call ahead, however, for the park is open only on weekends during the "shoulder" season).

DAY 1

Morning

Rise at the crack of dawn so that you can get there when the park opens at 10:00 A.M. Cedar Point is about two and one-half hours from Detroit. To get there, take Interstate 75 south to State Highway 2 and then continue straight east to Cedar Point. Highway 2 skirts Lake Erie, and although it's just two lanes, it's much more scenic than the anonymous Ohio Turnpike (it also generally has less construction). If your brood gets hungry once you're on the road, you'll find a number of fast-food restaurants along Highway 2 in Oregon, just outside Toledo. We usually stop at the McDonald's on Alexis Road just inside the Ohio border.

From Oregon you can't miss the signs to Cedar Point. You'll pass lots of restaurants and budget-level hotels in Sandusky, all good options if you're just looking for a place to sleep after a busy day. The Sandusky Visitors Bureau can supply you with a guide that lists the hotels if you opt not to stay within the park.

If you've got preschoolers, your first stop at Cedar Point will be the **Kiddy Kingdom** just past Main Street. With seventeen miniature rides, including a small-scale roller-coaster, bumper boats, and drive-it-yourself four-by-four trucks that look just like the grown-up models, the kids will think they're in heaven. If that's not enough, there's barnyard fun at the petting farm; the popular Berenstain Bear Country with tree houses, sand boxes, miniature train rides, and other themed fun; and an area with ball crawls, ropes, slides, and other playground favorites.

Afternoon

LUNCH: If you're smart, you'll pack a picnic lunch from home rather than buy the ubiquitous (and expensive) burgers, pizza, and chicken nuggets sold at stands throughout the park. (One exception is the French fries sold at a stand near the aquarium. They're good and greasy and best eaten smothered in malt vinegar.) An area near the park entrance has lots of tables on which to stow your stuff—most families leave their coolers covered with blankets while they explore the park and return throughout the day for breaks. You may also choose to bring something to tide the gang over until a late dinner so that you can plan to eat outside the park grounds.

DINNER: The nicest restaurant in the Cedar Point complex is the **Breakwater Cafe** at Sandcastle Suites (419–627–2107). This popular eatery at the northern tip of the peninsula serves breakfast, lunch, and dinner—all with breathtaking views. The cafe's cocktail lounge and patio are choice locations for viewing Lake Erie pleasure boats and the evening sun setting across Sandusky Bay. Moderate.

LODGING: If you're just staying one night or if money's no object, splurge with a stay at the historic **Breakers Hotel** (419–627–2106). The 1905 hotel underwent a $10-million facelift in 1995, and added the Breakers Tower in 1999; they also added 206 new units to this resort that once housed luminaries such as Abbott and Costello, Annie Oakley, and six U.S. presidents. With a sandy Lake Erie beach, two outdoor pools, whirlpools, and on-site restaurants, it's an elegant and convenient location. It also offers easy access to the adjacent park, so that you can come and go as you please throughout the day or be the first ones at the park each morning. Rates start at $195 per night.

The park also operates the new **Sandcastle Suites** (419–627–2107), which sit on a beach at the very tip of the Cedar Point peninsula facing Sandusky Bay and Lake Erie. Rates start at $165 per night. Both the Breakers and the Sandcastle Suites hotels offer getaway packages, which include discounted rates on accommodations as well as admission to the park, meals, and more. Ask for more information.

Soak City at Cedar Point invites plenty of wet and wild fun.

DAY 2

Morning

BREAKFAST: Fuel up for another fast-paced day with breakfast in one of the Breakers restaurants. Head back to the park if you missed some of the rides or if lines were too long on the first day. Otherwise, plan to spend the second day enjoying the wet and wild fun at the adjacent **Soak City Water Park**.

Soak City was added to the park late in the 1980s, partly as a way of keeping families at Cedar Point longer. It was recently doubled in size, with three new rides, including a gigantic, high-action water slide, featuring six-person rafts, an inner-tube river adventure, and two new playgrounds. *Note:* The two parks charge separate admission.

Afternoon

LUNCH: Head back to the hotel or grab something to tide you over at one of the concessions inside Soak City. Spend the afternoon in Soak City or in the adjacent **Challenge Park,** where you can live out your fantasies of being a race-car driver as you speed your go-kart to victory on the Grand Prix Raceway, tee off on two 18-hole miniature golf courses, or even experience the new RipCord, a bungee-jumping-like activity where you'll fall 150 feet and swoop through the air like a bird—all while safely anchored to a support structure, of course.

DINNER: Perkins Family Restaurant and Bakery (1530 Cleveland Road, Sandusky; 419–625–9234) is just outside the park grounds in the Best Western hotel. It's a family-style national chain but doesn't taste like a chain, with an on-site bakery, tasty sandwiches, salads for grown-ups, and an extensive kids' menu. Inexpensive. Another good bet is Italian-style **Fazoli's** on Route 6 near the Sandusky Mall. Although it's still fast food, it's better than most and is open until 11:00 P.M.

THERE'S MORE

Animals. Nearby Sandusky is also home to Lagoon Deer Park (1502 Martins Point Road, Sandusky, OH 44870; 419–684–5701), open from mid-April through mid-October. Here your family can get "up close and personal" with more than 250 animals from Europe, Asia, and North and South America. Hand-feed hundreds of deer and other tame species, feed fish, or cast your line in stocked lagoons and fishing lakes. Don't miss the famous "Dancing Chicken." There's also an attractive picnic area.

Carousels. The old-fashioned merry-go-round may seem a little tame after a day at Cedar Point, but it has a nostalgic charm that's perennially appealing—especially to toddlers and smaller children who may be a bit overwhelmed by Cedar Point's crowds and pace. The Merry-Go-Round Museum (West Washington and Jackson Streets, Sandusky, OH 44870; 419–626–6111) lets you relive the glory days of the carousel and other classic Americana with a tour of the museum, housed in the city's former 1920s post office. Highlights include a working Allen Herschel carousel from the 1930s (a free ride is part of the tour), a small turn-of-the-century English carousel, and a great gift shop that carries virtually every known carousel-related souvenir. There's also a charming full-time carver-restorer on the premises. Admission is $4.00.

Caves. Not far from Sandusky is Bellevue, where you can visit Seneca Caverns (15248 East Thompson Road, Bellevue, OH 44811; 419–483–6711). This 110-foot-deep cave—technically considered an earth crack—was discovered in 1872 by two boys hunting rabbits; it opened to the public in 1933. Today's visitors descend steps 110 feet underground through seven levels on hour-long tours. The cavern is fairly rugged—kids love it—and is one of the few in the country kept in its original, natural condition. Don't leave without panning for gems at the Sandy Creek Gem Mining.

Cruises. Sandusky is also home to a number of companies that offer day cruises in and around the Lake Erie Islands. Many offer meals as part of the package. The *Emerald Empress* (800–876–1907) is a 150-foot, three-deck cruise ship that accommodates up to 600 people on twelve itineraries. "Lazy Day" cruises head for Put-In-Bay and Kelley's Island, with continental breakfast and lunch en route. Lunch and dinner cruises include a one-and-one-half-hour sight-seeing cruise around the islands and Sandusky Bay and feature an on-board buffet. "Saturday Prime-Time" cruises include a hand-carved prime rib dinner and a dance band. There are also Sunday brunch cruises and "Lakebreak" sight-seeing cruises. Prices range from $5.25 to $29.95 per person. Popular island cruises are also offered on the *Goodtime I* (800–446–3140), docked at Jackson Street Pier. It includes full bar service, dance floor, and snack bar.

Inventions. About 13 miles south of Sandusky is the Thomas Edison's Birthplace Museum (9 Edison Drive, Milan, OH 44846; 419–499–2135). Would-be inventors find the simple seven-room, two-and-a-half-story home built in 1841 fascinating. The inventor of the phonograph and the lightbulb lived here from the time he was born in 1847 until he was seven years old, when the family moved to Port Huron, Michigan. Today the museum is still run by his great-grandson and furnished with many original family pieces. Don't miss the room honoring his many inventions, including phonographs, lightbulbs, and models of his movie studio and Menlo Park laboratory. The adjacent Milan Historical Museum (419–499–2968) has old-fashioned dolls and glassware, a blacksmith's shop, and a vintage general store.

Treats. A must-stop on any visit to Sandusky, Toft's Dairy (3717 Venice Road, Sandusky, OH 44870; 419–625–4376) has been serving up creamy confections since 1900, when it was founded as a small farm with a respected herd of dairy cattle. Since then it has moved three times and is the only locally owned and operated dairy on Lake Erie between Lorain and Toledo. Tours are offered daily. Afterward, sample favorite ice-cream flavors such as butter pecan and vanilla or newer additions such as Moose Tracks and Mother Lode, full of chocolate and caramel (kids may prefer the chewy Dinosaur Crunch).

SPECIAL EVENTS

April. Spring Bounty of Arts, Crafts, and Collectibles, Vermilion

June. Free Fishing Days, Lake Erie
Festival of the Fish, Vermilion

July. Arts and Crafts Show, Sandusky

October. Woolybear Festival, Vermilion

November. Santa's Arrival, Sandusky

OTHER RECOMMENDED LODGINGS

Sandusky

There is no dearth of family-friendly lodgings around the park, from barebones basic to top-of-the-line top-dollar. Dependable—if predictable—chain hotels include Holiday Inn–Sandusky/Cedar Point (5513 Milan Road, Sandusky, OH 44870; 419–626–6671), Comfort Inn–Sandusky (5909 Milan Road, Sandusky, OH 44870; 419–621–0200), Ramada Inn–Sandusky (5608 Milan Road, Sandusky, OH 44870; 419–626–9890). There are also a number of hotels and bed-and-breakfasts in nearby downtown Sandusky. For information, contact Sandusky/Erie County Visitors and Convention Bureau, 4424 Milan Road, Sandusky, OH 44870; (419) 625–2984 or (800) 255–3743.

Radisson Harbour Inn (2001 Cleveland Road, Sandusky, OH 44870; 419–627–2500) is the newest hotel owned by the park. The year-round resort offers 237 guest rooms and 45 suites, an indoor pool, and kids' center. Rates: $59–$139.

Camping: If you're bringing your own bed, Cedar Point has its own Camper village, with a store, laundry, showers, and beach access. Call (419) 627–2106. Rates: $38–$52 per night.

FOR MORE INFORMATION

Cedar Point Amusement Park & Resort, P.O. Box 5006, 1 Cedar Point Drive, Sandusky, OH 44871-5006; (419) 627–2350 or www.cedarpoint.com.

Cleveland

RENAISSANCE IN THE RUST BELT

2 NIGHTS

Theater • Restaurants • Rock and Roll Museum • Nightlife

Ohio's second-largest city, once jokingly referred to as "the mistake by the lake," is having the last laugh these days. Urban pioneers and envious city officials around the country—and especially in Detroit—are pointing to Cleveland as the comeback city of the century.

Today the city is a sophisticated midwestern metropolis and a fascinating family destination. Despite an admitted industrial bent, you'll find more than 19,000 acres of parkland and 90 miles of scenic Lake Erie shoreline, one of the country's finest art museums, and a renowned group of professional theaters for drama enthusiasts of all ages.

Clevelanders are proud of their city—a five-time recipient of the prestigious All-American City award. And they know how to have a good time—1996 was the city's two-hundredth birthday, and the entire population got into the swing with fireworks, parties, special events, even a giant traveling birthday card donated by American Greetings. Whenever you visit, however, you'll find a spirit of celebration that characterizes the new Cleveland.

DAY 1

Afternoon

Cleveland is about a two-and-one-half-hour drive from Detroit. You can take Interstate 75 to the Ohio Turnpike (I–90) or take the more scenic State Highway 2 east. Either way, plan to arrive in town in time to relax over dinner and

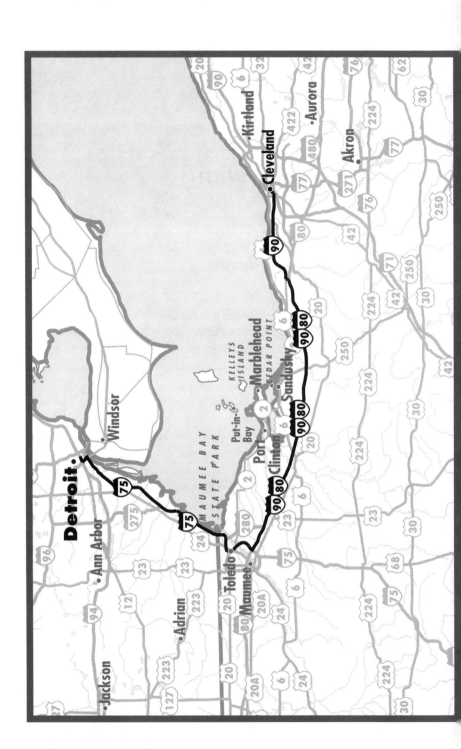

a little nightlife. Few areas in the city are as lively as **"the Flats,"** a renovated area not far along the Cleveland Memorial Shoreway. Once the home of hundreds of heavy industries, the Flats is now the city's premier entertainment district. An interesting blend of converted warehouses dots the east and west banks where the Cuyahoga River meets Lake Erie.

Here you'll find the popular **Nautica Entertainment Complex,** which covers some 28 acres on the river's west bank and includes an amphitheater, a riverfront boardwalk, and a floating restaurant. Anchored by two dramatic jackknife bridges, the complex has attracted millions of people since it opened in 1987.

DINNER: If you've brought the kids, check downtown's **Spaghetti Warehouse** (1231 Main Avenue, Cleveland, OH 44113; 216–621–9420), where you can pig out on pasta and even dine in a trolley car. If you were hoping for something a little less predictable, try **Watermark** (1250 Old River Road, Cleveland, OH 44113; 216–241–1600). It has what many consider the best seafood in town as well as riverfront patio dining in summer. Moderate.

Afterward, consider a nightcap and some jazz at **Sammy's in the Flats** (1400 West Tenth Street, Cleveland, OH 44113; 216–523–5560) or **Sammy's at the Arena** (100 Gateway Plaza, Cleveland, OH 44113; 216–420–2900), with high-tech style and an eclectic menu.

LODGING: The **Wyndham Cleveland Hotel** (1260 Euclid Avenue, Cleveland, OH 44115; 216–615–7500) was built in 1995 and is one of the city's newest hotels. Centrally located, the 205-room upscale hotel cost $28 million to build and is just steps away from the city's theater district. The spacious rooms all sport cable TV, voice mail, coffeemaker, and ironing board. Because of the hotel's proximity to the theater district, it was voted "The Place Most Likely to See Stars" by *Cleveland Magazine*. For a special treat, ask for one of the circular corner rooms, which feature a king-size bed and six floor-to-ceiling windows that overlook the theaters below. **Winsor's,** the hotel's restaurant, has a clubby, theater motif and is named after Winsor French, a popular 1920s gossip columnist. Rates: $129–$157 per night. Ask about the Theatre Package, which includes tickets and valet parking.

DAY 2

Morning

BREAKFAST: A great place for an impromptu and always-fresh breakfast is the historic **West Side Market** at West Twenty-fifth Street and Lorain Avenue in the neighborhood known as Ohio City. Duck inside the door of this vintage 1912 Old World–style market, one of the largest and last in the United States, and you'll be overwhelmed by the smells of fresh baked goods, exotic meats and cheeses, and more. Some one hundred indoor and outdoor merchants from various ethnic groups serve up anything you desire in a friendly, carnival-like setting. Highlights include **Farkas,** a Hungarian pastry shop, and **Athens Pastries and Imported Foods,** a Greek-style general store. Inexpensive.

Set aside the rest of the day for exploring downtown. Getting around is easy; most attractions are clumped together. Two good examples are the University Circle area and the North Harbor Coast. To get a better idea of what you can skip and what you won't want to miss, consider a swing around town on **Lolly the Trolley** (216–771–4484 for tickets and information). The bright red trolleys cover 20 miles and more than one hundred attractions.

If you'd rather go by sea (or, in this case, by lake), stow away on board the 1,000-passenger *Goodtime III* (825 East Ninth Street, North Coast Harbor, OH 44114; 216–861–5110). The city's largest charter boat offers sight-seeing and entertainment cruises along the Cuyahoga and Lake Erie from May through October. The *Nautica Queen* (Nautica Entertainment Complex, 1153 Main Avenue, Cleveland, OH 44114; 216–696–8888) also offers cruising and dining on its 300- to 400-passenger ships during warm-weather months.

Other would-be sailors head to the *William G. Mather* (1001 East Ninth Street Pier, Cleveland, OH 44114; 216–574–6262), a restored steamship that was originally christened in 1925. The former flagship of the Cleveland Cliffs Iron Company is docked at downtown's East Ninth Street pier and is now a floating discovery center. At 618 feet, it was built in 1925 to carry ore, coal, and grain throughout the Great Lakes but now houses exhibits and displays that focus on the history and lore of these "iron boats." Visitors are escorted through the pilothouse, the crew and guest quarters, and the galley as well as the guests' and officers' dining rooms. Tours are offered daily from June through August and on weekends in May, September, and October. The ship was the first landmark to open in the city's hot new "North Coast" district.

The *Mather* may have been the first, but it's certainly not the last, of the North Coast notables. The city's—some say even the country's—hottest ticket is the $92-million **Rock and Roll Hall of Fame and Museum** (1 Key Plaza, Cleveland, OH 44114; 800–493–ROLL). Put on your dancin' shoes and prepare to be swept off your feet by the stunning design and the toe-tapping tunes. I. M. Pei's controversial creation is a dramatic structure that includes a 165–foot tower rising from the water and varied geometric shapes exploding from the tower along with a shimmering, seven-story triangular glass tent. Pei, best known for his contemporary glass pyramid addition to the historic Louvre museum in Paris, wanted to "echo the energy of rock and roll" when he designed the museum. Opened in 1995, it houses 150,000 square feet of interactive exhibits, performance spaces, special programs, and displays. It attracted more than a million visitors in its first year of operation.

City leaders claimed that Cleveland was the most appropriate site for the new hall of fame because legendary disc jockey Alan Freed reportedly coined the phrase *rock and roll* here during a 1951 broadcast. In the museum the organizers hope to tell the story of rock and roll from its roots in country, blues, rhythm and blues, and jazz to the latest forms of hip-hop and rap. Among the more than 4,000 artifacts in the collection are Elvis Presley's black leather outfit worn in his 1968 TV special; John Lennon's "Sgt. Pepper's Lonely Hearts Club Band" uniform; handwritten lyrics by Chuck Berry and Jimmy Hendrix, even Roy Orbison's sunglasses and Jim Morrison's Cub Scout uniform. Other exhibits let you "host" a "live" radio broadcast and explore the recording booths where hit songs were made.

Afternoon

LUNCH: If all that excitement and energy makes you hungry (or tired!), take a break at the cafe on the museum's third floor. The menu changes monthly but always includes sandwiches, salads, and a daily hot entree special. There are also beer, wine, and gourmet coffee. Moderate.

Just steps away from the Rock and Roll Hall of Fame is the $54.9-million, 165,000-square-foot **Great Lakes Science Center** (601 Erieside Avenue, Cleveland, OH 44114; 216–694–2000). It opened late in 1996 and quickly earned a reputation as one of the most innovative science centers in the world.

Designed to provide a comprehensive learning center, it features 50,000 square feet of exciting hands-on exhibits that encourage visitors of all ages to learn and have fun. Features include a 20,000-square-foot gallery devoted to traveling and seasonal exhibits; a huge, 320-seat Omnimax theater, and another sure hit: a riveting replica of the NASA mission-control station in Houston. In addition, kids love Richard Scarry's Busy Town, full of lifting bridges similar to those found in the Flats, as well as the chance to pilot a blimp.

From the North Coast, head back into the heart of the city's downtown. Once a joke, Cleveland's downtown has made a startling comeback, with new shopping, sports, and entertainment complexes. In the heart of it all is Public Square, where the **Terminal Tower** (216–621–7981) rises 52 stories above the city streets. The lower level, once a train depot, was renovated in 1989 into an upscale shopping mecca known as "The Avenue." It now houses more than 120 shops, restaurants, and entertainment options. Don't leave the Terminal Tower without stopping in at the beautifully restored **Renaissance Cleveland Hotel,** one of the city's finest. It's also the site of **Sans Souci** (216–696–5600), an intimate restaurant that's always a good bet. It features hearty country fare from the Provence region in France; delicious but expensive. A forty-second-floor observation deck in the hotel offers a spectacular view of downtown and the Lake Erie waterfront.

DINNER: Linger at Sans Souci or grab an early bite at **Parker's** (2801 Bridge Avenue, Cleveland, OH 44115; 216–771–7130). It's considered one of the best restaurants in the city and is Cleveland's only Mobil four-star restaurant. It's in the recently resuscitated Ohio City neighborhood, about a five-minute ride from downtown. Pleasant and unpretentious, it features excellent Country French cuisine and an equally fine wine list. Try the five-course prix fixe menu, a bargain at about $40 per person. Moderate to expensive. Reservations recommended.

Afterward, take in a performance at one of the city's restored theaters. Cleveland is considered Broadway's home away from home, with many major shows either debuting or coproduced here. Recent productions have included *Phantom of the Opera, Grease,* and the family favorite, *The Nutcracker.*

The cornerstone of Cleveland theater is **Playhouse Square** (1501 Euclid Avenue, Cleveland, OH 44115; 800–766–6048), now the third-largest performing arts center in the country. With more than 7,000 seats and nearly a million patrons annually, Playhouse Square boasts four renovated theaters, all worth visiting for a tour even if nothing is on stage. The spectacular Ohio, State, Palace, and Allen Theaters were all originally built in the 1920s as vaudeville palaces. They were converted into movie houses in the 1950s and fell into disrepair in the 1960s. After a long fund-raising drive, they became home to five resident companies, including the **Cleveland Opera,** the **Cleveland**

Ballet, the **Ohio Ballet, Dance Cleveland,** and the **Great Lakes Theater Festival**. The Great Lakes Theater Festival was founded in 1961 to preserve classic theater and is one of a few companies left in the United States dedicated to this art form. For a schedule, pick up a copy of the *Cleveland Plain Dealer Magazine* on Friday or a free copy of the *Weekly Scene*.

If you're more into the roar of the crowds than the smell of the greasepaint, Cleveland is also a great sports town. Those traitor Browns may have moved to Baltimore, but plenty of all-star action is left. From the excitement of a buzzer shot at a Cavs basketball game to the frigid frenzy of a Lumberjacks hockey game, Cleveland offers enough thrills to satisfy sportaholics of any age.

Catch an Indians major-league baseball game at **Jacobs Field** (2401 Ontario Street, Cleveland, OH 44115; 216–241–8888) in the heart of downtown. This state-of-the-art facility holds 42,000 screaming fans who come to experience the thrills of America's favorite pastime while enjoying spectacular views of the field and skyline and the largest freestanding scoreboard in North America.

Jacobs Field is part of the city's world-class sports and entertainment complex that opened in 1994. The new **Gateway Sports Entertainment Complex** cost $362 million to build and is on the site of the city's Old Central Market. It has gained international acclaim for the visionary design of its two arenas—the aforementioned $161-million Jacobs Field and a $118-million, 20,000-seat indoor arena, home of the Cleveland Cavaliers NBA basketball team, the Lumberjacks hockey team, and the Thunderbolts arena football team as well as concerts and special events. Young fans love the on-site Kidsland, with a retail store, children-only concessions, and a restaurant with an eagle's-eye view of the playing field.

The ballpark is a mere five-minute stroll from most downtown hotels and is connected by a walkway to Tower City Center. With panoramic views of the skyline, a restaurant that looks out over the playing field, food courts, tempting team gift shops, and a colorful collection of public art by noted regional artists, Gateway is a sure hit with fans.

DAY 3

Morning

BREAKFAST: It's Sunday, therefore plan to indulge yourself with brunch at the **Ritz Carlton Cleveland** (1515 West Third Street, Cleveland, OH 44113; 216–623–1300). The hotel's Riverview Room is an elegantly paneled oasis that overlooks the Flats. Its brunch includes both breakfast and lunch special-ties, including waffles, eggs, smoked seafood, cheeses of all kinds, pastas, veg-gies, a carving station, and a delectable dessert bar. Expensive.

The city has been historically known for its grimy industrial image, but it has also long been a strong supporter of the arts. The majority of its cultural attractions are grouped in the **University Circle Area.** Just 4 miles east of downtown, it features the country's largest concentration of arts and cultural institutions—more than a half dozen in all. All are within easy walking dis-tance of each other and situated in a relaxing, parklike setting.

Your first stop is the respected **Cleveland Museum of Art** (11150 East Boulevard, Cleveland, OH 44106; 216–421–7340 or 888–CMA–0033). With more than 30,000 works of art spanning some 5,000 years, there's definitely something to suit every taste. The museum was founded by a group of civic–minded philanthropists "for the benefit of the people forever" and opened in 1916. True to the spirit of its founders, admission is always free—one of the few museums across the country to remain so.

Highlights of the collection include the ominous-looking swords, daggers, suits of armor, and other weapons of war (a favorite of young museumgoers), the exotic Egyptian galleries, with a rare statue of pharaoh Amenemhet III, a stunning collection of medieval art (including the famous golden Guelph Treasure), Old Master works from the thirteenth through the eighteenth cen-turies, and more modern masterpieces by David, Delacroix, Gauguin, Van Gogh, and Picasso. The surrounding fifteen-acre park has an outdoor sculp-ture court that's open to diners in season. There's also an indoor cafe when your feet and eyes get tired.

Afternoon

LUNCH: You've feasted your senses, now treat your stomach at the museum's restaurant. It offers hearty fare that includes soups, sandwiches, hot entrees, and more. Inexpensive to moderate.

More into dinosaurs than Dali? The nearby **Cleveland Museum of Nat-ural History** (1 Wade Oval Drive, Cleveland, OH 44106; 216–231–4600) is the state's largest natural-science museum. Regarded as one of the finest in North America, the museum is in a modern, 200,000-square-foot facility and draws some 400,000 visitors annually.

Many come to see the Foucault Pendulum in the main lobby, which demonstrates the earth's rotation. It's the world's only pendulum in which the electromagnet that keeps the 270-pound plumb bob moving is placed under-

The Cleveland Museum of Art is one of the country's top museums.

neath rather than mounted on top. Rock hounds of all ages appreciate the Gem Room, with an impressive collection of quartz crystals, opals, and diamonds in a rainbow of colors. The Barney set loves the dinosaurs and other prehistoric creatures as well as the birds, botany, and geology displays and the fascinating Hall of Man, home to "Lucy," the 3-million-year-old skeleton of the oldest-known human being. You can also see stars in the state's oldest planetarium, come nose-to-nose with native animals and wildlife in an outdoor environmental courtyard and rustic wood garden, or browse in the well-stocked gift shop, cleverly named the "Ark in the Park." Admission is free on Tuesday and Thursday afternoons; at other times it costs $6.00 for adults and $4.00 for young people ages five through seventeen. Children age four or younger always get in free.

More recent history can be found at the **Western Reserve Historical Society** (10825 East Boulevard, Cleveland, OH 44106; 216–721–5722), the city's oldest cultural institution. It was founded in 1867 to preserve and promote the area's rich heritage. Think you're a pack rat? You'll be amazed by the diverse collections here. Baseball, roller coasters, classic cars, bowling machines, airplanes, full-size log cabins, and more are crammed into this huge and fascinating space. Browse among the costumes, farming tools, manuscripts, and period rooms that re-create the area known as the Western Reserve from the pre–Revolutionary War era through early in the twentieth century.

The centerpiece of the museum is the Hay-McKinney Mansion, built in 1911 and designed by the son of President James Garfield. The ornate Italian Florentine villa is filled with important period furniture and decorative arts and was once part of the city's "Millionaire's Row" that stretched along part of Euclid Avenue (the mayor's home located here even boasted an indoor ice-skating rink). Tours take you "downstairs" to the servants' quarters for a starkly different perspective on nineteenth-century life.

Car buffs of all ages flock to the society's **Crawford Auto-Aviation Museum,** which houses more than 150 streamlined, vintage, and classic automobiles and aircraft, including a rare collection of Cleveland-built cars. It's considered one of the finest collections in the nation. Clotheshorses get equal time at the Chisholme Halle Costume Wing, where they can stroll down a street of re-created turn-of-the-century shops and imagine themselves dressed in nineteenth-century finery.

Two other small museums in University Circle are worth mentioning—and visiting. "Please touch" could be the motto of the innovative **Rainbow Children's Museum** (10730 Euclid Avenue, Cleveland, OH 44106; 216–791–5437). More like an activity center than a museum, it houses more than 100 displays that the whole gang will enjoy. Get wet—or at least learn about the properties of water—in "Water, Water Everywhere," which explores the mysteries of water and its cycles as kids pour and pump, carve riverbanks, work waterwheels, and enjoy racing a boat down a replica of Lake Erie. Prefer heights? You can enter a deep forest to check out "Tales in Tall Trees," let your kids' little hands work child-size bridges in the "Over and Under Bridges" area, or help them create a self-portrait in the "People Puzzle" area.

Looking for something really different? Check out the **Cleveland Health Museum** (8911 Euclid Avenue, Cleveland, OH 44106; 216–231–5010). This fascinating, 40,000-square-foot museum is the first of its kind in the United States. More than 200 permanent exhibits include Juno, the talking transparent woman; the world's largest tooth, which towers above your head at 18 feet; the family discovery center; and the theaters of Hearing, Sight, and Social Concerns. If you have kids and you've never been able to address the issue of the birds and the bees, check the "Wonder of New Life" section, which tells the story of reproduction in easy-to-understand cartoon style. The museum reopened in mid-1999 with a new expanded building and new exhibits as well as old favorites.

If you've brought the kids, let them stretch their legs a bit more before getting back in the car with a visit to the **RainForest at the Cleveland Metroparks Zoo** (3900 Wildlife Way, Cleveland, OH 44109; 216–661–6500). Just 5 miles south of downtown, it houses more than 3,000 animals. The RainForest is the big draw, however, with a simulated biosphere that features a two-story hydroponics plant wall, a 25-foot water curtain, and a tropical thunderstorm, complete with simulated lightning and melodic rain. After eight years of planning and nearly $30 million in expenses, the tropical netherworld opened in 1992 and remains one of the zoo's top attractions.. The newest exhibit is "Wolf Wilderness: Wildlife of the Great Lakes," which features these much-maligned mammals in their natural habitat.

THERE'S MORE

Amish Community. Ohio has the largest Amish population in the world. About 35,000 of these "plain people" live in the northeast part of the state, mostly in Holmes, Wayne, and Tuscarawas Counties. The region is known for its working Amish farms, down-home restaurants, and country crafts. For more information, call (800) 362–6474.

Amusements. Six Flags Ohio (1060 North Aurora Road, Aurora, OH 44202; 440–562–7131) is a classic summer park with one hundred wet and dry attractions. Adjacent to SeaWorld (see "Wildlife" section below).

Fishing. Wave Walker Sport Fishing Charters (216–641–2549) offers anglers the chance to fish for trophy-size walleye and steelhead trout from downtown Cleveland.

Flowers. The City of Cleveland Botanical Garden in Rockefeller Park (750 East 88th Street, Cleveland, OH 44113; 216–721–1600) and the Cleveland Botanical Garden (11030 East Boulevard, Cleveland, OH 44106; 216–721–1600), include acres of lush landscapes including Japanese, herb, rose, and wildflower gardens.

Golf. Fairway fans can try their luck at a number of public courses, including Cleveland Metroparks Big Met (4811 Valley Parkway; 216–331–1700),

Shawnee Hills, (18753 Egbert Road, 216–232–7184), or Manakiki (35501 Eddy Road; 216–942–2500).

Scenic Drive. Chagrin Falls is a charming historic village east of downtown with interesting boutiques and antiques, picturesque falls, a picnic area, and turn-of-the-century homes. The city's historical society (440–247–4695) offers a "Village Victorian" walking tour.

Skiing. Boston Mills/Brandywine Ski Resorts (7100 Riverview Road, Peninsula, OH 44264; 330–467–2242) operate seven slopes with six chair-lifts and two surface tows, as well as a popular beginners' program.

Trees. The Holden Arboretum (9500 Sperry Road, Kirtland, OH 44094; 440–946–4400), east of Cleveland in Kirtland, is the largest in the United States, with more than 3,000 acres of natural woodlands, horticultural collections, display gardens, walking trails, and open fields. Open year-round.

Wildlife. One of the top attractions in the Cleveland area is SeaWorld of Ohio (1100 SeaWorld Drive, Aurora, OH 44202; 330–995–2121 or 800–637–4266 in Ohio), a wildlife-centered water park that's also a family favorite. Here you can touch the smooth skin of a dolphin, enjoy the synchronized swimming of killer whales, and come face-to-face with the razor-sharp teeth of a shark in Shark Encounter, the largest shark display in the Midwest. New in 2000 was an exhibition exploring the myth and mystery of the Bermuda Triangle. Open mid-May through mid-October.

SPECIAL EVENTS

January. Winterscape

February. Autorama
National Home and Garden Show

March. Cleveland International Film Festival
World's Toughest Rodeo

April. Tri-C Jazz Fest

May. Great American Rib Cook-Off

June. Pepsi Country Music Festival

July. Cleveland Cook KidsFest

Festival of Freedom

August. Cuyahoga County Fair

Off-Shore Power Boat Races

September. Cleveland National Air Show

Oktoberfest

November. Downtown Holiday Lighting Program

OTHER RECOMMENDED RESTAURANTS

Great Lakes Brewing Company (2516 Market Street, Cleveland, OH 44113; 216–771–4404) has a friendly midwestern atmosphere, casual grub, and lagers and ales brewed on the premises. Moderate.

Li Wah (2999 Payne Street, Cleveland, OH 44114; 216–696–6556) serves dim sum from 10:00 A.M. to 3:00 P.M. and is open for dinner. Moderate.

Sokolowski's University Inn (1201 University Road, Cleveland, OH 44113; 216–771–9236) serves up fine Polish fare, including *nalesniki* (blintzes) and *pierogi* (dumplings). Moderate.

OTHER RECOMMENDED LODGINGS

Embassy Suites (1701 East Twelfth Street, Cleveland, OH 44114; 216–523–8000) has 268 suites, a heated indoor pool, and plenty of room to spread out. Handy location within walking distance of all the sites. Rates: $119–$199 per night.

The Ritz Carlton (1515 West Third Street, Cleveland, OH 44113; 800–241–3333) is the city's only Mobil four-star hotel, with 208 rooms, china cabinets in the halls, and a classically elegant atmosphere. Rates: $189 and up per night.

Renaissance Cleveland (24 Public Square, Cleveland, OH 44113; 800–468–3571 or 216–696–5600) is a huge, 491-room historic hotel connected to all the major city sights. It's a member of the Historic Hotels of America and has been rated four stars by AAA. Rates: $119–$259 per night.

FOR MORE INFORMATION

Greater Cleveland Convention & Visitors Bureau, (50 Public Square, Terminal Tower, Cleveland, OH 44133; 800–321–1004 or 216–621–5555.

Columbus

HELLO, COLUMBUS

2 NIGHTS

Historic Village • State Capitol
Avant-garde Arts • Sports • Shopping

To a University of Michigan Wolverines fan, suggesting a weekend getaway in Columbus, Ohio, home to the hated Ohio State Buckeyes, is akin to heresy. It's worth entering enemy territory, however, if you're looking for a weekend that offers the best of small-town America in a cosmopolitan setting. Once a sleepy governmental cow town, today's Columbus is a thriving city and the state's largest metropolis. And although the Columbus area boasts headquarters for thirty major American corporations and more than 16,000 hotel rooms, it has the pleasant feel of a much smaller city. Here you'll find the best of urban living without the hassles of modern urban life.

This is the place that *Newsweek* called "the gleam along the rust belt" and listed on its roster of the nation's hottest cities. For visitors, that translates into a suprisingly vibrant city, home of both German Village, one of the largest concentrations of restored historic structures in the state, and the mind-bending Wexner Center for the Arts, known for its cutting-edge modern-art exhibits.

Local author and cartoonist James Thurber said that "Columbus is a town in which almost anything is likely to happen and in which almost everything has." After a visit, you'll see what he meant.

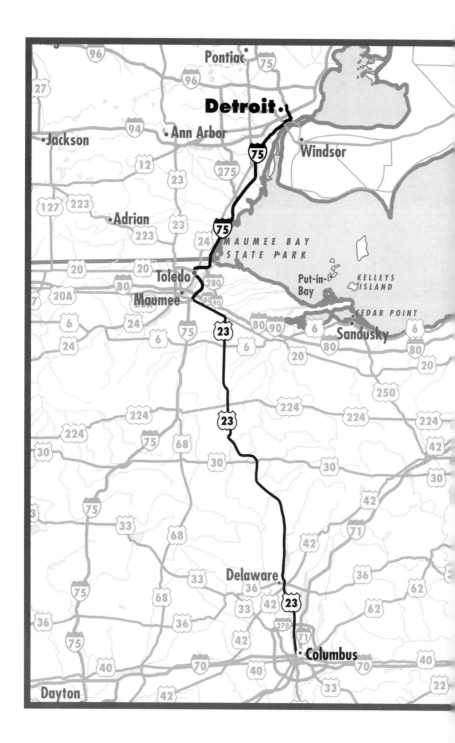

DAY 1

To reach Columbus from Detroit, take Interstate 75 to U.S. Highway 23 south, which cuts through downtown. It's a 186-mile drive, most of it uneventful, although a few interesting places lie along the way, such as the small town of Delaware, when you're ready to stretch your legs or get a bite to eat.

Afternoon

LUNCH: Fresh sushi in mid-America? If you like Japanese food, head for Columbus's **Sapporo Wind** (6188 Cleveland Avenue, Columbus, OH 43231; 614–895–7575), which has been voted the area's best sushi as well as one of the city's top ten restaurants by the *Columbus Dispatch*.

Use the rest of the afternoon to explore downtown. It's compact, easy to wander on foot, and boasts a number of things to see and do. The waterfront is home to two of the city's most popular parks. **Bicentennial Park,** at Rich Street and Civic Center Drive, is the site of the explosive "Red, White and Boom" fireworks display each July. The rest of the summer, it's a quiet and serene oasis, with beautifully landscaped grounds, a gurgling fountain, well-used bike trails, and the best skyline view in the city. **Battelle Riverfront Park** is another great picnic spot and also home to the flag-waving *Santa Maria,* a full-size, carefully crafted replica of Christopher Columbus's flagship. Built for the city's 1992 quincentennial celebration, the vintage vessel lets you experience life on board a historic sailing vessel. Don't miss it—especially if you have kids.

Back on dry land, a good place to get a feel for the pulse of the city—and the state—is the **Ohio Capitol Square Complex** (Broad and High Street, Columbus, OH 43215; 614–752–6350). First used in 1857, it's one of the oldest statehouses in continuous use in the United States and is affectionately known as the "Hot Box Capitol" because of its distinctive rotunda. It's considered one of the country's finest examples of Greek Revival architecture. Ironically, architect Frank Lloyd Wright considered it "the most honest of state capitols" although much of it was built by penitentiary inmates. This majestic structure was constructed of Columbus limestone after the city became the state's third capital in 1816. It's one of the few capitols that doesn't sport a dome and is decorated with 24-karat gold leaf. It took six architects twenty-two years to complete it at a cost of $1,359,121. On a tour, you can climb the Senate Building's 1901 Grand Staircase, watch restoration workers in more than sixty rooms, or sit a spell and just watch government in the making. The complex—which recently received a $114-million renovation—is open daily from 9:00 A.M. to 7:00 P.M.; tours are offered Monday through Friday from 9:00 A.M. to 3:00 P.M. On weekends, a guide is on-site from 11:00 A.M. to 4:00 P.M. for free impromptu tours.

If you're ready for a little all-American shopping, cross the street to the **Columbus City Center Mall** (111 South Third Street, Columbus, OH 43215; 614–221–4900), adjacent to the Hyatt Hotel. This downtown shopping center—one of the few in the country—has more than 150 stores for all budgets, including several of Columbus native and Limited founder Leslie's H. Wexner's stores. There are also a Marshall Field's, Jacobson's, and Ohio-based Lazarus department store as well as national restaurants and boutiques such as Gucci and Henri Bendel (the Columbus Bendel outpost is its first outside Manhattan). For something a little different, check the ever-tempting A Show of Hands gallery, which features the best of Ohio-made arts and crafts. Kids love the Imaginarium and the Great Train Store, which is overflowing with train memorabilia of all kinds.

DINNER: The Refectory (1092 Bethel Road, Columber, OH 43220; 614–451–9774) has pulled in the awards (everything from "Best Restaurant" from *Columbus Monthly* and "Top Ten" from the *Columbus Dispatch*) since it opened. One reviewer says it "may well be the finest restaurant in Ohio." The remodeled church with exposed beams serves the finest of French-inspired fare, including entrees such as sterling salmon and shrimp with mussel-butter sauce. Expensive.

If you're a drama fan, check out the **Ohio Theater** (39 East State Street, Columbus, OH 43215; 614–469–0939), a masterpiece on Broad Street. Lavishly restored by Loew's (one of the oldest theater families in the country) to the tune of $2 million, this 2,897-seat theater is adorned with gold-plated trimming and Tiffany chandeliers. Columbus residents raised funds to buy it just minutes—literally, as the bulldozer was driving down the street—before demolition began in the late 1960s. Since then it has become a lively showcase for the performing arts, with a full schedule of events, including the Columbus Symphony Orchestra, BalletMet Columbus, a popular Broadway-style series, and a well-attended summer movie program. Today, it's the busiest performing-arts facility in the state.

LODGING: The Westin Great Southern Hotel (310 South High Street, Columbus, OH 43215; 614–228–3800) is a beautifully restored downtown

The restored Ohio Theater was narrowly saved from the wrecking ball.

hotel adjacent to the City Center Mall, the Brewery District, and German Village. It was originally known as the Great Southern Hotel and was built in 1896 and renovated in time for its one-hundreth anniversary. The hotel's painstaking restoration is apparent as soon as you walk into the lobby. Marble floors, polished brass, and magnificent stained glass echo its opulence at the turn of the twentieth century, when the Great Southern Fireproof Building and Opera House was home to a theater, restaurants, shops, and apartments under its roof. James Thurber even lived here once. Today, the 196 guest rooms and suites are decorated with traditional furnishings, and have high ceilings and floral wallpaper. Rates start at $159 per night.

If you're looking for something a bit more modern, check the new **Lofts Hotel** (800–73–LOFTS), adjacent to the Crowne Plaza. Inside a former nineteenth-century wallpaper factory are 44 spacious loft-style rooms, all with different floor plans, 18-foot ceilings, Frette linens, and wet bars. Rooms start at $204 .

DAY 2

Morning

BREAKFAST: Juergen's Bakery and Kaffee Haus (525 South Fourth Street, Columbus, OH 43206; 614–224–6858) is a great place for a hearty omelette, French toast, or other sweet treat and some strong coffee to go along with it. The restaurant is well known for its German-inspired pastries and breads (don't miss the strudel) as well as for its sauerbraten, schnitzel, and bratwurst. There are also an on-site deli, a gift shop, even a bed-and-breakfast. Inexpensive to moderate.

Juergen's is part of **German Village,** a friendly neighborhood just six blocks south of the State Capitol via Third Street. It earned a spot on the National Register of Historic Places in 1975 because of the quaint brick homes set along its narrow cobblestone streets. German immigrants settled the 230-acre area in the mid-1800s; it was narrowly saved from a freeway expansion and the wrecking ball in the 1950s. If you're curious about old-time Columbus, this is the place to get an idea of how city residents lived in the nineteenth century. Today German Village is home to young urban professionals and others who prize its heritage and historic charm. Chic coffeehouses sit side by side with quilt shops, neighborhood pubs, and authentic German bakeries.

Wanderers in German Village find well-tended cottages and stately mansions with flower-filled window boxes and wrought-iron gates. Tours are offered in summer from the **German Village Meeting Haus** (588 South Third Street, Columbus, OH 43206; 614–221–8888), where volunteers are also available year-round to help you design self-guided tours.

Ideal for walking (but not always for parking), German Village is one of Columbus's major attractions and draws more than 100,000 visitors each year. More than just a pretty piece of restored Americana, this is a working neighborhood, with businesses that range from supermarkets and dry cleaners to antiques shops and bookstores. You can chew on spicy bratwurst at **Schmidt's Sausage Haus und Restaurant** (240 East Kossuth Street, Columbus, OH 43206; 614–444–6808), where they're also famous for their bet-you–can't-eat-it-all cream puffs. **Thurn's Bakery and Deli** (541 Third Street, Columbus, OH 43206; 614–221–9246) is an old-fashioned and still popular lunch counter.

Another landmark is **Diebel's Restaurant and Bierstube** (263 East Whittier Street, Columbus, OH 43206; 614–444–1139), where the spicy sausage and sauerkraut are legendary and where families get into the rollicking, good-time spirit of fun during weekly polka parties. It's also German Village's oldest restaurant. In the middle of it all is peaceful **Schiller Park,** 23 acres of greensward amid the district's tree-lined streets and home to many of the bed-and-breakfast inns.

Afternoon

LUNCH: Take a break from the streets with a picnic lunch from nearby **Katzinger's Deli** (475 South Third Street, Columbus, OH 43206; 614–228–3354), a landmark voted "Best Deli in America" by *Bon Appétit* magazine. You can't go wrong with the always-popular Reuben with piled-high corned beef. If the weather's uncooperative, try Thurn's, Juergen's, or Schmidt's.

If you're looking for an unusual souvenir of your stay, check the **Golden Hobby Shop** (630 South Third Street, Columbus, OH 43206; 614–645–8329). Housed in a 125-year-old brick school building, the shop sells crafts made by local senior citizens, from wooden shelves and hard-to-find old-fashioned toys such as tops and airplanes to intricately pieced quilts and beautiful hand-knits.

More goodies can be found in the nooks and crannies of the **Book Loft** (631 South Third Street, Columbus, OH 43206; 614–464–1774), where the store takes up an entire city block and where negotiating the thirty-two rooms of discounted paperbacks and hardcovers can require a whole afternoon and a map—or at least an unlimited credit card. Another fun shop is the quirky **Hausfrau Haven** (614–443–3680), also on Third Street, with unusual greeting cards, fine wines, and a renowned homemade fudge. If you've got kids in tow, keep an eye on them while you're in the store. Playful signs warn that UNATTENDED CHILDREN WILL BE SOLD.

You might even see lederhosen on some natives during special events. The neighborhood is the spotlight of the annual Haus und Garten Tour on the last Sunday in June as well as the Candlelight Garten Tour in August and a Merry Christmas Tour of Homes in December. The "village" also hosts the city's wildly popular Oktoberfest, ironically held in September, where you can stomp along to oompah-pah music and sample local brews. For more information on German Village, contact the German Village Society, 588 South Third Street, Columbus, OH 43215; (614) 221–8888.

DINNER: The city's best seafood can be found at **Engine House No. 5** (121 Thurman Avenue, Columbus, OH 43206; 614–443–4877) in German Village. The renovated 1892 firehouse is lively and affordable, with firefighting memorabilia as well as fresh seafood and steaks. Moderate.

DAY 3

Morning

BREAKFAST: Skip the bagel and coffee this morning and save room for the brunch at the **Plaza Restaurant** in the Hyatt Hotel on Capitol Square (75 East State Street, Columbus, OH 43215; 614–228–1234). Considered the best brunch in the city, it includes more than one-hundred items, including eggs, waffles, hash browns, made-to-order omelettes, French toast, and more for $24.95 per adult, $12.50 children five through twelve; free for children under five.

Set Sunday aside for museum hopping. Had enough history for a while? It's back to the future at the popular **Ohio Center of Science and Industry,** affectionately known as COSI (280 East Broad Street, Columbus, OH 43215; 614–228–COSI). It's hard to tell who's having more fun here, the kids or the so-called "adults." The COSI is dedicated to the conviction that science can be fun. After a visit, you'll be convinced, too. Ohio's only science center is one of just twenty-two centers worldwide. Its action-packed exhibits are spread out over three floors in a former 1906 Memorial Hall, now refitted with a modern solar addition. Visit the outer reaches of the solar system in the Planetarium. Lift a car . . . all by yourself. Touch a twenty-six-million-year-old concretion. Teach a computer to talk. The COSI challenges people of all ages to explore, invent, imagine, probe, discover, and experiment with more than 1,000 interactive exhibits. Where else can you climb aboard an authentic 1961 Mercury space capsule and prepare for launch, ride a high-wire bike to test the forces of gravity (with a protective net, of course), or pretend you're conducting laparoscopic surgery? Kids head for Familiespace, where they can play doctor at the COSI clinic, type in a make-believe office, walk on piano keys, even star in their own newscast or rock video (a concession sells videotapes so that you can record the performance for posterity). Hours are Monday through Saturday 10:00 A.M. to 5:00 P.M.; Sunday noon to 5:30 P.M. Admission is $20.00 per family, $6.00 for adults, $4.00 for children two through twelve and for seniors.

After the excitement of COSI you may want to wind down with a visit to the peaceful **Franklin Park Conservatory and Botanical Garden** (1777 East Broad Street, Columbus, OH 43215; 800–214–PARK or 614–645–8733), also on Broad Street. Located on 28 acres within the lush, 88-acre Franklin Park, the conservatory opened to the public in 1895. It underwent a dramatic change in 1992, when a $14-million expansion was built for AmeriFlora 92, a floral celebration marking Christopher Columbus's discovery of America.

This peaceful blend of glass and grace is home to approximately 10,000 plants representing more than 1,200 species. Displayed in six climatic zones—the Himalayan Mountain Room, the Tropical Rain Forest, the Desert, the Pacific Island Water Garden, the Tree Fern Forest, and the Cloud Forest—it's a pleasant place to relax and regroup after a busy day. It also has a nice shop featuring everything for the green thumb.

If you're looking for a little inspiration for your own front lawn, head for the downtown Topiary Garden on East Town Street, one block south of the Columbus Museum of Art (614–645–3550). This fanciful landscape created by sculptor James T. Mason depicts pointillist painter Georges Seurat's *Sunday Afternoon on the Isle of La Grande Jatte* and includes fifty-two larger-than-life human figures, eight boats, three dogs, and a monkey. It's the only topiary garden in the country to include human figures. Watch gardeners here snip and clip the figure into shape, and who knows what you'll decide to do with the bushes back home?

Afternoon

A spot you won't want to miss is the **Columbus Museum of Art** (480 East Broad Street, Columbus, OH 43215; 614–221–4848), Ohio's first museum. It's known for its innovative traveling exhibits and its small but excellent permanent collection, including the breathtaking $80-million Sirak Collection of Impressionist Art. The museum offers a relaxing respite from the city's streets and a well-rounded permanent collection that ranges from prehistory to modern times. While there, watch for works by two eminent Columbus natives, realist George Bellows and folk artist Elijah Pierce. The museum is worth a stop just for the well-stocked museum shop, which sells everything from unusual frames, greeting cards, and art books to innovative jewelry by local artists.

LUNCH: The museum also houses a restaurant that is a good place to grab a bite. Though small, it's a relaxing cafe eatery with fresh soups, salads, and changing specials. Inexpensive to moderate.

Not far from the museum is the **Thurber House** (77 Jefferson Avenue, Columbus, OH 43215; 614–464–1032). One-time home to James Thurber, it's now a lively writers' center and the popular site for summer "literary picnics" and the winter "Evening with Authors" series. You can wander in this modest home where Thurber lived during his college days with his parents, two brothers, numerous pet dogs, and an occasional relative. Artifacts and memorabilia from Thurber's long career fill the rooms. Many of his best-known stories (all available for sale in the small shop, once the dining room) are set here. It's open daily from noon to 4:00 P.M. for free self-guided tours.

Columbus prides itself on its strong support for the arts. One of the best places in the city to see cutting-edge visual arts is the 250,000-square-foot **Wexner Center for the Arts** (North High Street and Fifteenth Avenue, Columbus, OH 43215; 614–292–3535). Near the heart of the Ohio State University campus and dedicated to vanguard artistic activity, it opened in 1989 as a center for the presentation and study of contemporary arts.

With a multidisciplinary approach including exhibitions, media arts, performing arts, and education, the center encourages exploration. Four galleries host traveling exhibits from modern-art museums around the world, including the Museum of Modern Art in New York, the Walker Art Center in Minneapolis, and the Georges Pompidou Center in Paris, as well as a popular avant-garde film series.

More art can be had in trendy Short North, known as Columbus's Soho. Just north of downtown, it's worth an afternoon's wander, with good shopping, art galleries, and hip restaurants. A gallery hop is held on the first Saturday evening in each month.

DINNER: If you have time to squeeze in one more meal while you're in Short North, check **Rigsby's Cuisine Volatile** (698 North High Street, Columbus, OH 43215; 614–461–7888). Its cuisine is a little Italian, a little French, a little Greek . . . but all good. Don't miss any of the fish dishes or the delectable homemade gnocchi. Moderate.

THERE'S MORE

Academia. If you're visiting in fall, you can't miss a tour of the Ohio State University campus. One of the country's largest universities, OSU was designed by Frederick Law Olmsted of New York's Central Park fame. A free, two-hour tour departs from Drake Union and includes the residence hall, the main libraries, and the famous football stadium, long a home of gridiron glory. Tours depart from 1849 Cannon Drive; for more information, call (614) 292–3980.

Animals. The Columbus Zoo (9990 Riverside Drive, Powell, Columbus, OH 43065; 614–645–3550) is one of the best in the country, with more than 700 species and more than 11,000 animals and insects.

Bargains. Outlet shopping has become an American obsession. If you've been bitten, a good place to bag a bargain is the Prime Outlets, about a twenty-five-minute drive from Columbus. At the intersection of Interstate 71 and U.S. Highway 35 is the state's largest outlet mall, where you'll save 25 to 70 percent off retail prices at more than seventy-five stores. For more information and directions, call (800) 746–7644.

Baseball. Old-fashioned fun and the kind of baseball you remember from your childhood can be enjoyed at the city's Cooper Stadium, a 15,000-square-foot facility that's home to the Columbus Clippers, a AAA affiliate of the New York Yankees. Every night has a special event, including kids' night, ladies' night, fireworks night, and a Sunday "family day at the ballpark," when the whole gang is admitted for just $10.00. For tickets and other information, call (614) 462–5250.

Beer. Visit the world's largest brewery and view the making of their famous beers at the Anheuser-Busch Brewery Tour and Gift Shop (700 Schrock Road, Columbus, OH 43015; 614–847–6465).

Caves. Olentangy Indian Caverns (1779 Home Road, Delaware City, Columbus, OH 43015; 740–548–7917) is a good side trip and a sure hit with families. It offers three levels of caverns and is a spelunker's delight.

History. The Ohio Village/Ohio Historical Center (1739 North High Street, Columbus, OH 43211; 614–297–2300) is a museum and village complex that traces the fascinating history of the Buckeye State through acclaimed exhibits and costumed craftspeople.

Wet 'N' Wild. Wyandot Lake Amusement Park (10101 Riverside Drive, Powell, OH 43065; 614–889–9283) is the place to be in summer, with thirteen water slides, kid and adult rides, and a million-gallon wave pool as well as go-karts, miniature golf, and a video arcade. It's adjacent to the zoo and is open May through September.

SPECIAL EVENTS

May. Taste of Columbus, riverfront

June. Columbus Arts Festival, riverfront

Haus und Garten Tour, German Village

July. Red, White and Boom! riverfront

August. Candlelight Garten Tour, German Village

September. German Village Oktoberfest

December. Merry Christmas Tour of Homes, German Village

OTHER RECOMMENDED RESTAURANTS

Dick Clark's American Bandstand Grill (100 Hutchinson Avenue, Columbus, OH 43235; 614–785–1985) sports vintage photos, gold and platinum albums, rare posters, artists' contracts, and more from Clark's personal collection. You'll also see *American Bandstand* footage from the original TV series on screens around the restaurant. The cuisine is all-American, too— from Philly cheesesteaks and a classic burger and fries to spicy Santa Fe chicken fajitas. Open for lunch and dinner daily.

Handke's Cuisine (520 South Front Street, Columbus, OH 43215; 614–621–2500) is in the city's Brewery District, and it is built into the vaults of a nineteenth-century brewery. The restaurant, which has the state's only master chef, features American regional cuisine. Reservations suggested. Expensive.

Lindey's (169 East Beck Street, Columbus, OH 43206; 614–228–4343) has been one of the city's top restaurants for fifteen years and was voted "the city's most popular restaurant" by the *Columbus Dispatch*. It features progressive American cuisine, including steaks, chops, pastas, and more in a renovated mid–nineteenth-century structure. Expensive.

Spaghetti Warehouse (397 West Broad Street, Columbus, OH 43215; 614–464–0143), always a good bet with families, features fast and friendly service and a reliable menu of kid's pasta favorites.

Tapatio (491 North Park Street, Columbus, OH 43215; 614–221–1085) is behind the city's North Market, where their breads retail, and is known for upscale Caribbean and Mexican cuisine. Moderate.

OTHER RECOMMENDED LODGINGS

Courtyard by Marriott (35 West Spring Street, Columbus, OH 43215; 614–228–3200) is a good alternative for travelers on a budget who still expect attractive rooms and good service. The cheerful restaurant serves a hearty buffet breakfast with everything from cereals to croissants. Rates: $129–$139 per night.

Doubletree Guest Suites (50 South Front Street, Columbus, OH 43215; 614–228–4600) is an all-suite luxury hotel that is rated four stars by AAA. It's in Huntington Center, just across from the state capitol. Rates: $89–$135 per night.

Embassy Suites (2700 Corporate Exchange Drive, Columbus, OH 43215; 614–890–8600) offers spacious two-room suites with a refrigerator, microwave, wet bar, and coffeemaker as well as a free cooked-to-order breakfast each morning. A manager's reception nightly includes free beverages. Rates: $149 and up per night.

50 Lincoln (50 East Lincoln Street, Columbus, OH 43215; 614–291–5056) is a small, urban inn in the budding Short North district, with friendly accommodations and an award-winning chef. Rates: $129–$139 per night, including breakfast.

Hyatt Regency Columbus (350 North High Street, Columbus, OH 43215; 614–463–1234) has 631 newly decorated rooms in a location connected to the Greater Columbus Convention Center. Rates: $189 and up per night.

Bed-and-Breakfasts. If you're a B&B fan, the city has a number of options. For a list of the more than twenty inns in the city (including Henderson House, the only African American–run B&B in the state) contact the Central Ohio Bed and Breakfast Cooperative (180 Lansing Street, Columbus, OH 43215; 800–383–7839). Facilities range from urban-active to country-quiet.

FOR MORE INFORMATION

Greater Columbus Convention and Visitors Bureau, One Columbus, 90 North High Street, Columbus, OH 43215–3424; (614) 221–6623 or (800) 345–4386.

OHIO

Cincinnati

HAIL TO THE QUEEN (CITY)

2 NIGHTS

Chili Restaurants • Deco Hotel • Theater • Conservatory

English statesman Winston Churchill dubbed Cincinnati "the most beautiful of America's inland cities." More recently, it was "North America's Most Livable City." This big city perched high on the bluffs of the Ohio River is known for its small-town charm. It also has a vibrant and exciting downtown, with a 20-block elevated skywalk system that connects department stores, specialty shops, hotels, and even a museum. Cincinnati is also renowned for its restaurants, with eateries that range from five-star French to the city's signature five-way chili.

Cincinnati is also as far south as you can go in Ohio without hitting the renowned Kentucky bluegrass, just across the river. It's so close, in fact, that Covington, Kentucky, across the river, is considered part of Cincinnati and the two cities are marketed as an entity. And Cincy definitely feels more southern than midwestern—the pace is slower and accents are thicker. After a weekend in the Queen City, you're sure to agree with Churchill's assessment.

DAY 1

Morning

Plan to get an early start. From Detroit, Cincinnati is a straight shot (about 230 miles) south down Interstate 75. Most of the five-hour drive is an uneventful ride through flat Ohio farmland (watch for state troopers!), but a few places are worth stopping at along the way—including the **Neil Armstrong**

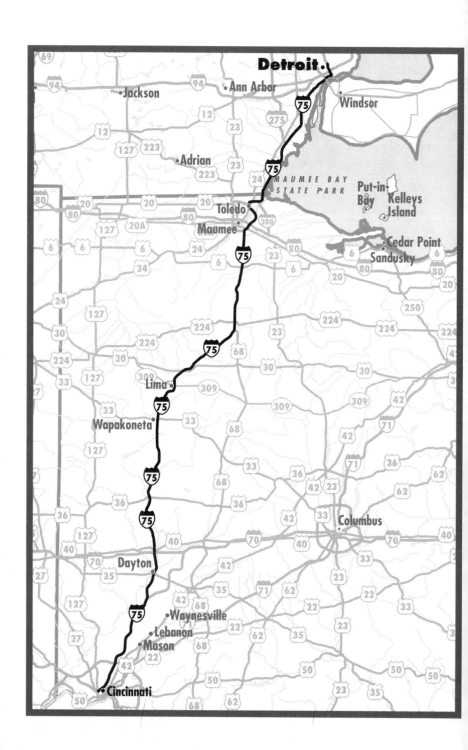

Museum (500 South Apollo Drive, Wapakoneta, OH 45895; 419–738–8811 or 800–282–5393), which honors the first man on the moon and the history of space exploration. (Armstrong was born here in 1930.)

LUNCH: You may also want to stop for a quick bite along the way (try Fazzoli's off I–75 and the Harding Highway, Lima, OH 45801; 419–222–2460 for quick yet tasty Italian specialties). Don't spend too much time lingering, however, for Cincinnati holds more than enough to fill a long weekend.

Afternoon

DINNER: Plan to arrive in town early enough for dinner. Cincinnati is known for its wonderful restaurants, and you won't want to miss the chance to sample as many as possible. A good one to try while you still have the car is **Grand Finale** (Sharon Road and State Highway 747, Glendale, OH 45241; 513–771–5925), north outside the city limits in historic Glendale. This once-dilapidated Victorian home was reputed to be haunted when owners Larry and Cindy Youse purchased it in 1975. Since then it has racked up awards ranging from "Best Outdoor Dining" and "Best Sunday Brunch" to "Best Desserts." The atmosphere is relaxed, the food is great (try the homemade Coquille St. Jacques crepes or the signature lobster linguine), and the desserts are to die for. Forget the diet—go ahead and splurge. Moderate to expensive.

LODGING: The magnificent **Omni Netherland Plaza** (35 West Fifth Street, Cincinnati, OH 45202; 513–421–9100 or 800–843–6664) is a local landmark and a stunning example of the French Art Déco style. It's worth spending a little extra to stay in this restored gem. Opened in 1931, the Omni antedated New York's Rockefeller Center by several years and was even compared to the grandeur of Solomon's temple. Pass through the impressive entrance of Roman Breche marble (look up and you'll see WELCOME TRAVELER inscribed on the ceiling in French), and you'll enter the elegance of another age. The hotel is also known for its Palm Court, with a ziggurat-shaped fountain made at the city's renowned Rookwood Pottery. Famous guests have included three presidents (Eisenhower, Truman, and Reagan) as well as Eleanor Roosevelt, Bing Crosby, and Winston Churchill, who was so taken with the yellow tile in his suite that he had it reproduced in his English country home. Rates: $119–$185 per night. Ask about weekend packages, which include breakfast and use of the health club.

DAY 2

Morning

BREAKFAST: Not long ago, **First Watch,** a popular suburban eatery, opened a downtown location (700 Walnut, at Seventh Street, Cincinnati, OH 45202; 513–721–4744). Lines can be long on weekends (try to get there early), but it's worth the wait for gourmet pancakes (try the fresh apple cinnamon and oatmeal), raisin bread, French toast, and their signature *crepeggs*—thin, sweet crepes combined with whipped eggs. Inexpensive to moderate.

Set the day aside for strolling downtown. A good place to get a grip on the city's psyche is **Fountain Square,** where the Genius of Water sculpture atop the Tyler Davidson Fountain surveys a broad, open plaza. In sunny weather you'll find shoppers and businessfolk brown-bagging it on the square or enjoying some of the city's famous chili while being entertained by people-watching and the open-air pavilion stage.

Paris has the Eiffel Tower, Chicago has the Sears Tower . . . Cincinnati has its own nosebleed section at the top of the **Carew Tower Observatory** (Fifth and Vine Streets, Cincinnati, OH 45202; 513–579–9735), where you'll be treated to excellent views of downtown as well as surrounding countryside from the top of the city's tallest building. Other great city views can be had in the stylish Mount Adams neighborhood, one of the city's liveliest. Though much smaller, it's often compared to San Francisco, as much for its annoying one-way streets as its breathtaking hilltop views. Here you'll find narrow row houses restored to their nineteenth-century glory as well as funky shops and interesting restaurants. You could easily spend days here wandering through the many tempting shops and boutiques.

Afternoon

LUNCH: The city's most unusual eatery must be the **Rookwood Pottery Restaurant** (1077 Celestial Street, Cincinnati, OH 45202; 513–721–5456), housed in the former pottery of the same name. Rookwood, active around the turn of the century through the 1960s, is known for its intricate glazes and beautiful designs and is highly prized by today's collectors. Vintage photographs, original pieces of pottery, and the rare chance to dine inside one of the three huge brick kilns that once reached thousands of degrees make this place a treat. Entrees include everything from a tasty Potter's Salad to a burger voted best in the city by *Cincinnati* magazine. Be sure to finish off your meal with a creamy concoction from the make-your-own sundae bar. Moderate.

Before leaving Mount Adams, trek over to **Eden Park.** When the sky-scrapers and the bustle get to be too much, city residents of all ages retreat to this well-loved greensward. This sprawling park boasts many of the city's most popular attractions, including its renowned art museum, two professional the-aters, and miles and miles of trails perfect for walking, hiking, biking, or Rollerblading (be sure to wear pads!).

If you prefer a slower pace, consider a stroll around the 88 galleries in the **Cincinnati Art Museum** (953 Eden Park Drive, Cincinnati, OH 45202; 513–721–5205). This was the first museum west of the Alleghenies built to be a museum; today its graceful halls house art dating back some 5,000 years. Founded in 1881, the museum opened to world acclaim and was heralded as "The Art Palace of the West." Not content to rest on its laurels, the museum has recently completed an extensive renovation. Collection highlights include Mary Cassatt's *Mother and Child* from 1889, the colorful *Red Rooster* by Marc Chagall, the collection of Rookwood Pottery, Andy Warhol's tribute to Cincinnati Reds great Pete Rose, and the mesmerizing Powel Crosley, Jr. sculpture by Korean artist Naim June Paik, which pays homage to the father of modern telecommunications.

Also in Eden Park is the respected **Irwin M. Krohn Conservatory** (Eden Park Drive, Cincinnati, OH 45202; 513–421–4086), one of the nation's largest public greenhouses. Wander through a tropical rain forest, duck while a spectacular 20-foot waterfall cascades overhead, or dry out in the desert greenhouses filled with prickly cacti and delicate multicolored orchids. All Cincy gathers here for seasonal events, which include festive holiday floral shows.

DINNER: Hungry yet? You can't leave the city without eating at its most famous restaurant. **Maisonette** (114 East Sixth Street, Cincinnati, OH 45202; 513–721–2260) has accumulated more Mobil stars than any other restaurant in the country. Reservations—well in advance—are a must. Maisonette is not only a critic's choice, but a people's favorite as well. It's known for impecca-ble service and outstanding entrees such as Grilled Quail with Champagne Mustard or Romantic Rack of Lamb for Two. Unlike its Gallic counterparts, however, it's also known for its friendly staff and warm midwestern welcome. Expensive. (A tip for the budget-minded: The restaurant's bistro-style lunches are very reasonable, about $15 for a selection that ranges from classic cassoulet to seafood crepes.)

Evening entertainment in Cincinnati has many forms. You might take in a play at the **Cincinnati Playhouse in the Park** (513–421–3888), one of the city's most intimate theaters (there's also a great view of the city from the parking lot). **Showboat Majestic** (513–241–6550) operates from the foot of Broadway and is one of the last original floating theaters. It shows dramas, comedies, and period melodramas Wednesday to Sunday from April to mid-October. Baseball fans who see red will want to head for **Riverfront Stadium,** one of the nation's most scenic ballparks and home of the world-famous **Cincinnati Reds,** the oldest team in the country (call 513–421–4510 for ticket information). Other options include the **Cincinnati Ballet** (513–621–5219), **Cincinnati Opera** (513–241–2742), even boot-scootin' at **Coyote's** (606–341–5150) in nearby Fort Mitchell, Kentucky, which has the largest dance floor in the Midwest.

DAY 3

Morning

BREAKFAST: The meandering Ohio River had a large part in Cincinnati's history and is one of the city's most scenic spots. Pay it proper homage with brunch on one of the few remaining riverboats, the *Mike Fink* (Greenup Street, Covington, KY 41011; 606–261–4212). Docked across the river in Covington, under the Queen City's famed Roebling Bridge (it was designed by the same architect and served as the prototype for the better-known Brooklyn Bridge), it's a floating restaurant popular for birthday or anniversary celebrations. The brunch spread includes egg specialties, meats, seafood, baked goods, and more.

Tired of being docked? Take to the river with a ride on one of the **BB Riverboats** (1 Madison Avenue, Covington, KY 41011; 800–261–8586 or 606–261–8500), the city's oldest and largest riverboat company. From the modern Funliner to the steamboat-era *Becky Thatcher* and the authentic stern-wheeler *Mark Twain,* BB offers more than thirty different cruises on four craft. They're docked at Covington Landing across from the Riverfront Stadium.

Afterward, abandon your sea legs for a walk on terra firma at the **Riverfront Park.** Bicentennial Commons at Sawyer Point is one of the city's newest and most beloved parks. Built in honor of the city's bicentennial, it skirts the river and boasts an impressive roster of recreational facilities and scenic overlooks. When you enter, look up and see the Cincinnati Gateway Sculpture, a whimsical three-dimensional work that pays homage to the city's history. (Interestingly, the sculpture was quite controversial. Many residents were offended by the bronze winged pigs—a reference to the city's onetime nickname "Porkopolis," because of its pork industry—but others loved them. Today the sculpture stands as a playful reminder to residents not to take themselves too seriously.)

While at the park, why not take a turn at the 21,000-square-foot roller-skating pavilion, a favorite of the city's in-line enthusiasts? Maybe you'd rather join in a game of sand volleyball or just wander the 4-mile riverwalk, where you can trace the city's past from prehistory and enjoy the great views of the graceful Kentucky antebellum mansions across the way.

The city's history is also the focus at the **Cincinnati Historical Society,** not far away in the Museum Center at Cincinnati Union Terminal (1301 Western Avenue, Cincinnati, OH 45203; 513–287–7000 or 800–733–2077). Some cities choose to honor their past by tearing it down piece by piece in the name of progress. Not so in preservation-minded Cincinnati, which, when faced with an unused Art Déco train station the size of fourteen football fields, decided to turn it into not one, but three fantastic museums.

Union Terminal was built in 1933 and once hosted up to 215 trains and 34,000 people daily. It closed in 1972, victim of America's love affair with the automobile. Now restored to its original grandeur, it stands as one of the country's most spectacular remaining examples of streamlined Art Déco architecture, with a magnificent rotunda filled with murals and other distinctive details. Inside the bright, soaring space—it covers some 500,000 square feet—are three popular attractions, including the Cincinnati Historical Society, the Cincinnati Museum of Natural History, and the Robert D. Lindner Family Omnimax Theater.

To survey the city's long and lively history, check the historical society first. Here you can trace the city's development from frontier river town to modern metropolis. Costumed interpreters escort you on a journey through time, from a frontier cabin to a 1940s-era gas station. Along the way, you can visit a settler's cabin, board an old-fashioned flatboat (a plaque nearby calls it the "moving van of the frontier"), and climb on to an original 1923 trolley used in the city until 1951.

Afternoon

If geology is your thing or you've brought the kids, the **Cincinnati Museum of Natural History** (513–287–7000 or 800–733–2077) captivates visitors of all ages. The emphasis here is on the natural and geological history of the Ohio Valley, including the Ice Age (where you can walk through a mock glacier), an exhibit on local caverns, and one exploring the dinosaurs that once walked the same soil. The popular Robert D. Lindner Omnimax theater takes movies to new heights. Your local multiplex will pale in comparison to this five-story, 72-foot domed screen. Special technology enables you to experience every scene and motion with gut-wrenching clarity. Past films have explored *Destiny in Space* and the natural wonders of *Yellowstone* and have even gone *To the Max* with the Rolling Stones.

LUNCH: Fuel up for the ride home with a taste of the city's famous chili. Sold all over Cincinnati (the city has more chili parlors per capita than anywhere else in the world), it's a favorite in the diner at the Museum Center. Have it your way or try the city favorite—served over a plate of spaghetti with diced onions, red beans, and cheddar cheese. For those who'd rather cool down than heat up, the train station's original **Rookwood Ice Cream Parlor** sells sweet treats in an atmosphere of glowing walls and floors of authentic locally made Rookwood tile.

Afterward, stop and shop at the three great stores in the Museum Center complex. The **Collector's Shop of the Cincinnati Museum of Natural History,** the **Children's Shop,** and the **Heritage Shop** of the Cincinnati Historical Society sell gifts and goods that make great souvenirs of your weekend visit to the Queen City.

THERE'S MORE

Animals. The Cincinnati Zoo and Botanical Garden (3400 Vine Street, Cincinnati, OH 45220; 513–281–4700) has been called "America's sexiest zoo" by *Newsweek* magazine. Among the world leaders in breeding endangered animals, it's a family favorite, with 67 acres of exhibits that range from tiny rare spiders to huge Komodo dragons, the world's largest and most dangerous reptile. Other highlights include Bagus and Rapunzel, the only breeding pair of Sumatran rhinos left in the world, and an ambitious cat house with rare, white Bengal tigers.

Antiques. Waynesville, about 20 miles north, is considered Southern Ohio's antiques capital and is a charming and picturesque side trip. Call (800) 433–1072 for information.

History. The Cincinnati home of Harriet Beecher Stowe, author of the famous *Uncle Tom's Cabin,* has been restored and now serves as a museum, gift shop, and cultural center. It's at 2950 Gilbert Avenue, Cincinnati, OH 45202; (513) 632–5120.

Scream Machines. If the kids are in tow, Kings Island (6300 Kings Island Drive, Mason, OH 45040; 800–288–0808) is just 24 miles north of downtown Cincy. One of the largest theme parks in the country, it features a replica of the Paris Eiffel Tower, seven areas with stage shows, thrill rides, and a 15-acre Waterworks park. More traditional thrills are found at Coney Island (6201 Kellogg Avenue, Mason, OH 45040; 513–232–8230), with a 500-foot-long waterslide, 180-foot roller-coaster, paddle boats, and mini-golf.

Ship Shape. Cincinnati is one of the many colorful ports visited by the *Mississippi Queen,* the *Delta Queen,* and the new *American Queen,* all part of the steamboat trips offered by the Delta Queen Steamship Company (800–543–1949). These overnight paddlewheel steamboats are the last to ply our nation's rivers and offer three- to sixteen-night cruises that explore "Mark Twain's America" and more.

Sun and Fun. The Beach (2950 Waterpark Drive, Kings Mills, OH 45040; 800–886–7946) is the state's largest water park, with thirty slippery slides and watery attractions spread out over more than 35 acres. It's conveniently located across from Kings Island. Surf Cincinnati (11460 Sebring Drive, Kings Mills, OH 45040; 513–742–0620) is also popular.

Washington Slept Here. Listed on the National Register of Historic Places, the Golden Lamb (27 South Broadway, Lebanon, OH 45036; 513–932–5065) is Ohio's oldest operating inn. Daniel Webster, Charles Dickens, Mark Twain, and ten U.S. presidents have slept here. The inn is also known for its hearty dinners and its impressive collection of Shaker and Victorian antiques on display throughout the inn. The charming town of Lebanon is a destination in itself, a great day trip with antiques shops, boutiques, and restaurants.

SPECIAL EVENTS

January. Travel, Sports, and Boat Show

February. Auto Expo

March. Home and Garden Show

April. Reds Opening Day

May. Delta Queen Homecoming
Taste of Cincinnati

June. KidsFest

July. Riverfront Stadium Festival

September. Oktoberfest Zinzinnati

October. Light Up Cincinnati

November. Festival of Lights

OTHER RECOMMENDED RESTAURANTS

The Diner on Sycamore (1203 Sycamore, Cincinnati, OH 45202; 513–721–1212) is a casual eatery set in an authentic 1950s diner, with a varied menu that includes seafood, meat, and fish entrees. Moderate.

La Normandie (114 East Sixth Street, Cincinnati, OH 45202; 513–721–2761) has been a downtown tradition for more than sixty years. It's next to the Maisonette downtown and is famous for its dry-aged steaks and fish. Expensive.

Main Street Brewery (1203 Main Street, Cincinnati, OH 45202; 513–665–4677). The city's first brew pub has a full-service restaurant and lively nightly entertainment. Moderate.

Montgomery Inn Boathouse (925 Eastern Avenue, Cincinnati, OH 45202; 513–721–7427) is one of the city's best-known barbecue joints, with a nice river view (and an endorsement from Bob Hope).

OTHER RECOMMENDED LODGINGS

The Cincinnatian Hotel (601 Vine Street, Cincinnati, OH 45202; 513–381–3000) is in the heart of downtown and is the area's only four-star hotel. It draws raves as one of the city's most luxurious and intimate hostelries, with personal service, a concierge, twenty-four-hour room service, and elegant guest rooms. Rates: $210–$265 per night.

Garfield Suites Hotel (2 Garfield Place, Cincinnati, OH 45202; 513–421–3355) is downtown's only all-suite hotel, with the city's largest suites and complimentary breakfast daily. Rates: $175–$325 per night.

Hyatt Regency Cincinnati (151 West Fifth Street, Cincinnati, OH 45202; 513–579–1234) has recently renovated guest rooms connected by the Skywalk to the Convention Center, restaurants, and more. Rates: $195–$275 per night.

FOR MORE INFORMATION

Cincinnati Convention & Visitors Bureau, 300 West Sixth Street, Cincinnati, OH 45202; (513) 621–2142 or (800) 543–2613.

Lake Erie Islands

ISLAND IDYLL

3 NIGHTS

Nature • Wineries • Nightlife • Water Sports

It doesn't take long to reach the Lake Erie Islands—just a short ferryboat ride from Port Clinton or Sandusky—but you'll swear you've traveled much farther. There's an otherworldly feeling about this string of islands 12 miles from Sandusky. The movie *Somewhere in Time* may have been filmed on Michigan's Mackinac Island, but it could easily have taken place here.

The islands' Victorian ambience is a large part of their charm. Other pleasures include sailing (the islands are a big destination for Great Lakes boaters), unspoiled scenery, lively waterfront restaurants, historic sites, and more. Each island tends to appeal to a different type of person, so that one is sure to be right for you.

DAY 1

From Detroit, the islands are a two-and-one-half hour drive. Take I-75 to I-280 to Route 2 or the Ohio Turnpike (Route 2 is more scenic, but has just two lanes). Plan to spend the first night in Sandusky or Port Clinton—you'll be up next day in time to catch the early ferry.

LODGING: A good choice in Port Clinton is the historic **Island House** (102 Madison Street, Port Clinton, OH 43452; 419–734–2166), which has occupied a corner of the city's main street for more than a century. Rooms are spacious and decorated with antiques and reproductions. Rates start at just $79 per night.

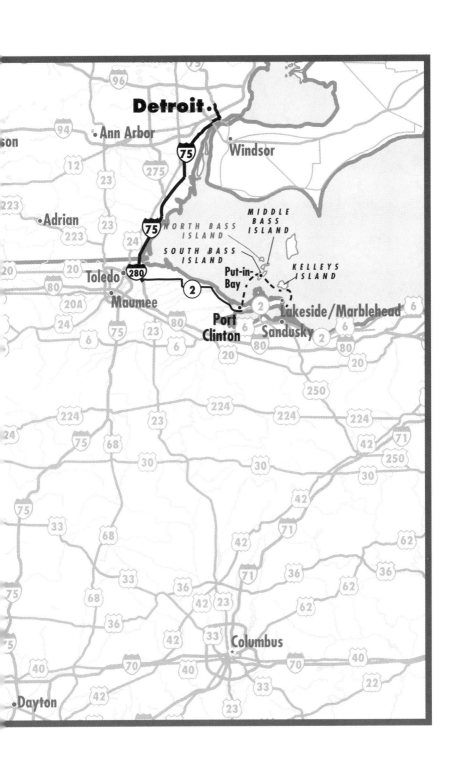

DAY 2

Morning

BREAKFAST: Grab a bite in the hotel's restaurant or the bakery down the street on Madison before catching the early ferry. From here it's just a short walk to the beach or to the ferry docks.

Your first stop is **Kelleys Island,** a short ride from the mainland. **Jet Express** (5 North Jefferson Street, Sandusky, OH 44870; 800–245–1538) or the **Island Hopper** (4 North Jefferson Street, Sandusky, OH 44870; 800–90–FERRY) make daily departures for Kelleys Island and Put-in-Bay.

Kelleys Island is the largest American island in Lake Erie, and vacationers have been relaxing here for more than a century. With lots of historic charm (the entire island has been designated a National Historic Landmark), the island is known for its waterfront, its charming shops and restaurants, and its abundant opportunities for bird-watching. The island was recognized in the Top 10 Undiscovered Places by *Vacations* magazine.

Spend the morning exploring the island's natural areas, including **Inscription Rock State Memorial,** on the south shore. Left by the Lake Erie Indians, these carvings of men, birds, and wildlife are estimated to be up to 400 years old. There is more to explore on the other end of the island at **Glacial Grooves State Memorial,** one of the world's largest examples of glacial scourings, left behind some 12,000 years ago. If you're a hiker, try the **North Shore Loop Trail** in 800-acre **Kelleys Island State Park** (419–746–2546). The park, nestled against the gorgeous North Bay, also has a number of campsites on a small bluff overlooking a sandy beach.

LUNCH: Bring along a picnic to enjoy in the park or head back in to town for lunch at the **Water Street Cafe** (101 West Lakeshore Drive, Kelleys Island, OH 43456; 419–746–2468). The restaurant serves lunch and dinner daily and is known for its tasty chicken Reubens and burgers. Inexpensive to moderate.

Afternoon

After lunch, explore the charming downtown via bike, golf cart, or your own two feet. The nostalgic **Lake Erie Toy Museum** (Main Street, Kelleys Island, OH 43456; 419–746–2451) has toys from childhoods long past, including stuffed bears and trains. It's a bargain at just $1.00 for admission.

Another highlight is the **Butterfly Box** (604 Division Street, Kelleys Island, OH 43456; 416–746–2454), where families can stroll through a butterfly greenhouse while North American butterfly species—many native to Ohio—flit about. Well-informed guides share facts about the insects habits and preferences, as well as tips on attracting these winged creatures to your own backyard. There's also a well-stocked gift shop that's fun to explore.

DINNER: The casual **Village Pump** (103 West Lakeshore Drive, Kelleys Island, OH 43456; 415–746– 2281) is the place to sample the area's famous fish, the walleye, found here fried, baked, or served up as a tasty sandwich. There's also perch if you aren't crazy about walleye, as well as a variety of soups, sandwiches, and salads. Inexpensive to moderate.

LODGING: On the island, B&Bs are the way to go. The best place to stay is **Kelleys Mansion Inn** (211 Lakeshore Road, Kelleys Island, OH 43456; 614–746–2273). With eleven rooms, it's one of the largest hostelries on the island, and has lots of period charm. Rates: $75 and up. Also recommended is **The Inn on Kelleys Island** (317 West Lakeshore, Kelleys Island, OH 43456; 419–746–2258), a historic Victorian inn with air-conditioning and a private beach. Don't worry if these two are full—the owners of the island's bed and breakfasts cooperate with each other and will call around for you to find out who has rooms available. Rates: $70–$90 per night.

DAY 3

Morning

BREAKFAST: The Island Cafe (across from Neuman's Ferry Dock, Kelleys Island, OH 43456; 419–746–2314) is a good place for breakfast in an open-air dining room with beautiful lake views. Inexpensive.

Had enough peace and quiet? An experience of another kind can be had at **Put-in-Bay,** where you may wish to "put in" overnight. In contrast to Kelleys's serenity, Put-in-Bay, on South Bass Island, is known for its partylike atmosphere. The bustling downtown is filled to overflowing with pubs, eateries, and revelers, most of whom arrive via private pleasure boats.

Every summer weekend, the celebration begins when the boats arrive from Toledo, Detroit, and Cleveland. Boaters mix with landlubbers, who come by ferry, and soon the scene rivals spring break in Florida. A number of regulars describe the atmosphere as a sort of "island fever," as partygoers crowd the bars and cafes such as The Other Barrel and Crescent Tavern and let their hair down.

A small carousel spins on Main Street, and playground equipment fills a harborside park. For the most part, however, this is an adult playground, with bars open late into the night. Stores and boutiques are filled with nautical-inspired giftwares and souvenirs. For more information, contact the Put-in-Bay Chamber of Commerce, 250 Delaware Avenue, Put-in-Bay, OH 43456; 419–285–2213.

LUNCH: The patio at **The Boat House Restaurant** (218 Hartford Avenue, Put-in-Bay, OH 43456; 416–285–5665) is perfect for watching the boats and the people in good weather. It's known for its seafood and, as in most eateries on the island, the atmosphere is casual. Moderate.

Afternoon

Put-in-Bay's bustling waterfront activities rarely spill over the rest of South Bass island, which is mainly residential. After lunch, check the island, including **Perry's Victory and International Peace Monument,** (419–285–2184), within an easy walk of downtown. At 352 feet, the tower offers a spectacular aerial view of the islands and the 25-acre park. A $3.00 elevator ride takes you to the top on an observation deck for a bird's-eye perspective. The site honors Commander Oliver Hazard Perry's victory over British forces in the Battle of Lake Erie during the War of 1812.

DINNER: Try the **Boardwalk** (419–285–3695), Put-in-Bay's only waterfront bar and restaurant, with everything from fresh seafood and live lobster to lake perch, burgers, tacos, and salads. Beyond the food and the view, it offers some of the island's best live entertainment. Moderate.

LODGING: **Parker's Inn at Put-in-Bay** (432 Catawba Avenue, Put-in-Bay, OH 43456; 416–285–5655), near downtown, has fifty spacious rooms as well as a full-service restaurant (one of the few hotels to have one on the island), gift shops, and more. Rates start at $65.

DAY 4

Morning

BREAKFAST: Catch a quick but hearty breakfast of fresh French toast or bacon and eggs in the hotel before setting out on the day's expedition.

Depending on how much time you have left, two other islands are well worth exploring. **Middle Bass Island** is often overlooked and is dominated by the historic **Lonz Winery.** Many people visit Middle Bass from South Bass via the *Sonny S* ferryboat, which shuttles between Put-in-Bay and the busy winery.

Middle Bass deserves more than just a morning visit. The famed French explorer René-Robert La Salle discovered it in 1679. He named it *Isle de Fleurs*—"island of flowers." A quiet island, it has little development, few cars, and no public transportation. The island is really two pieces of land joined by a narrow sandbar, with a magnificent marsh known for its lush flora and fauna. The narrow beach offers great swimming. Nearby are a handful of eateries and a few overnight accommodations.

Lonz Winery is situated on the southern tip of the island (419–285–5411). First opened during the Civil War as the Golden Eagle Winery, it was ranked in 1875 as the largest wine producer in the United States. Peter Lonz started producing wines in 1884, and his son, George, designed the magnificent Gothic structure that now rests on the original hand-hewn limestone cellars. Tours include a cellar visit and wine tasting. They are offered only on Wednesday and are free.

North Bass Island is lush and covered with vineyards. Private and open only to residents and guests, the island's remote beauty is enjoyed by boaters who cruise the secluded coast of the northernmost island. The south shore offers a protected basin that serves as a popular anchoring spot for boaters who fish, swim, and snorkel in the island's incredibly clear waters.

THERE'S MORE

Cruises. Several passenger boats depart from Sandusky for day-long island-hopping cruises, sunset dinner cruises, or mini-cruises around Sandusky Bay. The *Emerald Empress* (800–876–1907) offers varied special excursions, including a country music night, a luau cruise to Kelleys Island, and more.

Fishing. A number of charter boats take anglers out into Lake Erie to test their skill. A few to try: Shore-Nuf Charters (419–734–9999), C-Cat Charters (419–626–9342), or Speerfish Charters (800–735–1218). More information and names can be had by calling the Lake Erie Charter Fishing Association at (419) 734–9953.

History. Thomas Edison's birthplace and the nearby historical museum in Milan (exit 7 on the Ohio Turnpike, Milan, OH 44846; 419–499–2135) honor the man who gave the world the lightbulb and the phonograph.

Lighthouses. The lighthouse in nearby Marblehead is the oldest continuously operating light on the Great Lakes. Tours are conducted on the second Saturday in each month, June through September. Historic reenactments are presented at the Wolcott House, the first lightkeeper's home. For more information, call (419) 798–9777.

Serenity. Peaceful Lakeside, a gated Victorian community near Sandusky founded at the turn of the century, offers a historic hotel, regular concerts, and other events. It is a serene reminder of a kinder, gentler time. For more information, call the Lakeside Association at (419) 798–4461.

Thrills. Cedar Point (800–255–3743) is just minutes away, in nearby Sandusky. With 364 acres, the amusement park has been rated one of the best in the world. You'll find twelve roller-coasters, a water park, a sandy beach, and more. (See Ohio Escape Three.)

Wineries. Mon Ami Winery (3845 East Wine Cellar Road, Port Clinton, OH 43452; 419–797–4445) and Firelands Winery (917 Bardshar Road, Sandusky, OH 43452; 419–625–5474) are two well-known wineries worth a stop. Mon Ami has a restaurant with a popular weekend buffet and a Sunday brunch.

OTHER RECOMMENDED LODGINGS

Kelleys Island

Eagle's Nest (216 Cameron Road, Kelleys Island, OH 43456; 419–746–2708) offers cozy suites with private baths and air-conditioning in a wooded setting. Children are welcome. Rates: $55–$95 per night.

Himmelblau House (337 Shanon Way, Kelleys Island, OH 43456; 419–746–2200) is on the island's eastern shore, with a quiet atmosphere and spectacular sunrise views. Rates: $65–$75 per night.

The House on Huntington Lane (117 Huntington Lane, Kelleys Island, OH 43456; 419–746–2765) has air-conditioned rooms and continental breakfast, and is close to town and the ferry. Rates: $70–$85 per night.

Port Clinton

Our Guest Inn (2039 East Harbor Road, Port Clinton, OH 43452; 419–734–3000) has mini-suites with kitchenettes. Jacuzzi rooms available. Rates: $85 and up.

Phil's Inn (1704-08 East Perry Street, Port Clinton, OH 43452; 800–354–PHIL) has a well-known moderately priced Italian eatery adjacent to the inn. Rates start at $90.

FOR MORE INFORMATION

Ottawa County Visitors Bureau, 109 Madison Street, Port Clinton, OH 43452; (800) 441–1271.

Put-in-Bay Chamber of Commerce, 250 Delaware Avenue, Put-in-Bay, OH 43456; (419) 285–2213.

Sandusky/Erie County Convention and Visitors Bureau, 231 Washington Row, Sandusky, OH 44870; (800) 255–3743.

Kelleys Island Information Center, P.O. Box 783, Kelleys Island, OH 44870; 419–746–2360.

Ohio's Amish Country

TRAVEL BACK IN TIME

2 NIGHTS

Museums • Shopping • Restaurants • History

Each year, thousands of tourists follow the narrow back roads leading to Ohio's northeast counties hoping to travel back in time during a visit to Ohio's "Amish Country."

Not far from the state's big cities—Cleveland, Akron, and Canton—Holmes, Wayne, and Tuscarawas Counties are home to the world's largest community of "plain people," and to charming craft shops, hearty country-style restaurants, and more.

You'll pass Amish schools, homesteads, and old-fashioned buggies, all filled with the simple people who follow a life-style that hasn't changed since their forebearers settled here more than a century ago to escape religious persecution in Europe.

DAY 1

Evening

From Detroit, it's a two-and-one-half hour ride to Ohio's Amish Country. To get there, take I-75 to the Ohio Turnpike (I-90) and head east toward Cleveland until you get to I-77. Head south and follow the signs for Sugarcreek from there.

Once there, plan to spend your first evening relaxing and adjusting to the slower pace in Ohio's Amish Country. To best enjoy the atmosphere, plan to

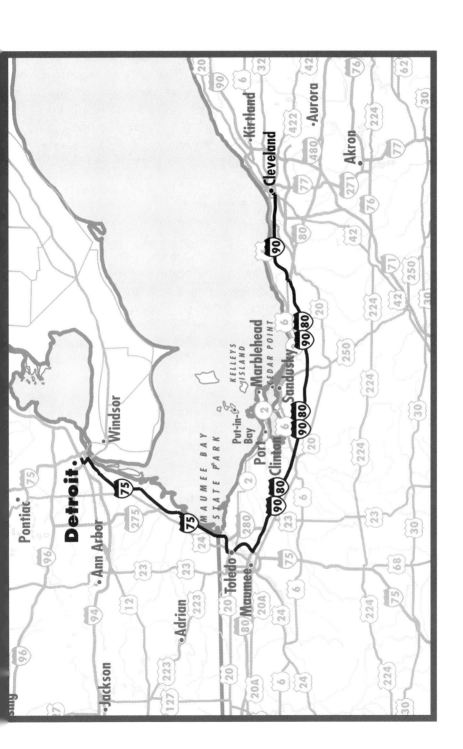

spend at least one night in one of the friendly bed-and-breakfasts. Many go to extra lengths to add Amish touches while retaining modern amenities.

One of the newest properties is the **Inn at the Amish Door** (1210 Winesberg Street, Wilmot, OH 44689; (888-AMISH-DOOR). Besides the comfortable, country-style rooms, it offers buggy rides through the surrounding countryside, beautiful views, and a hearty breakfast. There's even an indoor pool and business services.

DAY 2

Morning

After a hearty, home-cooked breakfast at the Amish Door, head for Berlin, heart of Ohio's Amish country. The town can be crowded with tourists on busy summer weekends, but the locals seem to take it all in stride, maintaining a consistently cheerful and welcoming hospitality. To avoid the congestion, visit in fall and winter, when the crowds are gone but the charm isn't diminished.

To get a better historic sense of the people who live here, begin your day at the **Mennonite Information Center** (5798 County Road 77, Berlin, OH 44610). "Behalt" is a 265-foot cyclorama illustrating the history of the Amish and Mennonites from the 1500s Anabaptist movement to the present Amish and Mennonite settlements. The cyclorama traces the Amish philosophy and values (*Behalten* means to hold, keep, and remember). Along with the display, there's a 15-minute informational video, Amish and Mennonite tour guides, and an on-site bookstore and gift shop.

Afterward, you may want to do some shopping and sightseeing. You can leave the driving to someone else on a **Country Coach** (800–619–7795) tour. Operator Carol Glessner is happy to share her experiences (and insider secrets) as she travels the area's back roads. Tours depart from the Carlisle Village Inn in Walnut Creek Monday through Saturday and last just over two hours.

Another worthwhile tour is that of **Yoder's Amish Home** (6050 State Route 515, Millersburg, OH 44654; 330–893–2541), which includes a guided tour (May through October) of a working Amish farm, including the family kitchen, living and sleeping room, and petting barn. A buggy ride is included.

LUNCH: Locals frequent **Boyd and Wurthmann Restaurant** (Main Street, Berlin, OH 44610; 330–983–3287), a landmark that opens at 6 A.M. and is known for its homemade specials and tasty desserts. Don't miss the apple pie. Inexpensive.

Afternoon

After lunch it's time to exercise the credit cards. Shopping is a popular pastime in Amish Country, where stores overflow with quilts, foodstuffs, and other tantalizing treats.

Among the most unusual is the **Wendell August Gift Shop and Forge** (7007 Dutch Country Lane, Berlin, OH 44610; 330–893–3713). Here, craftspeople create decorative items, including trays, plates, and coasters, from aluminum, pewter, and bronze. You can tour the workshop and observe craftspeople at work, shop in a gift area, then tour a small museum where forges and other tools are displayed. Closed Sunday.

Inspired to lead a simpler life? Pick up the trappings at **Lehman's Hardware** (4779 Kidron Road, Kidron, OH 44654; 330–857–5441), an old-fashioned hardware store that stocks items used by the Amish, including wood burners, gas refrigerators, old-fashioned nonelectric irons, pickle crocks, composting toilets, and other 19th-century staples.

Something for your bedroom can be had at the **Lone Star Quilt Shop** (County Road 77 in Mt. Hope, OH 44660), where Sara Yoder demonstrates the quilting techniques that have attracted clients from around the country (she has sold a number of pieces to Lands End, but prices are lower here). She and her daughter create original designs and also run Homestead Furniture (800–893–3702), behind the quilt shop.

Find other choices at **Helping Hands Quilt Shop and Museum** (330–893–2233), a nonprofit shop on Route 39 in Berlin that's filled with hand-quilted work by local Amish women. Store workers can be seen cross-stitching, hand quilting, or working on appliqué pieces. The adjacent museum displays several antique quilts and quilting tools.

Dolls star at **Ruth's Amish Dolls** on U.S. 62 in Winesburg. Here you can find original cloth dolls in various sizes as well as doll clothes and patterns for making your own. Also in Winesburg is **Winesburg Collectibles** for new and old furniture, accessories, and other Amish items. Hungry? If you stop before noon, you'll see the cheesemakers busy making their signature baby Swiss from secret ingredients at **Guggisberg Cheese** on Highway 557 just north of Charm.

DINNER: The Amish are known for beautiful homemade crafts, but they're also applauded for providing good, down-home comfort food. For visitors who want a home-cooked meal in an authentic Amish setting, Jayne Miller's **Amish Kitchen Tours** (330–674–4448) serve up dinner in privately owned homes. Miller works exclusively with tour groups, but individuals and families can call ahead to reserve a seat at the kitchen table along with other visitors. Typical fare includes roast chicken or beef, noodles, salad, dressing, and famous homemade desserts. The cooks and hostesses are happy to accept both questions and compliments.

LODGING: Inn at the Amish Door

DAY 3

Morning

If your last day is a Sunday, take a lesson from the Amish and slow down. Enjoy a relaxed breakfast at your hotel before visiting some of the natural highlights.

Work off part of your breakfast by hitting the trails—the new 5.5-mile **Holmes County Rails-to-Trails Coalition,** part of a proposed 29-mile bike path. The crushed-limestone path runs from Holmesville to Millersburg (cyclists can join the trail near Skip's Trail Depot Stop off Route 83 in Holmesville). But BYOB—bring your own bike, for no rentals are currently available.

Canoe fans find plenty to "wet" their appetite along the Mohican River. The river can get crowded, but it's generally empty at midweek and during one of the popular moonlight trips offered by **Pleasant Hill Canoe Livery** (800–442–2663) and **Mohican Canoe Livery** (800–MO–CANOE). In **Mohican State Park,** trails lead to a recessed cave, a gorge, and waterfalls and bridle paths, part of the adjacent Mohican State Forest.

OTHER RECOMMENDED RESTAURANTS AND LODGINGS

Der Dutchman Restaurant (Ohio 525 in Walnut Creek, OH 44687; 330–893–2981) is one of Amish Country's best-known restaurants. Diners line up for the homemade specials, and are welcome to wait in rocking chairs on the wide sweeping front porch.

Oak Ridge Inn (4845 Milo Drive, Walnut Creek, OH 44687; 800–723–6300) has spacious rooms that are perfect for families with children. Rates include snacks and breakfast.

The Inn at Honey Run (6920 County Road 203, Millersburg, OH 44654; 800–468–6639) is a contemporary and award-winning inn that is known for its excellent restaurant, serving fare fresh from the garden.

THERE'S MORE

Auctions: If you're lucky, you'll be in town during one of the regular auctions, which, held from Farmerstown to Sugarcreek, offer great deals and a great way to mingle with the Amish community. Depending on the season, you'll find everything from produce and baked goods to horses and livestock. Auctions generally start at midmorning and finish in the afternoon. Check the local papers and watch for signs.

Carvings: Warther Carvings and Gardens (331 Karl Avenue, Dover, OH 44622; 330–343–7513) illustrates the art of woodcarving and knife-making handed down through the Warther family. Intricate works by Ernest Warther, the eldest, are displayed along with his wife's more than 70,000-piece button collection. Their grandson, David, carries on the family tradition. Visitors can watch him work in his studio during a guided tour.

Nature Preserve: Take in nature's bounty at the Johnson Woods State Nature Preserve, 4 miles north of Orrville off Ohio 57. Here, a boardwalk leads through an old-growth and hickory forest filled with wildflowers and flora and fauna.

Trains: Shout All aboard! on the Ohio Central Railroad, which chugs along a scenic stretch from Sugar Creek to Baltic and back again. Along the way, the conductor points out Amish farms and other highlights. The 12-mile trips run May through October; call (330) 852–4676 for ticket prices and more information.

FOR MORE INFORMATION

Contact the Holmes County Chamber of Commerce and Tourism Bureau, 35 North Monroe Street, Millersburg, OH 44654; 330–675–3975, or the Mennonite Information Center, 5798 County Road 77, Berlin, OH 44610; 330–893–3192.

ONTARIO
ESCAPES

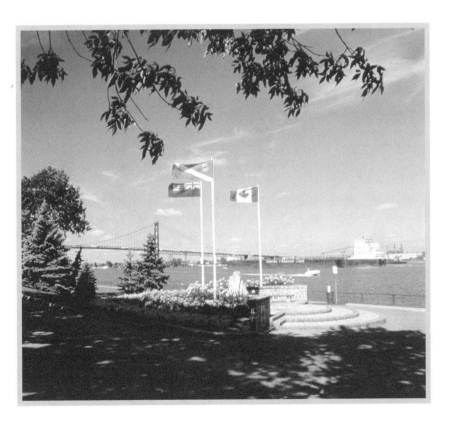

Windsor

BETTING ON WINDSOR

2 NIGHTS

Casinos • Restaurants • Shopping • Wildlife

Wander downtown Windsor's streets and you'll swear you're in another country. And you are—despite this city's proximity to Detroit (it's just a tunnel or bridge ride away), Windsor, Ontario, is very much a Canadian city. There's a certain European flair on the streets and in the cafes that you won't find across the border.

Detroiters have long enjoyed this city's rich and varied restaurant offerings—everything from Chinese to gourmet French. More recently, however, the city has become known as the gambling capital of Canada—the country's equivalent (albeit markedly tamer) to Las Vegas or Atlantic City. Casino publicity claims it has become the country's top commercial attraction. Since opening in 1994 it has attracted thousands of visitors from across the United States and Canada. With the recent opening of Detroit's three casinos, Windsor is working harder than ever to attract American greenbacks.

The strength of the American dollar doesn't hurt, either, making a weekend in Windsor a great deal as well as great fun. If you're looking for a quick trip that still gives you that delicious sense of being away from home, this is it. Windsor has plenty of family-friendly activities, but leave the kids at home if you're looking to gamble.

DAY 1

Afternoon

No need to leave early. From Detroit, Windsor is a fast tunnel or bridge ride away. Of the two, the four-lane Blue Water Bridge is more scenic, offering great views of the Detroit River and the Motown skyline from its 152-foot-high center span. It opened to traffic in 1929 and ranks as the world's longest international suspension bridge, stretching 1.75 miles between Canada and the United States. The recently renovated tunnel, however, is more convenient, whisking you right to the heart of downtown Windsor. Skip it if you're claustrophobic, however. It reaches a maximum depth of 75 feet beneath the surface of the Detroit River. Back-ups can be frustrating during peak times, such as rush hours.

DINNER: Windsor is known for its fine restaurants, many of which are housed in renovated historic structures. Friday night is generally less crowded at the tiny **Cook's Shop/The Pasta Shop** (683 Ouellette Street, Windsor, Ontario, Canada N8X 1K5; 519–254–3377), located in a former brownstone. Reservations aren't required, but they're usually a good idea. Specialties include the succulent rack of lamb and the pastas—all made on the premises. Moderate.

If you're interested in a few laughs, check out **Yuk Yuk's** (430 Ouellette Street, Windsor, Ontario, Canada N8X 1K5; 519–256–5233), Windsor's home of stand-up comedy. The lively club has hosted cut–ups such as Jerry Seinfeld, Jim Carrey, and Emo Phillips.

LODGING: If you're looking for convenience and plan to court Lady Luck into the wee hours, you can't do better than the **Radisson Riverfront Hotel** (333 Riverside Drive West, Windsor, Ontario, Canada N9A 5K4; 800–267–9777), next to the former casino. This modern chain hotel (it's called Doubletree in the United States) has 207 rooms (ask for one with a skyline view) and offers both a great location and reasonable prices as well as a "Stay, Play and Win" package that includes a cooked-to-order breakfast, twenty-four-hour tea and coffee, dinner at your choice of four first-class city restaurants (including taxes), $10 in casino tokens, free parking, a bottle of wine, and more—all for just $150 Canadian per night. There's also a tempting "Romance by the River" package at the same rate. The hotel's 5,000-square-foot Compri Club and its large health club offer stunning views of downtown Detroit across the way. Regular rates start at $129 Canadian.

DAY 2

Morning

BREAKFAST: Grab a quick bite in your hotel (a made-to-order breakfast from room service is included in your room rate) before setting out on foot to explore Windsor's downtown. Detroit's skyscrapers cast a long shadow over downtown Windsor, but that's the only reminder you'll have of your home across the way. Ouellette Avenue, the main drag, offers a bevy of sophisticated European-style boutiques and welcoming coffee houses and bistros, where your dollar is worth about 40 percent more (to get the best exchange, use your plastic).

From your hotel, wander along Ouellette. Skip the ordinary T-shirt and souvenir shops, but don't miss the deals at **Shanfield-Meyers** (119 Ouellette Street, Windsor, Ontario, Canada N9A 5K4; 519–253–6098), which has attracted Americans and Canadians alike for more than fifty years with great deals on fine porcelain, sparkling crystal (including an entire room devoted to Waterford), and other goodies. If you're looking for something to read while you're away, check **South Shore Books** (164 Pitt Street West, Windsor, Ontario, Canada N9A 5K4; 519–253–9102), which stocks a choice selection of American and Canadian titles as well as gambling how-to's such as *The Complete Idiot's Guide to Gambling Like a Pro.* A new addition to the city's literary scene is **Biblioasis** (519–256–7367). Owner Dan Owens stocks a widely varied Canadian and British literature, much of which is unavailable in the United States.

If you're curious about Windsor's history, stop at the stone **François Baby House** (254 Pitt Street West), in an 1812 structure that sits in the shadow of the nearby casino and Hilton Hotel. Its exhibitions trace the individuals, cultures, and events that contributed to the city's development.

Afternoon

LUNCH: Plunkett's Bistro-Bar (28 Chatham Street East, Windsor, Ontario, Canada N9A 2W1; 519–252–3111) is marketed as "a little bit of Toronto in downtown Windsor" and is an attractive urban eatery with many entrees, including soups, salads, and more creative fare. In summer, chic patrons prefer to sit outside on the patio that faces the street—the perfect vantage point for people-watching. Moderate.

After lunch, head down to the waterfront to **Dieppe Park,** where you can relax on one of the many benches and watch the huge freighters sporting colorful flags of many nations pass by (surprisingly, the Detroit River is the world's busiest international waterway).

After wandering around downtown, head over to the **Devonshire Mall.** Here the **Art Gallery of Windsor** (3100 Howard Avenue, Windsor, Ontario, Canada; 519–969–4494) holds court among more predictable shops and boutiques. Ironically, the art gallery once sat where the temporary casino is now (at press time no plans had been announced for the museum to move back to its former space). In a surprising blend of art and commerce, the museum decided for the interim to rent space in Devonshire Mall. To get there, just take Howard Street out of downtown and you can't miss it. At the gallery you'll find more than 2,500 pieces in the permanent collection, including an important gallery of Canadian art and a lively children's gallery that offers a view of art past and present. The museum also boasts more than thirty traveling exhibitions annually. Don't miss the gift shop, known as the **Uncommon Market,** which sells Canadian crafts and designs as well as the usual museum-shop books, note cards, and jewelry.

Most of the rest of the mall is predictable, with a lot of the same stores you'll find at home, although some merchandise is different, and you'll still enjoy the great exchange rate. One standout, however, is **Marks & Spencer** (519–966–1940), an outpost of the famous "Marks & Sparks" department store in London, England. Here you'll find all their signature clothing, as well as British foodstuffs such as distinctive teas, chewy toffees, frozen crumpets, steak and kidney pies, even a few frozen bangers (sausages). It's a fun place to pick up a few souvenirs or treats to enjoy once you're back home.

Afterward, head for Erie Street, home to one of the largest concentrations of Italians outside Italy. Located between Ouellette and Howard Avenues and also known as "Via Italia," it boasts more than sixty interesting specialty stores, small family restaurants, cafes, and tempting ethnic bakeries. Be sure to stop for a frothy cappuccino or tangy gelato to tide you over until dinner.

DINNER: Erie Street is also the home of one of the city's best-known restaurants. **Spago** (690 Erie Street, Windsor, Ontario, Canade N9A 3X9; 519–252–2233) is listed as one of the best restaurants in Canada in the well-known *Where to Eat in Canada* (Oberon Press). It's known for its veal, seafood, and homemade pastas; be sure to make reservations, however, for it fills up quickly on weekends. They also have simpler dishes such as tangy pizza and

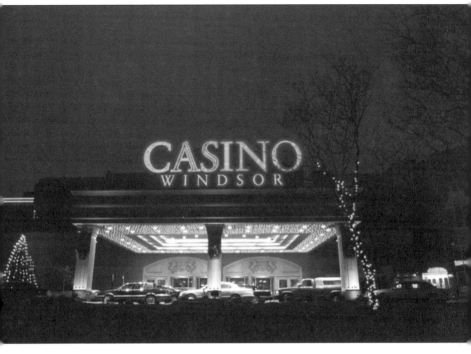

The new Casino Windsor attracts optimists from all over North America.

Italian-style sandwiches. The kitchen grows its own herbs, which are used extensively in the tasty cuisine. Moderate.

Afterward, there's still time for a night on the town. Casino Windsor is open twenty-four hours a day, seven days a week. Leave the tux and the glitter at home, however. The dress code here is casual, and you'll be more comfortable in a pair of pants and a sweater.

Casino Windsor (445 Riverside Drive West, Windsor, Ontario, Canada N9A 5K3; 800–991–7777) has become a local phenomenon. The first casino opened in 1994 with three floors (about 50,000 square feet) of gaming, including roulette, blackjack, baccarat, big six, pai gow, and Caribbean stud poker. The new casino, which opened in summer 1998, has twice as much gambling space, with 3,000 slots, blackjack, and Caribbean stud poker as well as its own glitzy hotel, restaurants, and entertainment.

If your idea of music is more symphonic than slots, the **Windsor Symphony** (519–252–6579) offers an extensive series of concerts at downtown's Cleary Auditorium throughout the year.

DAY 3

Morning

BREAKFAST: Skip the hotel's free meal and opt for a meal in the city's well-known **Chinatown,** not far from the University of Windsor. Here you'll find **Wah Court Restaurant** (1689 University Avenue West, Windsor, Ontario, Canada N9A 1C3; 519–256–4755), whose dim sum brunch has been attracting locals and in-the-know visitors for years. Foodies claim it's the best dim sum they've had outside of San Francisco. Inexpensive.

If you're looking for something a little more traditional, the brunch spread at the **Park Terrace Restaurant** in the Windsor Hilton is also a good bet and features meat, cheeses, and breakfast fare as well as a wide selection of Ontario wines.

Afterward, venture out for a Sunday drive to the wineries in nearby Essex County (see "There's More") or head for home. Before leaving, however, check the **Duty Free Shoppes** for a souvenir or two of your "time abroad." Here you'll find bargains on everything from Parisian perfumes to Spanish porcelains.

THERE'S MORE

Birds. "Let there be one place on earth where no money changes hands," wrote naturalist Jack Miner. To achieve that goal, he established the nearby Jack Miner Bird Sanctuary (Kingsville, Ontario, Canada N9Y 2K5; 519–733–4034) in 1904, primarily to help conserve migrating Canada geese and ducks. Since 1909, almost 100,000 migratory geese and 100,000 wild ducks have been tagged here. Today the sanctuary includes a museum, a nature stadium, and a pond where birds can be hand-fed. Admission is free, in accordance with Miner's will. The best times to visit, however, are October, November, and in spring. Birds are flushed out at 4:00 P.M. in daily "air shows."

Gardens. Colasanti's Tropical Gardens (1550 Read Street East, Ruthven, Windsor, Ontario, Canada N0P 2G0; 519–326–3287) has the largest selection of cacti and tropical plants in Southwestern Ontario, as well as exotic birds and gardens, domestic and miniature animals, wicker and crafts, even amusement rides for the kids. After wandering through the fifteen greenhouses filled to the brim with flora and fauna, head for the on-site restaurant and cafe, which serves everything from refreshing apple cider and homemade soups to chicken dinners and a famous Sunday brunch. Check with customs, however, if you plan to bring botanical goods across the border.

Parks. Point Pelee is Canada's most southerly mainland point, a slender tip of land that juts out into Lake Erie. It's accessible by ferry from March through December and is internationally known for its spring and fall concentration of migrating birds and for its fall migration of monarch butterflies. The trip takes about 75 minutes each way. Point Pelee National Park (519–322–2365) is a great place to hike, bike, swim, or canoe. Or you can just wander in the island's Heritage Centre (519–724–2291), which has exhibits on the rare flora and fauna as well as natural and human history and shipwrecks. If you'd like to check some of those wrecks for yourself, Wreck Exploration Tours (519–326–1566) offers adventures for novices as well as expert divers.

Wineries. If you think of venturing beyond the city limits, surrounding Essex County has a number of excellent estate wineries. Colio Estate Wines (1 Colio Drive, Harrow, Ontario, Canada N0R 1G0; 800–265–1322 or 519–738–2241) is known for its award-winning Vidal Ice Wines as well as for Pinot Gris and Rieslings Traminers. It offers daily tours of the winemaking and free samples at its Harrow location. D'Angelo Estate Winery (5141 Concession Five, RR4, Amherstburg, Ontario, Canada N9V 2Y9; 519–736–7959) grows more than seven varieties of vinifera and three types of French hybrids and offers year-round tours by appointment. The Pelee Island Winery (Kingsville, Ontario, Canada N9Y 2K5; 519–733–6551) dates back to 1865 and is the country's southernmost winery as well as one of its largest estate vineyards. Year-round, tours are offered three times daily.

SPECIAL EVENTS

May. Pelee Festival of Birds, Point Pelee National Park

June. Strawberry Festival, La Salle

Carousel of Nations, Windsor

Art in the Park, Windsor

July. International Freedom Festival, Windsor and Detroit

August. Harrow Peach Festival

Tecumseh Corn Festival

September. Via Italia Bicycle Races, Windsor

Ruthven Apple Festival

October. Oktoberfest, Windsor

November–December. Poinsettia Festival, Windsor

OTHER RECOMMENDED RESTAURANTS

Joseph's (345 Victoria Avenue, Windsor, Ontario, Canada N9A 4M7; 519–253–5218) is not far from the casino in a white nineteenth-century Victorian home complete with gingerbread. It serves homemade pastas and other continental favorites in a relaxed and elegant setting. Moderate.

La Cuisine (417 Pelissier Street, Windsor, Ontario, Canada N9A 37; 519–253–6432) is a tiny upstairs cafe with wonderful French food, including classics such as onion soup, quiches, and fancier fare at dinner. Inexpensive to moderate.

The Mini Restaurant (475 University West, Windsor, Ontario, Canada N9A 1C3; 519–254–2221) is one of the few authentic Vietnamese restaurants in Windsor and attracts diners from all over the region. Try the pan-fried noodles with mixed vegetables, the seafood with congee, or one of the daily specials. Inexpensive.

Shin-Shin (978 University West, Windsor, Ontario, Canada N9A 1C3; 519–252–1449) is the kind of local restaurant that the natives keep to themselves. It's known for its Szechwan and Peking specialties.

Tunnel Bar BQ (59 Park Street East, Windsor, Ontario, Canada N9A 37; 519–258–3663) has been a local favorite since 1941. It's across from the tunnel (of course) and is known for its tangy ribs and chicken as well as for its flaky homemade pastries. Try the mountainous coffee-cream walnut pie. Inexpensive.

OTHER RECOMMENDED LODGINGS

Quality Suites (250 Dougall Avenue, Windsor, Ontario, Canada N9A 7C6; 800–228–5151 or 519–977–9707) is the only all-suite hotel in downtown Windsor. Just a block from the casino, it offers attractive 450-square-foot two-room suites with king-size bed, large bathroom, and separate sitting area. No water views, but this is the place to stay if you brought kids. Rates start at $174 Canadian per night.

The 22-story Windsor Hilton (277 Riverside Drive West, Windsor, Ontario, Canada N9A 7C6; 800–445–8667) is more expensive than the other downtown hotels, but it offers some of the best vistas of the Detroit skyline (the hotel is angled so that each of the 303 rooms has a view). *Tip:* Be sure to ask for accommodations on one of the renovated floors. They're worth the little bit extra. The Park Terrace and River Runner Bar & Grill offer full-service cuisine on site. Rates start at $160 Canadian per night.

Ye Olde Walkerville Bed & Breakfast (1104 Monmouth Road, Windsor, Ontario, Canada N9A 5K4; 519–254–1507) is in a vintage 1903 home in the city's historic Walkerville district (so named for the huge Canadian Club plant that dominates it). Guest rooms are furnished with antiques and reproductions; common rooms include a comfy loft with TV, VCR, and stereo as well as a baby grand piano and a fully stocked bar. Rates: $79–$149 Canadian per night.

FOR MORE INFORMATION

Convention & Visitors Bureau of Windsor, Essex County, and Pelee Island, City Centre, Suite 103, 333 Riverside West, Windsor, Ontario, Canada N9A 5K4; (519) 255–6530 or (800) 265–3633.

Toronto

BROADWAY NORTH

AS MANY NIGHTS AS YOU CAN SPARE

Sports • Museums • Nightlife • Shopping
Restaurants • Theater

Not long ago, Toronto was considered one of North America's dullest cities. Its Sunday-closing laws were a national joke, and it was regularly compared with its chic French-speaking neighbor, Montreal, and found wanting. The city's transformation into the country's largest and most exciting metropolis is more than a little surprising. Today, once-tame Toronto is the Manhattan of Canada—center of the country's fashion, publishing, and art worlds. It's also called "Hollywood North" because of the volume of film and television production done here. In North America, only Hollywood and New York serve as locations for more film and commercial work than Toronto. Feature films shot in Toronto include *Sea of Love, Three Men and a Baby,* and *Moonstruck,* made by Toronto resident Norman Jewison.

This once-stodgy enclave of Scottish bankers and British expatriates has become a booming metropolitan area with a population of 3.5 million, including burgeoning Chinese, Taiwanese, Thai, Sikh, Portuguese, and Caribbean Islander communities. It's also a big draw for visiting Americans, who find its *joie de vivre* exciting and the strong U.S. dollar an added bonus.

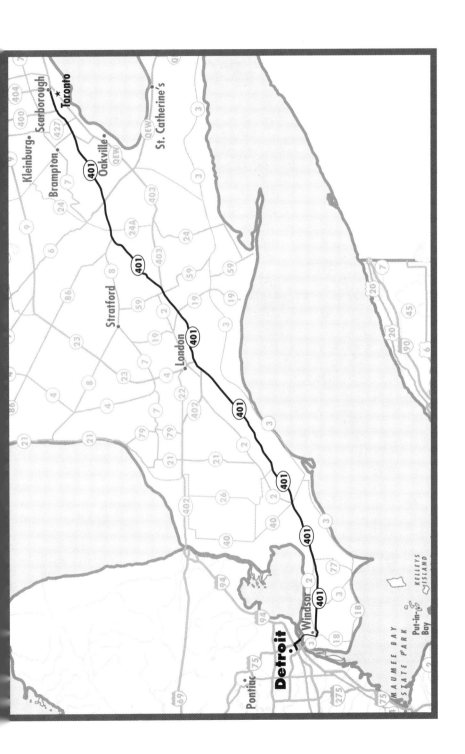

DAY 1

Afternoon

Toronto is a four-hour drive from Detroit. Simply take I-94 to the Blue Water Bridge to Queen's Highway 401. You'll probably want to take off Friday to get in a full three-day stay. Plan to get out of town as early as possible to make it to Toronto in time for lunch. You might even want to stay through Monday for a full-fledged mini-vacation. If you do, be sure not to leave visiting the museums until the last day, because most are closed Monday.

If you'd like to leave the driving to someone else and enjoy the ride along the way, you can ride the rails to Toronto. **VIA Rail Canada** offers service from Windsor, Ontario, across from downtown Detroit for about $125 Canadian round-trip in economy class. For an additional $100 you can treat yourself to the special service and fine dining offered in VIA 1 first class, which includes a three-course meal, larger seats, cocktails, and more. For reservations and ticket information, call (800) 561–9181.

There's plenty of time for serious sight-seeing on Saturday and Sunday. Save your first day for chilling out, Canadian style. Wander around the neighborhood near your hotel, cool your road-weary heels over a glass of wine (try one of the great local Ontario vintages) or a cappuccino at a charming bistro, or explore one of Toronto's ethnic enclaves such as China Town, the Greek-inspired Danforth, or Little Italy.

Little Italy is the center of the city's Italian neighborhood, its largest ethnic group. It's a bit more of a melting pot now (Canadians prefer to call it a mosaic), but it still has genuine trattorias and outdoor cafes as well as small gatherings of old Italian men smoking cigars or drinking dark red wine and playing bocce ball. It's also the place for perfectly prepared pastas and other kinds of heartwarming comfort food, Italian style. Three restaurants worth a try at dinnertime include **Cafe 82 Diplomatico** (594 College Street, Toronto, Ontario, Canada M6J 2N9; 416–534–4637), **Trattoria Giancarlo** (41 Clinton Street, Toronto, Ontario, Canada M6J 2N9; 416–533–9619), and **Sotto Voce** (595 College Street, Toronto, Ontario, Canada M6J 2N9; 416–962–0011). Depending on what time you arrive in town, they're also good choices for lunch.

If you'd like to take in a little nightlife, Toronto offers plenty of choices. As in any other city, the club and bar scene can be fickle, and clubs come and go like fashion trends. The **Warehouse District** at Richmond,

Adelaide, and John Streets is always a sure thing, with clubs such as Syn, Atlas, Whiskey, and Fluid Lounge Saigon consistently packing in the crowds. One of the newest hot spots is the **Joker** (318 Richmond Street West, Toronto, Ontario, Canada M6J 2H1; 416–598–1313), a $1.5-million, four-floor extravaganza complete with a palace and court jester. This 20,000-square-foot showpiece houses up to 1,000 hipsters each night and also has six bars, an Internet to surf, pool tables, and dance floors.

LODGING: Toronto has thousands of nice hotel rooms. For about the same price as a regular room in the other hotels, however, you can enjoy a spacious suite at **Cambridge Suites** (15 Richmond Street East, Toronto, Ontario, Canada M5C 1N2; 416–368–1990). All 231 well-decorated suites have a living and dining room, a separate bedroom, an oversize bathroom, a minibar with microwave, and extra-nice amenities. Rates: $180–$210 Canadian per night, including breakfast.

DAY 2

Morning

BREAKFAST: Cambridge Suites has a better-than-usual continental breakfast consisting of yogurts, cereals, fruits, fresh breads, bagels, juices, and coffee. If you're still hungry, however, head for the **St. Lawrence Market** near the harbor, a mecca for foodies and galloping gourmets. Housed in a vintage brick building are hundreds of butchers, bakers, and sausage makers, each with a fragrant food stall filled with tasty treats of all varieties. Even if you're not hungry, the market is a sight to see.

Once you've had your fill, you may want to get your bearings with a guided tour of the city. Scores of companies offer standard sight-seeing tours, all of which provide a good introduction to the city's many attractions.

A few favorites include **National Helicopters, Inc**. (416–361–1100) for bird's-eye views; and any of the dozen or so companies offering harbor and water tours; or the always reliable **Greyhound Tours** (416–594–0343). For something really unusual, however, sign on for a tour by bike, rickshaw, or underground. **Neighbourhood Bicycle Tours** (416–463–9233) offers city cycling adventures; **Rickshaw Walas, Inc.** (416–703–4469) lets you ogle the city's hot spots via authentic rickshaw; **Toronto Underground City Tours** (905–886–9111) takes you deep into the city's subterranean world. If you're curious about the city's historical inhabitants, sign on for a tour of haunted Toronto with **Ghostwalk** (416–501–0615).

Whatever your interest or mode of transportation, you'll want to explore Yonge Street during your weekend stay. Yonge is listed in the *Guinness Book of World Records* as the longest street in the world. It begins at the city's lakeshore and runs an incredible 1,178 miles to Fonda, North Dakota, before it ends. In Toronto, the famous strip is both fun and flashy, with a blend of sleaze and sophistication found nowhere else.

Afternoon

LUNCH: Marche Movenpick (42 Yonge Street, Toronto, Ontario, Canada M5E 1T1; 416–366–8986) is a European market transported to Toronto's busiest street. Inside this cavernous restaurant are ten or more food stations where diners are free to wander and take their pick from hundreds of food and drink choices. Sushi, seafood (try the bouillabaisse or the pasta with smoked salmon), pizza, pastries, ice cream, bakery goods, and gourmet items to take back to your hotel make this a must-stop when strolling Yonge. Lines can be long at dinner but move quickly. Inexpensive to moderate depending on how much you eat.

Yonge Street is also home to **Eaton Centre** (Yonge and Dundas Streets, Toronto, Ontario, Canada M5B 1C8; 416–343–2111), the city's largest shopping center. With 350 stores, including the flagship **Eaton's**, it's a favorite with Americans and Europeans out to take advantage of the exchange rate. Another popular place is the **CN Tower** (301 Front Street West, Toronto, Ontario, Canada M5V 2T6; 416–360–8500), reportedly the world's tallest free-standing structure. On a clear day you can see Blue Mountain and the Toronto Islands. Whatever the weather, you can enjoy futuristic pinball and laser tag games, explore virtual reality at the Ecodek, or dine in the world's highest revolving restaurant. Craving an adrenaline rush? Take in the outdoor observation deck, where you'll walk on air—or at least on a glass floor that's 1,122 feet above street level. The tower was recently renovated and now includes a cafe and arts-and-crafts market.

Plan on an early dinner so that you can catch a show at one of the city's famous theaters. In 1962, Toronto had only two professional theaters; today it boasts more than 140 and is the third-largest theater center in the English-speaking world (it ranks behind only New York and London). Big splashy musicals such as *Sunset Boulevard* and *Phantom of the Opera*—the latter running since 1989—have earned the city the nickname "Broadway North." Repertory companies include the **Royal Alexandra Theatre** (260 King Street West, Toronto, Ontario, Canada M4P 2E7; 800–461–3333 or 416–872–1212), the longest-running theater in downtown Toronto, and the **Canadian Stage Company** (416–368–3110), which presents contemporary Canadian productions as well as classics at a number of venues. Another sure crowd-pleaser includes the hilarious satire, *Forbidden Hollywood,* at the **Atlantis Complex** at Ontario Place (955 Lakeshore Boulevard West, Toronto, Ontario, Canada M6K 3B9; 416–260–8000).

If you're looking for something really different, sign on for a tour of the **Elgin and Winter Garden Theatre Centre** (189 Yonge Street, Toronto, Ontario, Canada; 416–872–5555), the last operating doubledecker theater in the world. A Canadian National Historic Site, it includes the opulent Elgin Theatre and the Winter Garden, the world's only fully restored roof-garden theater. At night, shows include plays and performances as notable as the theaters themselves. If you're feeling lucky, try for half-price tickets on the day of the performance at the T.O. Tix outlet outside the Eaton Centre on Yonge Street.

Not a theater fan? Toronto is also a fanatical sports town. The National Hockey League's Toronto Maple Leafs play in historic Maple Leaf Gardens. In hockey, only the rival Montreal Canadiens have won more Stanley Cups. Hockey fans (especially die-hard Detroit Red Wings fans!) will want to visit the **Hockey Hall of Fame** at the foot of Yonge and Front Streets in the BCE Place (30 Yonge Street, Toronto, Ontario, Canada M5E 1X8; 416–360–7735). The Toronto Blue Jays, part of major-league baseball's American League, prove that the boys of summer are not just an American phenomenon. The team won the Eastern Division title in 1985, 1989, 1992, and 1993 as well as the World Series in 1992 and 1993. Since moving into their new home, the SkyDome, the Blue Jays have drawn more than 3 million fans and have sold out practically every game.

DINNER: The **Centro Grill** (2472 Yonge Street, Toronto, Ontario, Canada M4P 2H5; 416–483–2211) is an intimate, four-star eatery with a façade of etched glass, granite, and marble and a welcoming interior featuring huge blowups of owner Franco Prevedello's hometown, Asolo, Italy. Massive columns, a bright blue ceiling, and salmon-colored walls are a backdrop for the creative cuisine, which features specialties such as rack of lamb with tomato, garlic, Spanish capers, eggplant, and salsa. All baking is done on the premises. Moderate to expensive.

DAY 3

Morning

BREAKFAST: Enjoy continental breakfast at Cambridge Suites, then head out to market. The American dollar is at such a premium in Canada that it would be a shame not to take advantage of the exchange rate. One ever-tempting place to do so on the weekend is the **Sunday Market** (416–410–1310), at which more than eighty antiques vendors take over St. Lawrence Market and hawk their wares in an arena reminiscent of Bermondsey Market in London. Another 150 or so dealers can be found at the city's **Harbourfront Antique Market** (390 Queen's Quay West, Toronto, Ontario, Canada M5J 2G8; 416–973–3000), just south of SkyDome. Canada's largest antiques market, it's open daily year-round but has more exhibitors (and therefore more goodies) on the weekend. You'll find lots of British imports, many dating back centuries.

Torontons are a fashionable lot. Many of the shops have a decidedly European flair and carry designers' and brand names unavailable at home. If you'd like to import a few fashions to yours, head for **Hazelton Lanes,** a chic enclave in the picturesque high-rent district known as Yorkville. Here you'll find tiny storefronts jammed with the latest in everything from cigars to clothing, handmade papers to homemade pastas. A few of the more famous outposts include Polo/Ralph Lauren, Cache (April Cornell in the United States), Gianni Versace, Chanel, and the Provence-inspired Pierre Deux, but there are also many local boutiques and shops unique to Toronto.

Afternoon

LUNCH: Yorkville has many wonderful restaurants and bistros. One of the best, however, is **Studio Cafe** in the elegant Four Seasons Hotel (21 Avenue Road, Toronto, Ontario, Canada M5R 2G1; 416–928–7330). The AAA voted Truffles, the hotel's fancier restaurant, best in Canada, but the Studio Cafe offers lighter, more informal, and equally accomplished dining in a modern, avant-garde atmosphere. The fish and pasta dishes are excellent. Moderate to expensive.

It's no surprise that this fashionable district is home to two of the city's best museums. The **Royal Ontario Museum** (100 Queen's Park at Avenue Road, Toronto, Ontario, Canada M5R 2G1; 416–586–8000) is one of the city's—and the country's—best, with a wing dedicated to European decorative arts and a fascinating working paleontology lab. Don't miss the popular galleries dedicated to Ancient Egypt or dinosaurs or the rare Bat Cave and Chinese Tomb. Not far away is the **George Gardiner Museum of Ceramic Art** (111 Queen's Park, Toronto, Ontario, Canada M5R 2G1; 416–586–8080). The Gardiner is North America's only specialized ceramics museum. It houses a beautiful collection of Italian majolica, English Delftware, Meissen figurines, and other priceless pieces.

If you're museum-hopping, one you won't want to miss is the **Art Gallery of Ontario** (317 Dundas Street West, Toronto, Ontario, Canada M5R 2G1; 416–979–6648). One of the largest and finest art museums in North America, its fifty galleries display an encyclopedic collection, from pre-Columbian to contemporary Canadian. Don't miss the smooth and sinuous Henry Moore Sculpture Center, which houses the largest collection in the world of the artist's important works. The adjacent Grange is Toronto's oldest standing brick house, a Georgian mansion built in 1817 and the Art Galleries' first home. It's now a living museum of nineteenth-century Canadian life. Entry to the garden is included with the $7.50 per person admission fee to the art gallery.

If you're into shoes, put your best foot forward and head to the **Bata Shoe Museum** (327 Bloor Street West, Toronto, Ontario, Canada M5J 2N5; 416–979–7799). You may have thought that Imelda Marcos had the most shoes under one roof, but that dubious distinction belongs to this well-heeled museum. It even looks like a giant shoe box, and is filled with 10,000 items and more than 4,500 years of shoe history, all collected by Sonja Bata, whose husband has shoes manufacturing plants around the world. Displays range from papyrus sandals worn during biblical days to rocker Elton John's nose-bleed-inducing platforms.

Before jumping back on Queen's Highway 401 and heading home, plan a stop at **Ontario Science Centre** (770 Don Mills Road, North York, Ontario, Canada M3N 1X1; 416–429–4100) just outside the central city in North York. A hit with scientists and nature lovers alike, it gives you the chance to walk through a steaming tropical rain forest, make a fool of your-self in a shadow tunnel, and enjoy a bird's-eye view in the city's first Omni-max theater. Open year-round.

THERE'S MORE

Amusements. Paramount Canada's Wonderland (9580 Jane Street, Vaughan, Ontario, Canada L4L 8P5; 905–832–7000) is a huge, 300-acre theme park with more than 140 attractions, including Splashworks Water Park, Kid's Kingdom play area, Canada's largest wave pool, *Star Trek* and Hanna-Barbera characters, and more. Open weekends in May and fall; daily from late in May through Labor Day.

Animals. The Metro Toronto Zoo (361A Old Finch Avenue, Scarborough, Ontario, Canada M1N 1T5; 416–392–5900) is one of the world's best zoos, with 5,000 animals in seven tropical pavilions. A must-see if you have kids.

Art. The Group of Seven are well-known Canadian painters. Their work is featured at the McMichael Canadian Art Collection (10365 Islington Avenue, Kleinburg, Ontario, Canada; 905–893–1121). Also featured are Inuit, First Nations, and contemporary Canadian works. There are also an on-site restaurant and gift shop.

Castles. Casa Loma (1 Austin Terrace, Ontario, Canada M5R 1X8; 416–923–1171) was built for financier Henry Pellatt. It features unusual architecture, elegant furnishings, secret passageways, and an 800-foot tunnel connecting the mansion to its luxurious riding stables. The adjacent gardens are a lush oasis of dancing fountains, sculpture, and floral displays.

Cruises. A number of companies offer boat and yacht tours around Toronto harbor and the nearby Toronto islands. The *Empress of Canada* (416–260–5547) is the city's newest, with large panoramic windows and a contemporary decor. At the other extreme is the Great Lakes Schooner Company (416–260–6355), with the 96-foot, three-masted schooner *Challenge* that sails daily for one- and two-hour sailing tours. If you've something more southern in mind, check the *Oriole* (416–203–0178), a 120-foot river showboat with sweeping staircases, Tiffany lamps, spacious dance floors, and on-board dining.

Entertainment. Ontario Place (955 Lakeshore Boulevard West, Toronto, Ontario, Canada M6J 3B9; 416–314–9900), the province's well-known park dedicated to entertainment, celebrated its twenty-fifth anniversary not long ago. Since opening it has been known for its Cinesphere IMAX films, rides (including the Rush River Raft Ride), other attractions, restaurants, and the colorful children's village. The park is open from mid–May through Labor Day; admission is $12 Canadian at the gate.

Golf. Toronto has seven respected courses, including Glen Abbey in Oakville (905–844–1800) designed by Jack Nicklaus; Lionhead Golf & Country Club (905–455–8400), with two championship courses; and St. Andrews Valley (905–727–7888), the country's highest-rated public golf course. Public courses include Centennial Park, Don Valley, Felmingdon, Scarlett Woods, and Tam O'Shanter.

History. Fort York (100 Garrison Road, Toronto, Ontario, Canada M5B 192; 416–392–6907) is an early-nineteenth-century fort that re-creates the drama in the War of 1812 and the history of early Toronto. Open year-round, it includes tours, displays, and military reenactments.

Skiing. Blue Mountain (Rural Route #3, Collingwood, Toronto, Ontario, Canada L9Y 3Z2; 705–445–0231) is the best-known local ski area and Ontario's largest four-season resort. It features the highest ski vertical, with thirty trails and sixteen lifts.

Snowmobiling. Want to really chill out? Sign on for one of the tours offered by Canadian Snowmobile Adventures (800–465–7378). The company takes the adventurous on guided snowmobile treks along 20,000 miles of groomed trails and through thick Canadian forests.

Theater. What began in 1961 as a weekend event in postcard-pretty Niagara on the Lake is now an annual summerlong event. The Shaw Festival (P.O. Box 774, Niagara on the Lake, Toronto, Ontario, Canada L0S 1J0; 800–267–4759) features top-notch plays by George Bernard Shaw and his contemporaries in three theaters. The Stratford Festival (55 Queen Street, P.O. Box 520, Stratford, Ontario, Canada N5A 2R3; 800–567–1600) presents Shakespearean classics as well as modern drama and comedy against the bucolic backdrop of Stratford, Ontario (for more on Stratford, see Ontario Escape Four). Both venues are a 90-minute drive from downtown Toronto.

Water Wonderland. Wild Water Kingdom (7855 Finch Avenue West, Brampton, Ontario, Canada L6W 3J3; 905–369–9453) is Canada's largest water theme park, featuring a half-acre wave pool, tube and river rides, kids' watery playground, batting cages, and miniature golf. Open summer only.

Wineries. The Wine Council of Ontario (110 Hanover Drive, St. Catherine's, Toronto, Ontario, Canada L2R 1A2; 905–684–8070) operates a number of vineyards within a two-hour drive of Toronto. Acres of vineyards produce some of the finest grapes in the world, with many wineries opening their doors and cellars for tasting and tours. Contact the council for more information.

SPECIAL EVENTS

January. International Boat Show

February. Canadian International Auto Show

March. Canadian Music Festival

April. National Home Show

May. Toronto International Pow Wow
Lilac Festival

June. Symphony of Fire Fireworks Festival
Downtown Jazz Festival
Taste of Toronto

July. Canada Day Celebration
Caribana Fest

August. Canadian National Exhibition
Canadian International Air Show

September. Toronto International Film Festival

October. International Festival of Authors
Canadian Ski Show
Autumn Artsfest

November. Royal Agricultural Winter Fair

OTHER RECOMMENDED RESTAURANTS

Chiaro's (37 King Street East, Toronto, Ontario, Canada M5R 2G1; 416–863–9700) is in the opulent King Edward Hotel. Specialties including Dover sole, New York steaks, rack of lamb, and other French-inspired cuisine served in a plush gray dining room. Expensive.

Joso's (202 Davenport Road, Toronto, Ontario, Canada M5R 1J2; 416–925–1903) is the place to be if you're a member of the international artistic community. Owner Joso Spralja is an artist, musician, and restaurateur and has filled his two-story restaurant with sensual paintings and large, intriguing wall hangings. Food is unusual and healthy, with a number of Italian and seafood specialties. Moderate to expensive.

North 44 Degrees (2537 Yonge Street, Toronto, Ontario, Canada M5R 1J2; 416–487–4897) refers to the city's latitude and to this trendy modern eatery. Specialties inside the metallic-looking dining room include rack of lamb, angel-hair pasta, and a mixed appetizer platter. You'll also find a popular wine bar on the upper level and entertainment on weekends. Expensive.

Truffles (21 Avenue Road, Toronto, Ontario, Canada M5R 2G1; 416–964–0411), in the Four Seasons Hotel, is best known for its wonderful wine list, which features rare European and North American vintages. Murals, paintings, and ceramics by local artists decorate the dining room, which serves cuisine based on the gastronomic offerings of Provence, France. Specialties include Quebec duck and a rack of lamb with mustard seed sauce. Pastries are made on the premises. Expensive.

OTHER RECOMMENDED LODGINGS

Downtown

Clarion Essex Park Hotel (300 Jarvis Street, Toronto, Ontario, Canada M5B 2C5; 416–977–4823) has 102 recently renovated guest rooms and suites in an intimate, European-style hotel within walking distance of Eaton Centre. The on-site Bistro Restaurant offers three meals daily. Rates: $99 and up Canadian per night.

The Delta Chelsea Inn (33 Gerrard Street West, Toronto, Ontario, Canada M5G 1Z4; 800–243–5732 or 416–595–1975) is centrally located near the theater district and downtown shops and restaurants. It's especially popular with families, with an innovative Delta Dolphin swim program for kids and a drop-off Children's Creative Center. An added plus: Kids age five or younger eat free; kids ages six through eleven eat at half off. Rates: $120 and up Canadian per night, although package deals are often available.

Royal Meridien King Edward Hotel (37 King Street East, Toronto, Ontario, Canada M5C 1E9; 416–863–9700) is one of the Leading Hotels of the World and an elegant European-style inn. Built in 1903, it was remodeled early in the 1980s and boasts a vaulted ceiling, marble pillars, and palm trees in its lobby. The 312 guest rooms are well furnished, with sumptuous marble bathrooms. Rates: $225 and up Canadian per night for weekends.

Novotel Toronto Centre (45 The Esplanade, Toronto, Ontario, Canada M5E 1W2; 416–367–8900) has 262 rooms close to the Harbourfront, theaters, and the St. Lawrence Market. Facilities include health club, whirlpool, restaurants, and more. Rates start at $185 Canadian per night.

Radisson Plaza Hotel Admiral (249 Queen's Quay West, Toronto, Ontario, Canada M5J 2N5; 416–203–3333) is a well-run 157-room hotel near the Harbourfront and St. Lawrence Market. Its Commodore's Dining Room is rated four diamonds by CAA/AAA. Rates: $129–$165 Canadian per night.

The stately Royal York Hotel (100 Front Street West, Toronto, Ontario, Canada M5J 1E3; 416–368–2511 or 800–441–1414) is a huge landmark hotel across from Union Station. It has 1,365 rooms as well as a health club and ten on-site restaurants. Rates: $159 and up Canadian per night.

Yorkville

Four Seasons Toronto (21 Avenue Road, Toronto, Ontario, Canada M5R 2G1; 416–964–0411) is in the heart of the fashionable Yorkville district and is Toronto's only five-diamond hotel. Rates: $285–$345 Canadian per night.

Bed-and-Breakfasts

If you'd like to experience the warmth of a bed-and-breakfast inn, the city offers many options. B&B Homes of Toronto (44 Yonge Street, Toronto,

Ontario, Canada M5B 192; 416–363–6362) represents twenty homes in many of the city's best neighborhoods. The competing Bed & Breakfast Guest Houses Association (416–368–1420) represents a large selection of distinctive Victorian homes in downtown Toronto.

FOR MORE INFORMATION

Tourism Toronto, 207 Queen's Quay West, Toronto, Ontario, Canada M5J 1A7; (800) 203–1990 or (416) 203–2600.

Ste. Anne's
Country Inn and Spa

SYBARITIC SPA WEEKEND IN ONTARIO

2 NIGHTS

Spa • Country Inn • History • Elk Farm

"The things I won't do in the name of research," I thought to myself as I dipped a tentative toe into the bath filled with inky mud. I hadn't played in the mud since I was a kid and was definitely out of practice.

I have to admit my skin did feel smoother afterward, although the mud bath had a strange feel to it, sort of like sitting in a warm chocolate pudding, according to my technician, Lucie. Yoga classes, long walks in the surrounding Ontario countryside, and relaxing gourmet meals are all just a part of a weekend at **Ste. Anne's Country Inn and Spa,** just an hour outside of Toronto in Grafton, Ontario. With the American dollar almost 50 percent stronger than Canadian currency, both the price and the pampering are right.

DAY 1

Ste. Anne's Country Inn and Spa is about four-and-a-half hours from Detroit. Take I-94 to the Blue Water Bridge to Queen's Highway 401. There are plenty of places to stop along the way, including tiny Canadian towns full of tea houses and antiques shops bursting with British imports. Plan to get to the inn in time for dinner, however. You won't want to miss any of the excellent meals prepared by chef Aram Saillian.

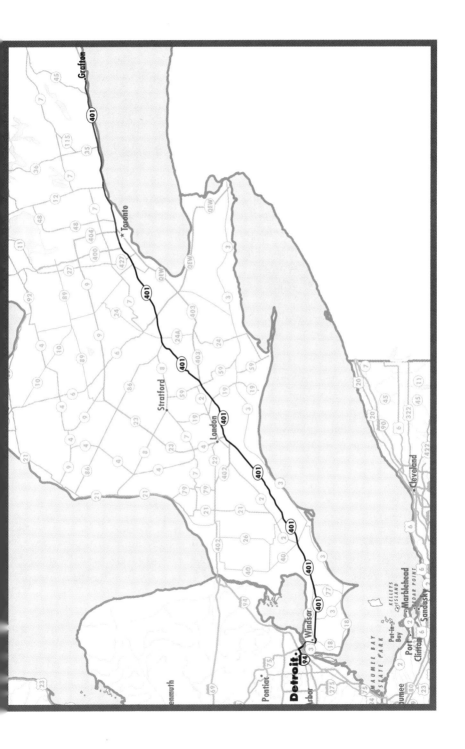

Afternoon

DINNER: Dinner is the only time you can't wear your white spa robe. You'll be glad you didn't, as a hostess ushers you into a cozy dining area overlooking the countryside. Though spa food usually brings to mind meager portions arranged artfully on a plate, Ste. Anne's chooses to emphasize the property's inn, rather than spa, persona during meals. Guests can opt for more health-conscious cuisine, but few do.

The first night, I chose smoked duck salad, followed by marinated monk-fish with sun-dried tomato and spinach ragout. My dessert was a decidedly "undiet" chocolate mousse cake, topped with a spun-sugar sculpture. While I ate, I chatted with other guests, who ranged from a mother-daughter pair from Ottawa, Ontario, to a couple from Long Island, New York—the only other Americans besides myself.

After dinner, guests can choose to relax in the living room, where a variety of magazines, books, and a continuing puzzle await. You can also try the spa's hot tubs or basement steam room. There are no televisions or phones in the guest rooms, although both are available on request.

LODGINGS: Ste. Anne's has ten regular rooms and five off-site guest houses. My room was the West Suite—a large, airy space with a cathedral ceiling, big comfy couch, and roaring fireplace. Because Ste. Anne's is an Aveda Concept Spa, the large bathroom was well stocked with Aveda sample-size toiletries, all of which smelled heavenly. After a quick soak in the hot tub, I slept peacefully in the four-poster bed and awoke early next morning ready to explore.

DAY 2

Morning

BREAKFAST: Because I had a treatment planned for morning, I opted to wear my robe to breakfast. I wasn't the only one, and once I got over the strangeness of wearing a robe in front of people I had never met, I actually enjoyed it. Breakfast was a luscious meal of French toast served with fresh strawberry compote and rich, dark coffee.

After breakfast, I decided to accept marketing director Marijo Corcoran's offer of a tour of the property. Ste. Anne's is housed in a sprawling fieldstone structure in the Northumberland Hills overlooking 560 acres and Lake Ontario. It was built in 1857 by Samuel Massey, a well-known maker of farm implements. In the 1930s, the property was purchased by Robert and Sarah Blaffer, oil tycoons from Texas who used it as their summer retreat. They added towers, archways, and a walled garden hoping to make Ste. Anne's look like a mini Scottish castle. Sarah Blaffer named it Ste. Anne's in honor of an English finishing school she had attended.

In 1981, the estate was purchased by the Corcoran family. By then, harsh Canadian winters had taken their toll on the property. Empty and neglected, it took years of restoration and rebuilding before the Corcorans were able to reopen the gracious country inn in 1983. Spa services were added in 1991.

In addition to the spa, the Corcoran family owns an adjacent 560-acre elk farm, where animals are raised for the velvet inside their horns, which is sold to the Korean market as an aphrodisiac. There is also an on-site mineral-water–bottling plant. In summer, you can swim in these therapeutic waters, which are used to fill the Olympic-size pool on the grounds.

After the tour, I joined an exercise class in the spa's sunlit workout room, where classes include everything from Tai Chi to low-impact aerobics. I tried out the treadmill and chatted with a few guests before heading to lunch.

Afternoon

LUNCH: Lunch was a delicious meal of chicken-stuffed ravioli with a sauce of sun-dried tomatoes and crunchy garlic bread. There go the calories I burned in the exercise class, I thought with chagrin.

Afterward, I visited the inn's impressive full-service spa, carved out of the estate's former cellar. Here you can choose from more than twenty treatments, including a standard manicure or pedicure and more unusual options such as lymphatic drainage or a seaweed body masque. A spa veteran, I decided to try a couple of things I had never experienced, including a soothing skin polish.

During the skin polish, a grainy substance made of freshly ground walnut shells was rubbed on with a soft brush, followed by a massage with a high-pressure "Scotch Hose." It was followed by an application of a wonderfully smooth lotion made of lavender and hibiscus oils. Between that and the scalp treatment I received the next day, I felt like a new woman, which was the idea behind escaping to Ste. Anne's in the first place.

Carl Corcoran, father of Ste. Anne's owner, Jim Corcoran, said that the spa business is a happy one. "This is a great business because everyone feels good while they're here. It's like owning a hospital where everyone is cured."

DINNER: Dinner on the second night consisted of butternut squash soup as an appetizer and a strip loin steak in red wine with fresh tarragon. The only signs of more typical spa fare were the raw veggies presented with the appetizer. *Note:* Ste. Anne's does not have a liquor license, and so if you'd like a glass of wine with your meal, you must bring your own. Many guests did just that during my stay, and one even shared a glass with me while we were talking.

DAY 3

Morning

BREAKFAST: After another night of uninterrupted sleep (a rarity for this mother of two young children), I enjoyed a tasty omelette made from the inn's fresh herb garden and fresh fruit. Afterward, I joined three other guests for the morning walk, which took us on a 3-mile hike across the inn's rolling acres. The friendly elk on the nearby farm moseyed up to the fence for a look as we power-walked by, accompanied by Highway, Ste. Anne's resident black lab.

Afternoon

LUNCH: Before I knew it, it was time for my last lunch. I opted for a breast of chicken served on home-grown greens with a raspberry vinaigrette and homemade bread.

Lunch was followed by the aforementioned mud bath. The gooey bath was made up of $2,000 worth of rare Moor mud mined from deep beneath the Ontario landscape. Rich in nourishing vitamins and minerals, it was historically renowned for detoxifying the system and reviving winter-weary skin. The treatment is all the rage in Europe, but Ste. Anne's is the only place in Ontario that offers it.

Therapeutic benefits aside, it still felt like mud. I have to admit I got a kick out of the Polaroid they gave me of myself, lolling around in the ooze (a similar souvenir is given to each bather). Afterward, I decided that the mud bath was something everyone should try at least once. After all, how often do you have the chance to float in a bath of warm chocolate pudding?

THERE'S MORE

Antiques. The charming town of Port Hope, about 15 minutes west of Grafton on Route 401, has a number of antiques shops and is a good place to while away a morning. It also has a number of charming bed-and-breakfasts.

Other Fountains of Youth. Ste. Anne's is just one of Ontario's many wonderful spas. Another one is High Fields (905–473–6132) in Zephyr, Ontario, about a one-hour drive from downtown Toronto. Like Ste. Anne's, it emphasizes pampering and nurturing in contrast to more regimented exercise and diet programs.

T-Town. Because Ste. Anne's is just an hour from Toronto, you could easily make it part of a longer getaway. A few days at Ste. Anne's in mid-week, when it's cheaper, could be followed by a weekend in cosmopolitan Toronto. For more on what to see and do in the Queen City, see the chapter on Toronto.

FOR MORE INFORMATION

Room rates for the spa plan at Ste. Anne's start at $225 Canadian and include all meals, a $65 spa credit, and accommodations in one of the spa's ten regular rooms or five off-site guest houses. They also offer a number of packages, including a two-night retreat with aromatherapy, a Moor mud bath, pedicure or manicure, and mini-facial. You can also choose a five-night, totally indulgent "Total Transformation" package. For more information, contact Ste. Anne's at Rural Route 1, Grafton, Ontario, Canada K0K 2G0 or call (905) 349–2493 or (888) 3–INNSPA (466–772). The Web site address is www.steannes.com.

Stratford

"THE PLAY'S THE THING"

2 NIGHTS

Drama • History • Gardens • Restaurants

Is the London stage a stretch for this year's travel budget? Consider a trip to Stratford, Ontario, just two hours away by car. You almost expect to see Shakespeare himself strolling along the streets and rivers in this charming Canadian town. If it weren't for the Ontario license plates, you'd swear you were in Merrie Old England.

Nestled in the countryside between London (Ontario) and Toronto, this town of 28,000 people is best known as the home of the celebrated **Stratford Festival,** which attracts internationally acclaimed thespians to three stages. The wildly popular festival began under a tent in 1953 and today ranks among the three greatest English-speaking theater festivals in the world. The 26-week season includes both Shakespeare's classics and more contemporary works.

The twelve-play repertory season runs from May through November. Stratford also has lots of historic buildings to explore, boutiques to browse in, and art galleries where you can pick up a few masterpieces to take home. In short, there's enough to do even if you're not a thespian.

DAY 1

From Detroit's Ambassador Bridge, Stratford is an easy, two-and-one-half-hour drive. Take I-94 to the Blue Water Bridge to Queen's Highway 401. Then take 59 north to Route 8 west to Stratford.

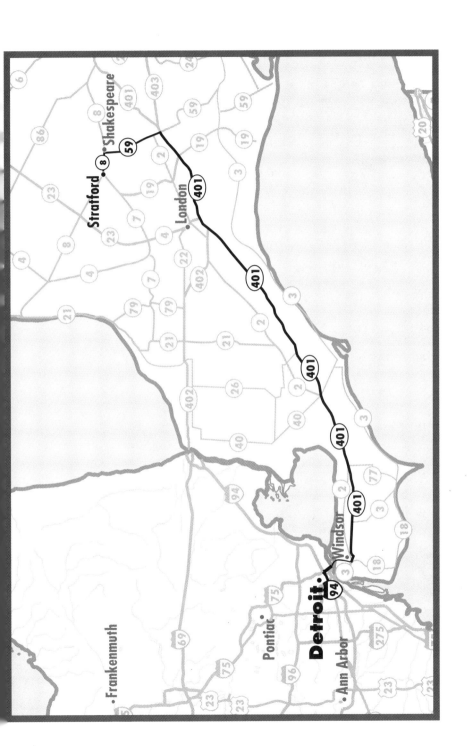

Afternoon

DINNER: Plan to arrive in time for a late, pub-style meal at **Bentley's** (99 Ontario Street, Stratford, Ontario, Canada N5A 6V2; 519–271–1121). This cozy inn and restaurant has seventeen beers on draft, darts, and British-inspired favorites such as steak and kidney pie. Moderate.

LODGING: There are plenty of places to stay and play, including British-style bed-and-breakfasts and small, family-run inns. One of the best is the **Victorian Inn on the Park** (800–741–2135), just five minutes from the Festival Theatre. With 115 rooms, it's one of the largest hostelries in town. Despite the name it's not particularly Victorian, although it does boast a great view of the Avon River. Rooms are freshly decorated and were renovated in 1998. Rates start at $120 Canadian.

DAY 2

Morning

BREAKFAST: Grab a bite at the **York Street Kitchen** (York Street, Stratford, Ontario, Canada N5A 6V2; 519–273–7041) before getting an early start. This unpretentious eatery, a few yards from the river, has home-cooked daily specials and just thirty seats. Try it for lunch or dinner if it's too crowded at breakfast. Moderate.

First stop: one of the city's **Historic Walking Tours,** offered Monday through Saturday in July and August, and on Saturday only in May, June, and September. The tour starts at the city's Visitors Information Center.

If you get up late or prefer to schedule your own itinerary, don't miss Stratford's many worthwhile sights. One tour that everyone loves is the 45-minute peek inside the **costume warehouse,** which stores props and colorful wares from 45 years of Stratford productions. Also popular are the Sunday-morning backstage tours of the **Festival Theatre,** informal discussions with actors held on Wednesday and Friday mornings, and **Table Talk,** a series of lunch lectures designed to give playgoers insight into the many productions.

LUNCH: Soltar (161 Ontario, Stratford, Ontario, Canada N5A 6V2; 519–271–1400) is a lively bistro celebrating the cuisine and decor of Santa Fe. It's definitely the place to go if you get tired of that clubby, British-inspired style and fare. Moderate.

Afternoon

Spend the afternoon enjoying the smell of the greasepaint. Because there are three distinctive theaters, you can take in up to three performances in a well-planned weekend. Be sure to get schedules ahead of time so that you can be assured of getting seats at your favorites.

The **Festival Theatre** stage has 1,820 seats with an intimate, wraparound stage. Despite the theater's size, actors often seem close enough to touch. The **Tom Pearson Theatre** has just 487 seats and a long, narrow stage. In the heart of town is the more traditional **Avon Theatre,** which holds 1,089 seats and a large stage.

You could easily spend the weekend hopping from play to play, but try to squeeze a little shopping between curtain calls. Good bets include the **Gallery Indigena,** filled with art of the Inuit, North Pacific Coast, Iroquois, and Cree peoples. Not far from the festival theater is the **Gallery Stratford,** which showcases Canadian visual and theater arts. Another fun stop is the Theatre Store, located in the Festival Theatre Lobby, the Avon Theatre lobby, and 96 Downie Street. All have theatrical-inspired books, music, and souvenirs. Antique lover? Check **Gregory Connor** and **Hidden Treasures.**

DINNER: Antiques, Windsor chairs, chintz fabrics, and a cozy fireplace make **Mrs. Carter's** (Downie Street, Stratford, Ontario, Canada N5A 6V2; 519–271–9200) a comfortable choice. The smoke-free atmosphere offers a peaceful retreat from the crowds outside. New menus feature trout fillet and fresh pastas. The restaurant is open late on theater nights, making it a good spot for a late-night cappucino or dessert. If you're looking for something a bit more casual, consider **Keystone Alley Cafe** (Brunswick Street, Stratford, Ontario, Canada N5A 6V2; 519–271–5645). Bright art on the walls and wonderful daily specials such as steamed mussels, pastas, fish, and Yorkshire pudding make this a local favorite.

DAY 3

Morning

BREAKFAST: Start your last day in town with brunch at the **Caesar Restaurant** (800–741–2135) in the Victorian Inn on the Park. The traditional brunch overflows with pastas, omelettes, waffles, and other tasty hot and cold entrees. For dessert you can load up at the sundae bar. It's a great way to end a great weekend and is well priced at just $14.95 per adult; $7.95 per child.

Tired of sitting in small theater seats? Stretch your legs and wrap up your stay by exploring Stratford's natural side. An extensive park system surrounds the city's Avon River and ends at the **T. J. Dolan Natural Area,** a marked trail that follows the river for a beautiful walk under a canopy of maple and pine trees.

If it's raining, check the **Stratford–Perth Museum** (182 King Street, Stratford, Ontario, Canada N5A 6V2; 519–271–2311). This civic museum recounts the city's history and includes many interesting displays, including one honoring Jennie Kidd Trout, Canada's first licensed female physician.

THERE'S MORE

Antiques. The nearby town of Shakespeare is regarded as one of Ontario's antiques capitals. More than ten shops filled to the brim with Canadiana and British and American imports tempt collectors. An in-town tea room bakes its own tempting treats.

Fresh Produce. Stratford is the site of a Saturday Farmer's Market from 6:30 A.M. to noon at the fairgrounds. Wares include baked goods, fish, cheese, flowers, and various crafts.

Gardens. Storybook Gardens (Springbank Park, London, Ontario, Canada N5A 6V2; 519–661–5770) are a children's fantasy theme park with storybook characters, a playground, and petting zoo. Adults even like it, too.

History. Fanshawe Pioneer Village (100 Clarke Side Road, London, Ontario, Canada N6B 1S2; 519–457–1296) re-creates a nineteenth-century community, with more than twenty original buildings and costumed interpreters.

Music. Are you a Guy Lombardo fan? The famous bandleader and his Royal Canadians are honored by videos and memorabilia in the Guy Lombardo Museum (205 Wonderland Road South, London, Ontario, Canada N6B IS2; 519–473–9003).

Shopping. Major mall action and charming downtown boutiques can be found in nearby London. Richmond Street, from Oxford to Carling, is full of small shops offering local crafts, clothing, and other goodies.

OTHER RECOMMENDED RESTAURANTS

The Church (70 Brunswick Street, Stratford, Ontario, Canada N5A 6V6; 519–273–3424) is a romantic yet relaxed restaurant housed in a restored church. At dinner, check the five-course prix fixe menu. Moderate to expensive.

The Old Prune (151 Albert Street, Stratford, Ontario, Canada N5A 3K5; 519–271–5052) is, despite the name, an elegant, semiformal eatery featuring innovative cuisine based on natural ingredients. There's also a nice selection of Ontario wines. Expensive.

Rundles (9 Cobourg Street, Stratford, Ontario, Canada N5A 3E4; 519–271–6442) is the place to go to splurge, and it is one of Stratford's most formal restaurants. Overlooking the lake, it features a contemporary decor and a sumptuous, three-course, prix fixe dinner. Expensive.

OTHER RECOMMENDED LODGINGS

Stone Maiden Inn (123 Church Street, Stratford, Ontario, Canada N5A 2R3; 519–271–7129) has fourteen rooms in a restored 1872 Victorian inn. Some rooms feature fireplaces and canopy beds. Rates start at $135 Canadian.

Woods Villa B&B (62 John Street, Stratford, Ontario, Canada N5A 6K7; 519–271–4576) has six rooms in an elegant 1879 home that once belonged to Magistrate James Peter Woods. Check the funky collection of antique coin-operated musical devices in the parlor. Rates: $90–$165 Canadian.

FOR MORE INFORMATION

Tourism Stratford, 88 Wellington Street, Stratford, Ontario, Canada N5A 6W1; (519) 271–5140 or (800) 561–7926.

INDIANA
ESCAPES

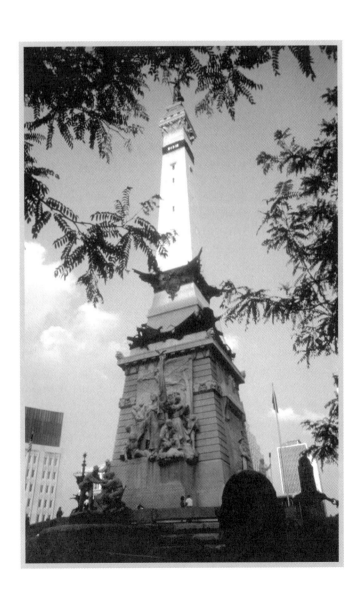

Indianapolis

HOOSIER HOSPITALITY

2 NIGHTS

Museums • Sight-seeing • Speedway • Theater
Amateur and Professional Sports

For many Detroiters, Indianapolis seems like just another notch on the midwestern rust belt. Dismissing the nation's twelfth-largest city so easily, however, would be a mistake. Today's Indianapolis has built a reputation for its sporting facilities, world-class attractions, performing and visual arts, and legendary Hoosier hospitality. There's more than enough to fill a weekend.

Residents are quick to point out that Indianapolis, not Detroit, was the first automobile capital. Early in the 1900s, more than sixty car makes were produced here, including Duesenbergs, Marmons, and Stutzes. Detroit's assembly-line production soon replaced Indy's custom-made vehicles, however, and by the mid-1930s only three auto manufacturers were left. Today Indianapolis manufacturers produce automotive parts rather than finished cars. The city's most famous connection to cars is the annual **Indianapolis 500** automobile race, which draws about 400,000 spectators.

And though Detroit is still working on its renaissance, one is in full bloom in Indianapolis. A sure sign is the impressive Circle Centre Mall, which opened in fall 1995 and is linked by skywalks to downtown hotels. Anchored by tony Nordstrom's and the Parisian's, the mall has about one hundred stores, as well as nightclubs and movies. It's a source of pride for local downtown boosters and popular with both residents and visitors. Indianapolis is also a mecca for sports lovers of all varieties. Besides the Indy 500 for auto-racing fans, there are professional football (Colts) and basketball (Pacers) teams. The

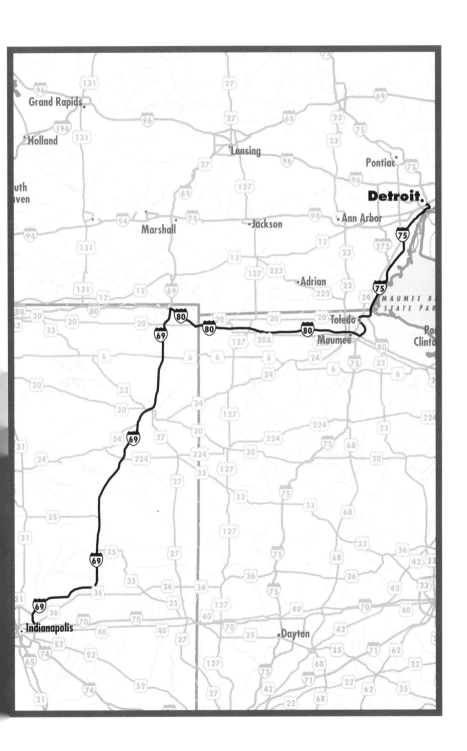

new Victory Field is home of the Indians minor-league baseball club. As *TV Guide* put it, "Indianapolis never met a sport it didn't like."

DAY 1

Morning

Indianapolis is 284 miles from Detroit, a drive of about five hours. To get there, take Interstate 75 south to Interstate 80 west and then continue to Interstate 69 south, which goes right into downtown Indianapolis.

The city is easy to get around in. Architect Alexander Ralston, who worked with Washington, D.C., planner Pierre L'Enfant, laid out the city on a mile-square grid. At its center is **Monument Circle,** the starting place for four diagonal spoke streets. The circle, in the heart of downtown, is home to a number of historic landmarks. The best-looking one is the 284-foot Soldiers and Sailors Monument, completed in 1902 as a Civil War tribute (a new Civil War museum is also planned for the site). For a bird's-eye view of the city, take the elevator or stairs to the top of the 284-foot obelisk. In summer, you'll be able to see picnickers and people-watchers on the circle below; in winter, it's home to both carolers and Christmas lights.

The modern heart of the city, however, is **Circle Centre Mall** (49 West Maryland Street, Indianapolis, IN 46204; 317–681–8000), a sparkling new mall that epitomizes the new Indianapolis. City leaders had the foresight to save three blocks of landmark stores and office façades, some dating to the 1800s. When the buildings were demolished, their fronts were stored and later incorporated into Circle Centre Mall, thereby preserving the original look of downtown. The $314-million shopping center, with Nordstrom's and the Parisian as its anchors, has revitalized the city's heart since opening in 1995.

This is power shopping at its best. Besides the big department stores, the mall is home to more than 100 smaller boutiques, including the first-floor **Back Home Indiana** (317–630–4663), chock full of paintings, furniture, books, and other items by Indiana artisans. The most unusual spot is the fourth-floor virtual world, billed as the world's first digital theme park. Here you can don a headset and travel to Mars or compete against pilots in a space race known as "Red Planet." The mall is linked to the respected Arts garden, six hotels, and the Indiana Convention Center, and it also houses restaurants and entertainment, including **Flashbaxx** (317–630–5483), a funky tribute to the 1970s disco scene. After a visit, you'll never again think all malls are alike.

The Indianapolis skyline rises like a beacon above the surrounding plains.

Afternoon

LUNCH: *Indianapolis Monthly* voted the **California Cafe** (Circle Centre, 49 West Maryland Street, Indianapolis, IN 46204; 317–488–8686) "Indy's Hippest Eatery." It has a California-cool interior and a menu that features lighter fare such as seasoned fish and an eclectic daily special. You'll feel as if you've been transported from the heartland to the West Coast. There are also a separate espresso bar and an in-house bakery. Moderate.

One of the highlights in a weekend here is a trip to the **Children's Museum of Indianapolis** (3000 North Meridian Street, Indianapolis, IN 46204; 317–924–5431). With more than five floors of hands-on adventure for explorers of all ages, it's a family favorite. It's even fun if you don't have kids. Plan to arrive early, for lines can be long for the most popular exhibitions and displays, including the turn-of-the-century hand-carved carousel. During your visit, you'll barter for goods in an eighteenth-century fur-trading post, sit behind the wheel of a roaring race car, and explore a limestone cave. The antique doll and model-train collections are the largest in the country. Be sure to stop and let the kids spend the allowance in the "Kid Stuff" shop, which features goodies all priced $5.00 or less. If you have preschoolers, there's also an expansive playscape. Admission can be steep if you have a large family ($8.00 for adults; $3.50 for kids ages two to seventeen; under two free), but it's worth every penny. You may decide to visit on Thursday night from 5:00 to 8:00 P.M. when the museum is free.

DINNER: Louisiana Street Restaurant and Bar (123 West Louisiana Street, Indianapolis, IN 46225; 317–631–2221) in Union Station has been called the city's best-kept secret by the *Indianapolis Star*. It specializes in spicy Creole cuisine, with an excellent blackened swordfish. If you're up for some fun, try **Buca di Beppo** (35 North Illinois, Indianapolis, IN 46217; 317–632–2822). The city's alternative weekly called it "part comic opera, part Roman orgy." It was also voted one of America's best new restaurants by *Bon Appétit*. Whatever you order, you'll receive huge portions of what they call "Southern Immigrant" fare. Moderate.

LODGING: If you've decided to splurge, the place to do so is the **Canterbury** (123 South Illinois Street, Indianapolis, IN 46225; 317–634–3000). This elegant British-style hotel features 99 rooms with four-poster beds (adjacent to Circle Center and the Convention Center), Chippendale reproductions, and marble baths. Public rooms—including the parlor, with its carved wooden fireplace—are spacious and sophisticated. Rates: $200 per night and up. The hotel's restaurant is known for its Dover sole, rack of lamb, veal dishes, and its to-die-for dessert souffles. Expensive.

If you've brought the family, the **Crowne Plaza Union Station** (123 West Louisiana Street, Indianapolis, IN 46225; 317–631–2221 or 800–2–CROWNE) has affordable weekend packages and offers the rare chance to sleep in one of 26 Pullman train car rooms. Opt for one of the 276 regular rooms if you're claustrophobic, however. All rooms are centrally located adjoining Union Station and are near Circle Centre Mall. Rates: $129–$179 per night.

INDIANA

DAY 2

Morning

BREAKFAST: Le Peep (301 North Illinois Street, Indianapolis, IN; 317–237–3447) has been voted one of the city's best breakfast spots since 1988. Specialties include frittatas, French toast, overstuffed omelettes, and four types of casserole-like "pampered eggs." Inexpensive.

No trip to Indianapolis would be complete without a visit to the **Indianapolis Motor Speedway Hall of Fame and Museum** (4790 West Sixteenth Street, Indianapolis, IN 46224; 317–484–6747), just west of downtown. This is mecca to motoring fans: You can take a $3.00 bus ride around the famous 2.5-mile track or ooh and aah at the adjacent museum, which features one of the world's largest and most varied collections of racing, classic, and antique cars as well as more than thirty Indy winners. You'll find also a half-hour film on the track's history, plus racing memorabilia, a great gift shop, and more.

Afternoon

LUNCH: The **Rathskeller** (401 East Michigan Street, Indianapolis, IN 46204; 317–636–0396) is housed in the Athenaeum, which was designed by the grandfather of well-known native son Kurt Vonnegut, Jr. It's an Old World–style eatery that serves up dark German beer along with German specialties from brats to sauerbraten. There's also a full menu of American favorites. Moderate.

You may know the city best for its motor sports, but Indianapolis's "other" history takes center stage at the **Indiana State Museum** (202 North Alabama Street, Indianapolis, IN 46204; 317–232–1637). A frequent stop for Smithsonian traveling exhibitions, this showplace in the original City Hall concentrates on the state's natural and cultural history. Popular displays include an ancient glacier, city streets from 1910, and—of course—a section on the world of modern sports. Admission is free.

DINNER: If you're into meat and potatoes, you won't do better than the **St. Elmo Steakhouse** (127 South Illinois Street, next to the Circle Centre Mall, Indianapolis, IN 46204; 317–635–0636), a city landmark since 1902. It has been voted the best downtown restaurant for five straight years by readers of

Indianapolis Monthly. Specialties include a hefty twenty-ounce New York–cut sirloin steak, a carnivore's dream, and a fiery shrimp cocktail. The restaurant's excellent wine cellar has been cited with an Award of Excellence from the *Wine Spectator,* every year since 1991. Expensive.

Indianapolis is credited with having some of the oldest and best jazz clubs in the country. After dinner, check the **Chatterbox Tavern** (435 Massachusetts Avenue, Indianapolis, IN 46220; 317–636–0584); or the **Jazz Cooker** (925 East Westfield Boulevard, Indianapolis, IN 46220; 317–253–2883); or the **Slippery Noodle Inn** (372 South Meridian Street, Indianapolis, IN 46220; 317–631–6974), where blues rules. It opened in 1850 and is the state's oldest bar.

DAY 3

Morning

BREAKFAST: Grab an eye-opener at your hotel, but save room for brunch at the **Garden on the Green Restaurant** (317–926–2628), part of the Indianapolis Museum of Art. For just $10.00 per person ($6.75 for kids) you'll choose from a buffet that includes enticing hot and cold breakfast dishes (including a wonderful cheese strata) and lunch items. Reservations are required.

After brunch, don't miss the **Indianapolis Museum of Art** (1200 West Thirty-eighth Street, Indianapolis, IN 46208; 317–923–1331), one of the oldest in the country. Set on 152 lush acres, it includes four pavilions featuring African, medieval, and Renaissance art, plus eighteenth- through twentieth-century European painting and decorative arts in period settings. Other attractions include a beautiful botanical garden, shops, greenhouses, a concert hall, a theater, and more.

Western art in the middle of the heartland? At the **Eiteljorg Museum of American Indians and Western Art** (500 West Washington, Indianapolis, IN 46204; 317–636–9378), seeing is believing. The adobe Eiteljorg is home to one of the nation's finest collections of American western and Native American art and artifacts. Highlights include works by Charlie Russell, Frederic Remington, and Georgia O'Keeffe as well as Native American objects. The museum was a gift to the city from a coal baron and is part of the **White River State Park** (317–634–4567). There are also daily films and demonstrations and a large museum store. This is one museum kids love as much as adults do.

THERE'S MORE

Antiques. The Historic Fountain Square neighborhood (317–686–6010), not far from downtown, boasts 150 antiques dealers in three malls. You can also dine at three vintage lunch counters, an old-time soda fountain, even a restaurant featuring classic southern cookin'. The Midland Arts and Antiques Market (317–267–9005) occupies 40,000 square feet in a renovated warehouse.

Cultural Center. The Madame Walker Urban Life Center (617 Indiana Avenue, Indianapolis, IN 46204; 317–236–2099) was named for the country's first black woman millionaire. Originally used as a vaudeville stage, the 1927 Art Déco building fell into disrepair after World War II and received a $3-million facelift in 1988. It now serves as an arts and cultural center for Indianapolis's African-American community as well as the site for the popular weekly "Jazz on the Avenue" concerts.

Sports. Professional, semipro, amateur: Whatever your pleasure, Indy has something for you. The Pacers tip off at Market Square Arena (300 East Market Street, Indianapolis, IN 46204; 317–639–6411) and the Colts kick off at the Hoosier Dome (100 South Capitol Avenue, Indianapolis, IN 46204; 317–297–7000). For information on both, call (317) 239–5151. Baseball fans can check the AAA affiliate Indianapolis Indians, a farm team of the Cincinnati Reds. For tickets, call (317) 269–3545.

SPECIAL EVENTS

May. Indianapolis 500

June. Talbot Street Art Fair
Midsummer Fest

July. Indiana Black Expo, Indiana State Fairgrounds

August. Indiana State Fair, Indiana State Fairgrounds
Brickyard 400 Race

September. Penrod Arts Fair

OTHER RECOMMENDED RESTAURANTS

Bazbeaux Pizza (334 Massachusetts Avenue, Indianapolis, IN 46202; 317–636–7662), in the Broad Ripple area, is known for its homemade doughs and sauces as well as fifty-two tasty toppings. Inexpensive.

Essential Edibles (303 North Alabama, Indianapolis, IN 46202; 317–266–8797) is an award-winning gourmet vegetarian restaurant in the basement of a former Catholic girls' school near theaters and art galleries. It features specialties such as the Wander India sampler plate and the veggie burger as well as a popular carry-out market. There's live jazz on Friday and Saturday nights. Moderate.

The Majestic (47 South Pennsylvania Street, Indianapolis, IN 46204; 317–636–5418) features fresh seafood such as stuffed Florida pompano and bluepoint oysters in a vintage 1895 building. Moderate to expensive.

Palomino Euro Bistro (49 West Maryland, Indianapolis, IN 46204; 317–974–0400) has a Mediterranean/Northwest Italian menu with fresh pastas and Roman-style pizza. Moderate.

The Porch (in the Hyatt Regency Indianapolis; 1 South Capitol Avenue, Indianapolis, IN 46204; 317–632–1234) offers dark woods and contemporary art in a setting inspired by midwestern architect Frank Lloyd Wright. Specialties include steaks and pastas as well as a scrumptious Sunday brunch. Moderate to expensive.

OTHER RECOMMENDED LODGINGS

Embassy Suites (1100 West Washington Street, Indianapolis, IN 46204; 317–236–1800) has 360 all-suite rooms connected to the Circle Center Mall and the Artsgarden. Rates start at $169.

Hampton Inn (105 South Meridian, Indianapolis, IN 46225; 317–261–1200) is a new downtown hotel across from City Centre. The 180 rooms are nicely appointed; continental breakfast is included. Rates: $94 and up.

Westin Indianapolis (50 South Capitol Avenue, Indianapolis, IN 46204; 317–262–8100) has 573 rooms as well as a heated indoor pool, Jacuzzi, and health club. It's adjacent to the Hoosier Dome and Convention Center. Rates: $175 per night.

FOR MORE INFORMATION

Indianapolis Convention & Visitors Bureau, 1 RCA Dome, Suite 100, Indianapolis, IN 46225; (317) 639–4282.

INDEX

ABOUT THE AUTHOR

Khristi Sigurdson Zimmeth is senior editor of *Michigan Living* magazine and a regional editor for *Better Homes & Gardens* design publications. She is also a former editor of *Travel & Leisure* magazine and *The Magazine of the Detroit Institute of Arts*. Khristi has traveled in and around Detroit extensively and currently lives in Michigan with her husband and two children.